LIQUIDITY STRATEGIES FOR FINANCIAL INSTITUTIONS AND CORPORATES

THE ART OF CASH MANAGEMENT

By John Bertrand

Searching finance

Published under licence 2012 by Searching Finance Ltd, 8 Whitehall Road, London W7 2JE, UK

ISBN: 978-1-907720-47-5

Typeset and designed by: Deirdré Gyenes

LIQUIDITY STRATEGIES FOR FINANCIAL INSTITUTIONS AND CORPORATES

THE ART OF CASH MANAGEMENT

By John Bertrand

Searching finance

About the author

John Bertrand has over 30 years' expertise in banking; cash management, payments and technology, gained at Citibank, IBOS, ALLTEL and Misys in the USA and UK.

In this time John has created, developed, implemented and sold technology for front, middle and back offices in both banks and corporates. This includes redefining core banking for over 300 banks, developing cash management consulting, netting schemes, third party cash management, pooling and foreign exchange.

John has also worked with the financial authorities in the US (Federal Reserve), UK (Financial Services Authority) and Sweden (Finansinspektionen).

John is a Freeman of The City of London and has an MSc from Warwick University in marketing and financing and a BSc (Hons) from City University in Civil Engineering.

About Searching Finance

Established in 2010, Searching Finance publishes books and reports on economics, politics and finance.

www.searchingfinance.com

CONTENTS

TABLES AND FIGURES

PREFACE

WELCOME TO LIQUIDITY STRATEGIES. This book is the distillation of many years in the financial services industry. The intent is to take the complexity out of cash management and to make it as simple as possible. The aim is to enable all businesses to make the most of their assets and liabilities now and going forward in the new age of transparency and rapid access to information.

In Liquidity Strategies you will find diagrams that show the financial flows visually. This will help you understand what you need to do and give you the knowledge to ask the right questions. It is the knowledge of the details and structures that is important. Without looking at these it is difficult to assess the right approach that will avoid mistakes and confusion.

Throughout my career I have met many wise and knowledgeable people, including Bert Morris and Tom Jones. Bert, a career banker with Nat West, rose through the bank to Main Board and along the way, introduced the UK population to direct debits. Bert also had a key role in the founding of the UK's Clearing House (BACS) and its ruling body, the Association of Payment Clearing Services (APACS). I was with Citibank when I first met Bert as a business associate and since then gone he has become a good friend and mentor.

Tom Jones is another good friend and mentor. Tom left Citibank as Chief Accounting Officer to become Vice Chairman of the International Accounting Standards Board (IASB). He provided great insight into many intricate accounting methods and how to deal with them. Tom created the time whenever it was needed to explain the nuances of the situation.

Both Bert and Tom endorse the current environment of transparency. The IASB, with its patronage from Paul Volker, has an open forum so any decisions can be seen from all sides. One such decision – the need to mark-to-market derivatives and the like (value securities at today's market price) – caused an uproar prior to 2007. Since the financial crisis, the need to know the value of your position has became paramount and the uproar has died away. In fact, it has gone the opposite way: banks and corporates want to know what their assets are worth, and more importantly, how quickly they can be exchanged for cash.

Regulators around the world are not only supporting mark-to-market, but are assessing the liquidity of those assets. This technique of risk weighting assets is now the flagship of Basel II, and Basel III will ensure that by 2019, all banks meet the minimum capital requirements on a global basis. The financial crisis has clearly shown no-one can work in isolation, but even if they do, they will still be affected.

It is this global wave of fiscal irregularity that has resulted in the need to know where you are financially, right now. Smartphones have been influential in facilitating the immediacy of information flows. These devices will continue to shape and facilitate the flow of financial information.

Liquidity Strategies enables the structure and use of various techniques that start out simple and build in sophistication to give a real-time view of your organisation. Knowledge is control, and control is power. By applying this across various sectors of the business, both you and your business will be well placed to survive and prosper in the stringent current financial climate.

INTRODUCTION

CASH MANAGEMENT is a broad term which covers the usage of cash across a wide range of activities which includes, at the basic level, paying or getting paid by someone. It is the use of cash on hand or of cash due that can bring prosperity, or if not looked after, that can cause misery. As Charles Dickens wrote over 100 years ago:

> *"Annual income twenty pounds, annual expenditure nineteen six, result happiness. Annual income twenty pounds, annual expenditure twenty pound ought and six, result misery.."*

This remains true today: only the amount of the annual earnings and expenditures have changed. As Dr. Evil from the 'Austin Powers' movies said:

> Dr. Evil: "Here's the plan. We get the warhead, and we hold the world to ransom for ... ONE MILLION DOLLARS!!"
>
> No.2: "Ahem ... Well, don't you think we should maybe ask for more than a million dollars? A million dollars isn't exactly a lot of money these days. Virtucon alone makes over nine billion dollars a year!"
>
> Dr. Evil: "Really?"
>
> No.2: "Mm-hmm."
>
> Dr. Evil: "That's a number. Okay then. We hold the world ransom for ... One hundred ... BILLION DOLLARS!!"

Even $100 billion Dr. Evil was asking for is starting to look insignificant compared to the Greek, US and UK bail outs. The proposed Greek bailout of $172 billion is just to keep the country going and with it comes austerity measures that will cause widespread unhappiness. In addition, private holders have signed up to a voluntary Greek bond swap of some 200 billion euros of Greek bonds and are to take a loss of 50%. This will cut Greece's debt from 160% of gross domestic product to 120% by 2020.

The other mass bailout was of US banks in the form of Troubled Asset Relief Program (TARP) for $700 billion. The UK, Ireland and others also bailed out their banks which were caught up in the sub-prime mortgage schemes, often to the tune of billions. This has created an implicit notion that banks cannot fail. The bankers themselves seem wedded to the past, expecting the status quo to remain. Their behaviour concerning retaining their privileged life style funded by bonuses, is at odds with the reality of government hand-outs to prevent a global financial collapse.

Managing cash flow

Regardless of the size of the cash flow, it needs to be managed. Not managing it or managing it badly creates negativity and stress. Managing it well brings extra rewards and increases well-being and positivity. It also can be the divide between success and failure with all aspects being equal.

In addition, banks have changed their approach towards how money is managed. Gone are the days of tolerance and flexibility. They are approaching cash management with a zero tolerance attitude that would make a police state smile. No arrests, only big fines for the smallest transgressions. For example, moving more money out of your account than is present could easily result in a hefty fine, sometimes 10 times the amount moved. So watch out, as it is not going to get easier.

Five key events have pushed cash management to the forefront of attention in the world today:

1. Liquidity concerns and cash cushions;
2. No growth economies (especially in Europe);
3. Tight credit markets;
4. Recapitalisation of banks to meet new global standards (Basel III);
5. New legal regulations and compliance.

The Aberdeen Group reported in January 2012 that 82% of companies have increased their focus on cash management. The PwC Global Treasury Survey 2010 noted the proportion of participants rating cash management as highly important has doubled from 35% to 70%.

The top 20% performers in Aberdeen's cash management study have the following characteristics:

- 28% align the Treasurer with the management team, often reporting to the Board;
- 53% are less likely to rely on manual procedures and spreadsheets;
- 69% are more likely than their peers to have Straight Through Processing (STP);
- 88% are likely to have automated reconciliation of the bank accounts.

One of the most neglected aspects of cash management is accurate cash forecasting. According to a Schmidt CS Survey, 79% of companies polled still used spreadsheets for cash forecasting. HSBC's own survey of its corporate customers found that 42% rely on manual forecasts, something with which 80% are dissatisfied.

The focus on cash is on the rise since the financial crisis and has propelled company cash balances to new record heights. Cash and equivalents in the top 1,000 European companies for 2010 increased 18% over 2009, as noted by REL Consulting. The cash holdings ot the Top US 1,000 companies increased by 6% in 2010 over 2009. The 2010 US cash figure of $850 billion was 75% higher than 2007, the beginning of the financial crisis. In addition, since 2008, cash in the supply chain has increased by €183.5 billion as debtors have slowed payments by an average of 4.3 days of sale. Companies are creating their own cash cushions.

Banks create their own cash cushions

Under the Basel III proposals, banks need to create a cash cushion of 2.5% included in the capital structure. The difference between Basel I and Basel III looks like an additional 25% in new capital for most banks. Wells Fargo in the case study (see Chapter 16) noted its Tier 1 capital ratio is reduced by 26% under Basel III. The choice of measures for Wells Fargo is to: i) raise the new capital by 26%; ii) reduce lending by 26%; iii) sell assets; or iv) a combination of the three. Whichever approach is taken, Wells Fargo needs an extra $24 billion by 2019. For Wells Fargo, given its the 3rd quarter 2011 results showed an increase of $3.1 billion in Tier 1 for the quarter, that figure looks very achievable.

But for other banks, especially in the eurozone, the task looks more daunting. The regulators want the European financial institutions to raise $145 billion by June 2012. One of the first banks to approach its shareholders is UniCredit, which is looking to raise $10 billion but which saw its share price drop 40% in the first week of January 2012. It does not help that UniCredit is based in Italy, whose sovereign debt rating is looking downwards with the euro under market pressure.

This does not bode well for credit availability from banks. Banks with a 10% capital ratio can lend 10 times their capital base. As an illustration, having raised $1 billion in new capital, the bank could lend $10 billion. The new capital increase is to shore up the existing position; therefore the only new lending capabilities come from the maturing of debt. A new capital ratio of 15% reduces the amount of credit a bank can offer from $10 billion to $6.7 billion, a loss of lending of $3.3 billion to the community.

Cash and liquid instruments are king. The challenge is where to keep the cash and make money off that money. This is becoming harder, as in January 2011 Germany sold six-month bills at a negative interest rate yield. The investment pyramid ranks risk against return, with the safest and most liquid at the base. The higher up the pyramid, the higher the risk and the lower the liquidity (see Chapter 8). At the top of the pyramid liquidity is virtually nil. Any forced move to take liquidity out of those assets held at the top will result in the assets being sold at a heavy discount to the market, hence the phrase 'fire sale'. For longer-term cash cushions, Cash Managers should consider strong currencies and gold with the appropriate stop-losses. Both are highly liquid and have shown past appreciation rates in double digits.

The move towards non-banks

The key for cash management now is to make absolutely certain that accounts do not go negative. Most banks charge fees for credit provision, often up to 20% per annum, that are completely disproportionate to the interest they pay, which is often less than 0.5% per annum. Banks have also taken a zero tolerance approach to credit, with many reducing the credit line available and/or increasing the interest rate being levied. Credit from banks is becoming scarce, and this is opening doors to non-banks to provide credit. These include asset-based financing, pledged collateral and short-term loans with funding coming from the non-bank sector. Often this sector is funded by banks which are taking the risk on one company. This company lends out to many companies at a higher interest rate. The cost of these types of financing can often exceed 20%, with the shorter loans exceeding 100%.

This move away from the banking community to non-banks is beginning to accelerate across the bank product range. For example:

- Credit is being offered by new companies offering secured and unsecured loans especially through asset finance, with rates with rates often much higher than the traditional bank rates. The reason is banks historically were the first port of call for credit and if there was no credit forthcoming then the business sentiment is that the risk of default must be really high;
- Savings: Sweden permits new companies to offer certificates or bonds backed by callable assets and these are paying 6% against the banks;
- Payments: Warehouse account companies such as PayPal allow payments to be made at any time, with credit to a bank account in a maximum of three days. In the UK, Barclays has just allowed payments to be made from a smartphone on a virtually instantaneous basis. Both PayPal and Barclays use existing banking infrastructures to make payments easy and convenient.

Technology and ready access to data is driving the product sets away from banks and managing cash requires anyone to find the best and safest product. Banks can no longer believe that while they have the bank account they have the business.

This book steers through the myriad of complications and complexities of cash management, enabling at least happiness, if not fun.

CHAPTER 1

THE THREE LEVELS OF CASH MANAGEMENT

Questions for the CFO, Treasurer or Cash Manager

- What is the cash position now?
- How many bank accounts are being maintained?
- How many banking relationships are being maintained?
- Are any of the accounts running near to or below zero?

Key considerations

- Cash management starts off simple and then increases in complexity;
- A couple of weeks' of overdraft charges can wipe out a year's worth of interest;
- Free bank accounts are becoming rare and account fees are growing;
- Technology is becoming a significant part of the process.

Introduction

The three levels of cash management are:

1: Domestic cash management;

2: International cash management; and

3: Global cash management.

Cash management starts simply enough and then grows in complexity as the company grows and changes. The first bank account is usually registered in a single currency; this may be followed by development steps to meet the increasing globalisation of people and businesses. The first step is local cash management, often referred to as 'domestic cash management'. Once another currency becomes active, the step becomes 'international cash management', followed by the final step of 'global cash management'.

Within each level, there are several stages of functionality and complexity that have developed to meet the organisation's requirements and growth stage, from a simple transactional bank account for accounts payable and receivable, through to sophisticated and bespoke cash management services for global corporates.

- Stage 1: Simple bank account;
- Stage 2: Bank account with technology;
- Stage 3: Bank account with investment rules;
- Stage 4: Bank account with overdraft facilities;
- Stage 5: Multiple banks with more than one bank account in the same currency;
- Stage 6: International cash management services with more than one currency account;
- Stage 7: Global cash management.

Domestic cash management

Cash management starts very simply with a bank account. A company opens the account with a bank to begin business. For a company, the initial reason is to pay suppliers (creditors) and receive funds from sales (debtors). These two activities are termed the 'accounts payable' and the 'accounts receivable' and are the financial centre of the company.

Figure 1.1: Simple domestic cash management

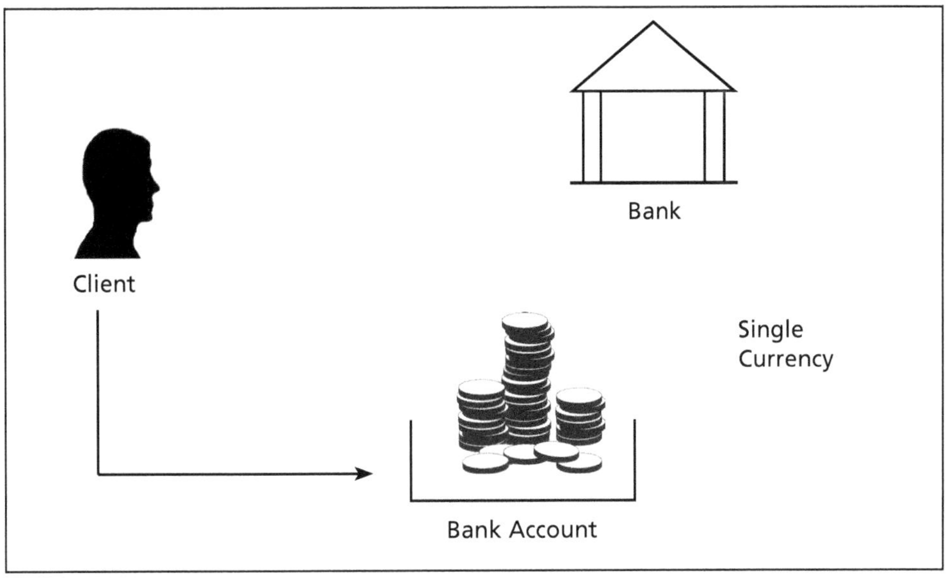

Source: IBS Publishing

Bank charges on the rise

In the US and elsewhere, banks historically have given their customers free banking. But now bank charges are being made for accounts, and this trend looks like it will continue and spread. Examples in the US include:

- Wells Fargo – $5 per month for using cheques and $6.95 for online bill payment;
- Citicorp – $8 per month if five transactions or more are made;
- Chase – $12 per month if the customer does not maintain $1,500 in the bank account, or $5,000 across deposit accounts or does not make a minimum of $500 in deposits.

Similarly in the UK, fees for bank accounts are being introduced. The terms and conditions along with benefits are reflected in the monthly charges that range from £5 to £19.50 per month.

Table 1.1: Features of UK bank accounts 2009, 2010

	2009	2010	Change
Average interest rate paid on £1,000	0.87%	0.61%	+30.00%
Number of banks NOT paying interest	23.00%	59.00%	+157.00%
Average authorised overdraft rate per annum	14.10%	14.90%	+6.00%
Number of paid packaged accounts	54.00%	69.00%	+28.00%
Average monthly fee for packaged accounts	£13.62	£15.37	+13.00%

Source: Defaqto

One in five adults in the UK now has a packaged account – the regular bank account surrounded by a group of services such as travel insurance, shop discounts, etc. that the bank offers for monthly fee. Since 2010, the UK banks have paid 30% less interest on the accounts still carrying interest; 60% of accounts do not pay interest, up from 23%, packaged services has grown by 28% and the price of these packages has grown by 13%. The average authorised rate for overdrafts looks set to rise by 35% as the major UK clearers raised the interest level to just under 20% throughout 2011. The response to these trends by the UK population is remarkably low; just 3.8% changed bank accounts in 2011 according to the Independent Commission on Banking. This is less than half the rate of switching in the US of 8.7%, according to JD Power and Associates 2011 US Retail Bank New Account study.

The ICB and the Payments Council in the UK have agreed to bring in a guarantee scheme by September 2013 that bank accounts will be moved within seven business days; the current barriers to account switching mean that it takes a minimum of seven days at present. The guarantee includes:

- The old account remains open, and the customer uses it in exactly the same way, until the end of the seventh day. On the eighth working day, their new account will be fully operational, and any remaining credit in their old account transferred across;
- The customer will receive whatever they need to operate the new account, like a debit card, PIN and cheque book within those seven working days;
- The customer's new bank will arrange for all their incoming and outgoing payment instructions to be redirected from the old account to the new one;
- The customer's balance will be transferred to the new account;
- Any payments sent to the old account on or after the seventh working day will be automatically 'caught' and moved on to the new account;
- The customer will not suffer if there are any bank errors;
- The old current account will be closed at the end of the process.

In addition the ICB is aiming at increasing competition between the four existing banks which dominate the local UK banking market.

Bank accounts are not free any longer and companies tend to pay more than consumers for them. Most companies are offered bank accounts based on a package of services, with a transaction price list tied to volume and type of payment.

Given the disparity in interest rates for savings (0.61% per year against 20% on an authorised overdraft limit – and unauthorised overdrafts are even more expensive than that), it is also clear that a couple of weeks' of overdraft charges can wipe out a year's worth of interest

Consequently, today's cash management ethos is to make certain that the probability of a bank account going into an overdraft position is virtually zero.

The bank account is the payment gateway to the banking community's payment infrastructure and the start of any cash management is the opening of a bank account. The bank account is the gateway to the local bank's payment and clearing systems and a bank's correspondent banking network for international payments. Under their banking licence, banks are permitted to pay and credit accounts from their pool of money. The pool is a combination of everyone's money in the bank. Each bank can lend up to a certain amount before being restricted by capital requirements. Capital requirements for banks have been increasing over the years. Under Basel II, the banking regulators were looking for 8% (2006); now under Basel III (2012 onwards), the requirement is 10.5%. This is the amount of capital banks have to keep on hand to cover unexpected financial conditions.

Figure 1.2: Account opening process

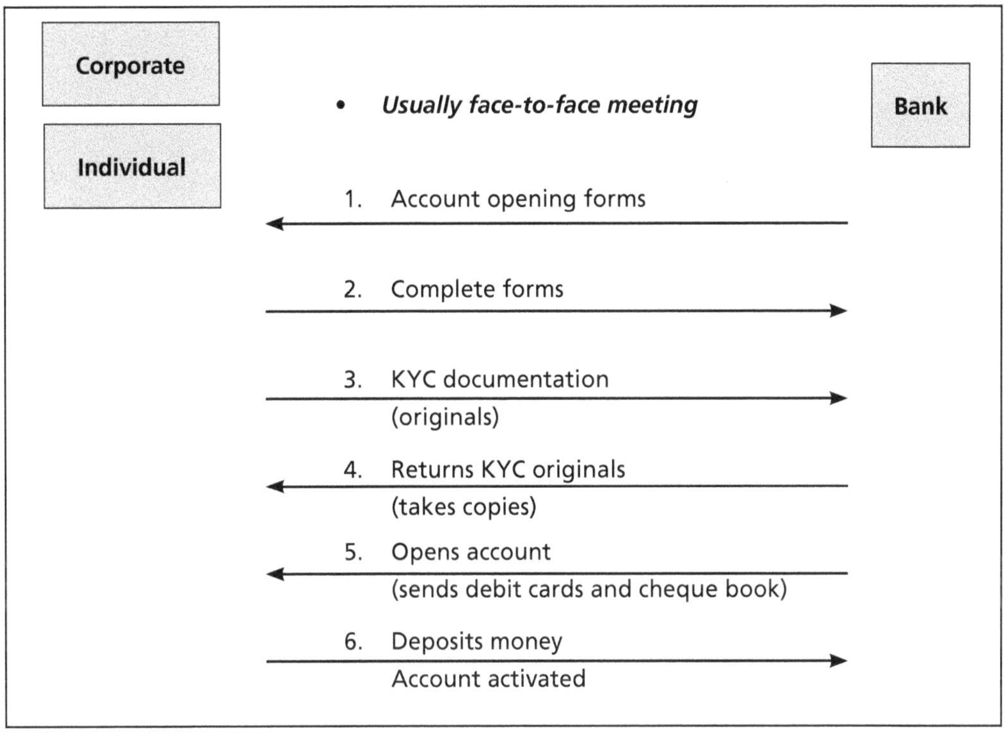

Source: Author

Domestic cash management stages

Domestic cash management covers stages 1–5 and provides increasing levels of complexity of features.

Stage 1: Simple bank account

Key features:

- Account in a single currency;
- Access through the branch;
- Ability to collect money;
- Ability to pay money if cash is in the account;
- Payments made by cheque, electronic transfer or Automated Clearing House (ACH);
- Branch foreign exchange rates offered for any infrequent currency movements.

The bank account is in a single currency and opened at a branch or bank business office. Banks handling corporate banking often have separate areas for their corporate clients. The need to deposit payment by cheque leads the corporate to use the local branch of the bank where it's bank account has been opened. The account allows the corporate client to use the domestic clearing system and the bank's correspondent network for international payments.

Figure 1.3: Simple bank account – domestic

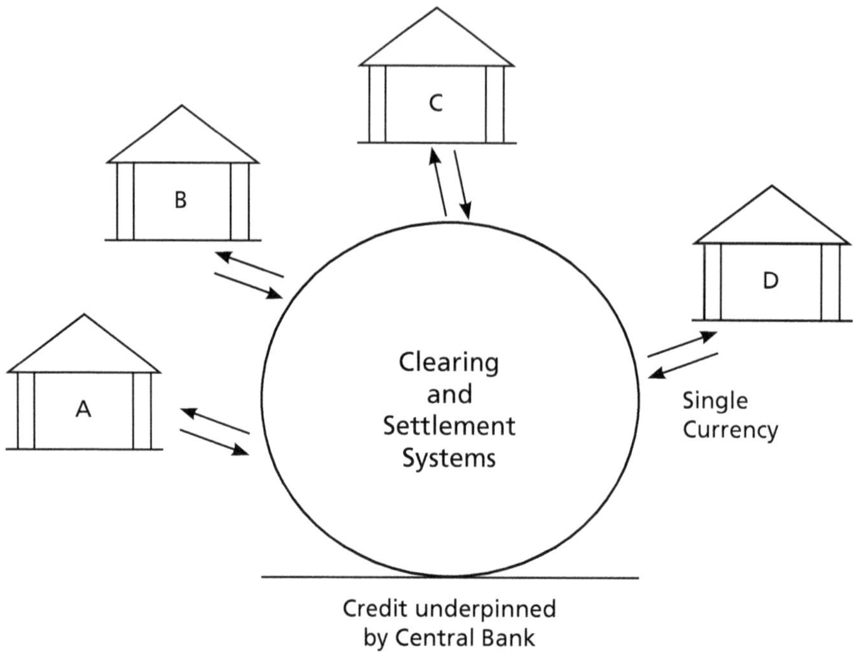

Source: IBS Publishing

Figure 1.4: Simple bank account – international

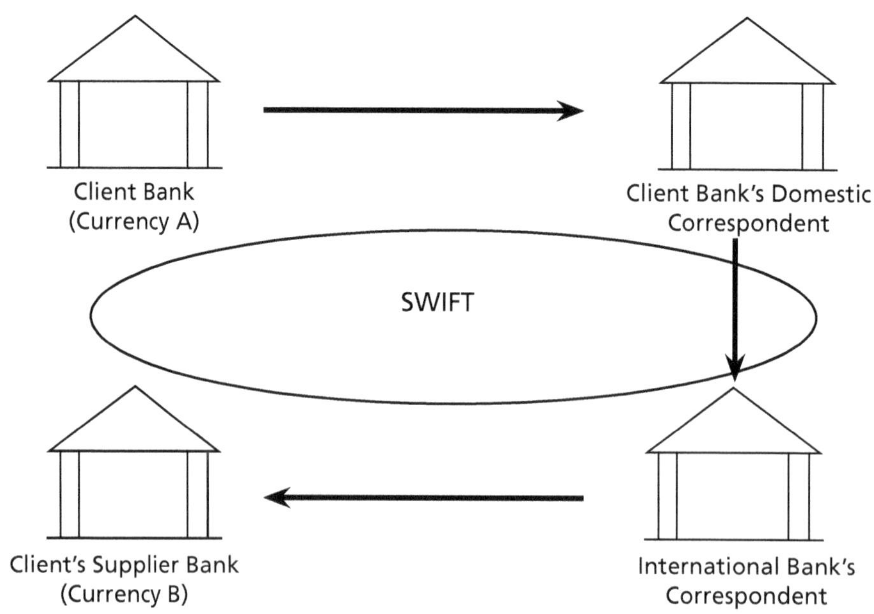

Source: IBS Publishing

Stage 2: Bank account with technology

Key features:

- As Stage 1 with:
    - E-banking software – either internet or proprietary channels;
    - Mobile banking using smart phone (m-payments).

E-banking now the preferred approach

The US was probably the first to start electronic banking (e-banking) closely followed by Europe. Europe was the first with Automatic Teller Machines (ATMs). ATMs and e-banking were the first products to enable the bank account to become 'self-service'; i.e., people other than bank staff could access the account.

The use of e-banking started in the 1980s with priority systems from each of the major corporate banks. These systems were expensive to build and maintain, but they met the corporate market need to look after their money. It is still startling that most companies fail not though poor products, management or business strategy, but through cash flow. Consequently, the need for cash management has been a growing concern for both domestic and international businesses.

The internet has replaced the need for priority communication networks, which the major banks used as their competitive edge in the 1980s and 1990s in offering cash management business. The sheer scale of telecommunication growth and usage has enabled any bank to enter the e-banking market.

Historically the larger banks held the skills to create their own e-banking and cash management software. Now many software companies are using XML and open software computer languages and can provide these services on a licence or as an Application Service Provider (ASP) using internal or cloud technology. Cloud technology is starting to absorb ASPs, making the application and infrastructure a single purchase. In addition, smartphone applications – iPhone, Blackberry and Android – are starting to appear; one app, for example, can help see bank balances held at a number of banks.

Smartphones

Banks prefer e-banking as the information comes and goes in a fully automated format. This makes it easier to receive and deliver information from and to the client. In addition, smartphones are becoming the device of choice for many customers. A study by Accenture in February 2011 showed that:

- Nearly half (45%) of the most active mobile device users would welcome the opportunity to pay for goods and services using their mobile phone;
- 73% expressed significant privacy and identity theft concerns;
- 69% of survey respondents in Asia indicated they favoured using mobile phones for most payments, broken down as –
    - Chinese consumers (76%)
    - India (75%)

- Korea (56%)
- Japan (47%).

Outside Asia, the next highest positive response was in Brazil, where 70% of consumers favoured using mobile phones for most payments. In the US and Europe combined, however, only 26% of respondents favoured using mobile phones for most payments.

In the UK, it is estimated that by 2013 up to 20% of a bank's activity will come via the mobile phone. The trend among a number of banks is to add m-banking to their e-banking offering so the client has one interface, regardless of device.

In February 2012 Barclays UK launched Pingit, an app that allows an owner of a Barclays bank account who also has a smartphone to send up to £300 ($450) per day to another bank account. Non-Barclays customers with a current account can only receive payments at this time. In its first two days, the app was downloaded 20,000 times. The British Bankers Association (BBA) noted that there were 43.6 million internet bank registrations in the UK (up from 32.1 million in 2007).

The UK Payments Council has commissioned VocaLink, the UK manager of the local ACH, to build a central database that will allow bank customers to link their mobile phone number to their account for person-to-person mobile payments. This will offer a standard service to current bank account holders, allowing intra-operability across the banking sector. Unlike e-banking where each bank has a proprietary standard, mobile payments in the UK will have a common and secure database.

Today the smartphone has more functionality than most desktop computers. In the UK, 50% of the UK population has a smartphone. Smartphones now dominate the market, with Android (50%) and Apple (25%) as its leaders. (Source: Kantor) The remainder of the market is taken by Windows phones (Microsoft and Nokia) and Blackberry (the first phone to push email to the user). Gartner estimates the smartphone has increased 75% year-on-year in terms of percentage of sales in the 2nd quarter 2011.

Stage 3: Bank account with investment rules

Key features:

- As Stage 1 with:
  - Interest paid on certain balances, often in a separate savings account;
  - Higher interest paid on higher yielding 'market' instruments;
  - Time-extended investments based on account balances for greater yield.

Stage 4: Bank account with overdraft facilities

Key features:

- As Stage 1 or 2 with:
  - Overdraft facility allowing the account to be overdrawn to a set level;
  - Loan facilities after 'credit review'.

Stage 5: Multiple banks with more than one bank account in the same currency

Key features:

- As Stage 1, 2, or 3 with:
  - More than one account in the local currency;
  - Account consolidator, especially sweeping, topping and zero balances.

Multibanking occurs as the corporation grows. A growing company attracts different banks. As the late Steve Jobs, CEO of Apple, noted: "When JPMorgan sent people to meet me, I knew Apple had joined the big boys". Neither the bank nor the corporation wants to be reliant solely on each other. Consequently, multinational and very large national companies have more than one bank.

Regardless of country, banks offer some form of the above under the general term of domestic cash management. The switch to electronic access (e-banking) is based on the e-readiness of the country (see Table 2:2, Top 20 country e-readiness scale) and those banks that have invested in electronic cash management. Where the electronic infrastructure does not exist or is not used, then companies use physical receipt and delivery, usually around the bank's branch or business offices.

Table 1.2: EIU 2010 digital economy rankings and scores

1.	Sweden	8.49/10	11.	Canada	8.05
2.	Denmark	8.41	12.	Taiwan	7.99
3.	United States	8.41	13.	South Korea	7.94
4.	Finland	8.36	14.	United Kingdom	7.89
5.	Netherlands	8.36	15.	Austria	7.88
6.	Norway	8.24	16.	Japan	7.85
7.	Hong Kong	8.22	17.	Ireland	7.82
8.	Singapore	8.22	18.	Germany	7.80
9.	Australia	8.21	19.	Switzerland	7.72
10.	New Zealand	8.07	20.	France	7.67

Source: Economist Intelligence Unit

The banks that have invested in e-banking have done so in such a way that the interface between the bank and the customer is unique to that bank. Consequently, using more than one bank means that consolidation at the company needs two or more interfaces. Few countries have insisted on a multibank format/interface standard, with the exception of Germany. German banks operate in a multibank environment so only one interface is needed for their banking community. The need to build interfaces restricts the flow of information within a country; this tends to result in companies focusing banking activity on to one bank for ease of use.

Complexity increases as the company grows

As the company grows, the need for additional bank accounts becomes a necessity. The accounts are opened for a variety of reasons, but the need to make the most out of the money is still there. It is here that the complexity of cash management begins to increase and banks begin to specialise. The first step is to bring the accounts of the company together. In the simplest form it is the mailing-out of the bank accounts to the same address, or showing the accounts on e-banking as separate accounts. The bank does not try to work with the accounts as if they belonged to one company.

Technology and processes

It is here the technology and processes being applied by certain banks within a particular country that start to earn them a name for cash management. In addition, the availability of inexpensive software to assist companies in reconciling their bank accounts has made companies keener to have the banks develop more sophisticated techniques. This has lead to competition from banks outside the domestic country for the larger companies' banking business. The key technique is the automated movement of funds between all the accounts so that no one account generates overdraft charges should one of the accounts become overdrawn when another has more than enough to cover the shortage. It is similar on the investment side when consolidating the money enables the company to generate a greater level of interest payment.

Figure 1.5: More than one company bank account (single currency) – simple

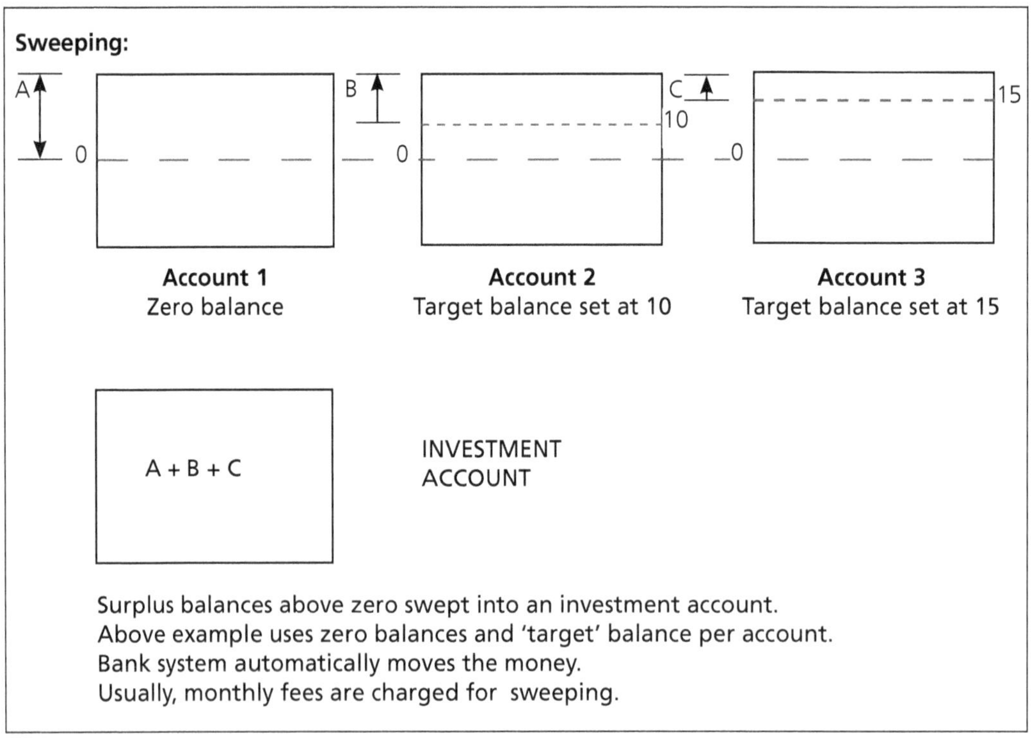

Source: IBS Publishing

Figure 1.6: More than one company bank account (single currency) – alternative

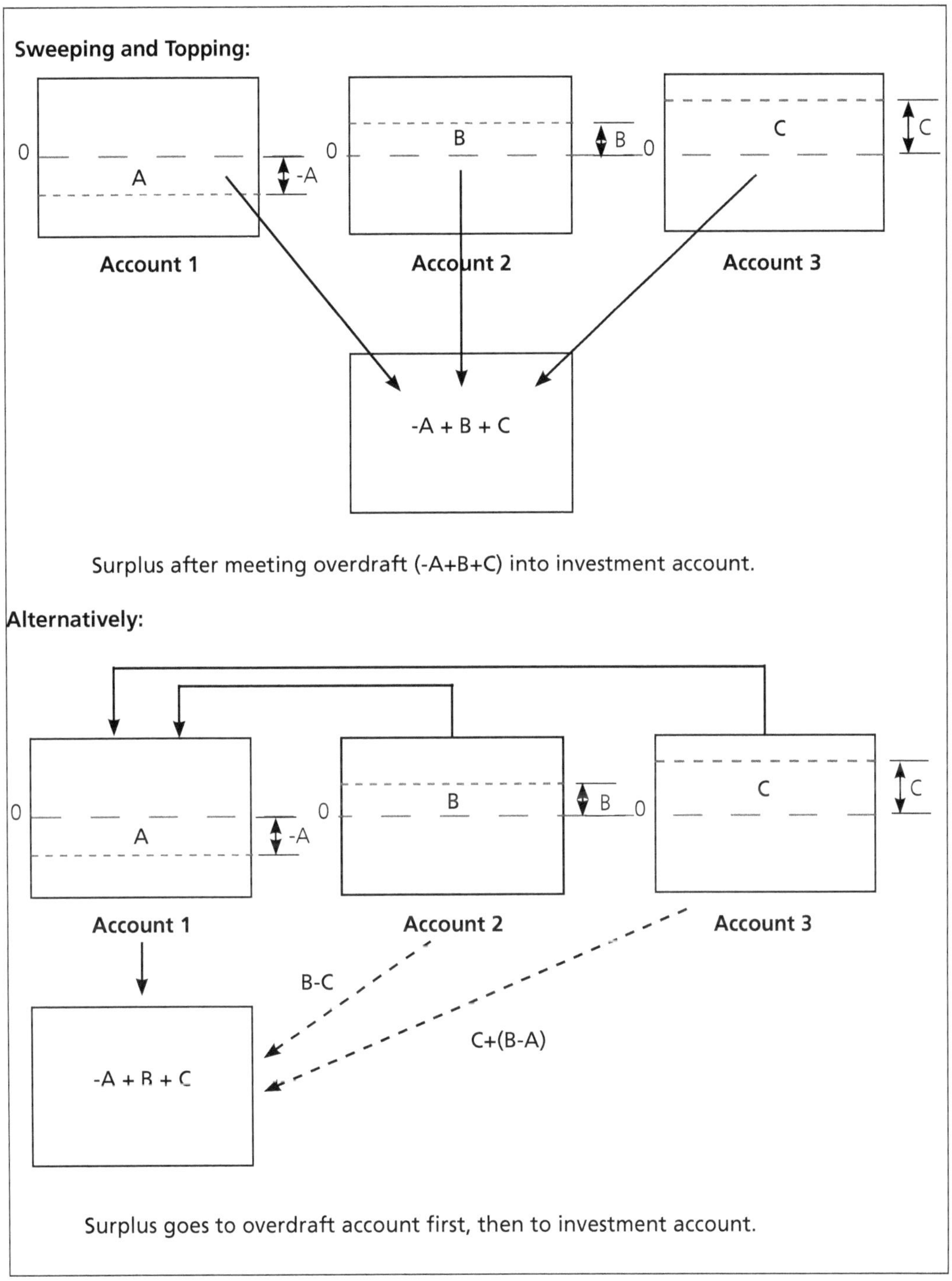

Source: IBS Publishing

The account consolidation also manages the billing. The levels of transactions by accounts are totalled and matched against an agreed to level of transaction charges. It is these companies with strong transactional business that are valuable to banks. These corporates, providing the credit situation between them and the bank is not locked, can offer their banking business for competitive bids.

Competitive bidding for banking business

The competitive bidding process starts with a RFP (Request for Proposal), which is prepared by the company or its consultants. The RFP covers the transactional volumes and the details of when, where and how they occur. Details are also provided on the types of payment channels being used. The RFP will include SLAs (service level agreements) and the corporate will expect the bank to sign up to them, with penalties should they fall below the set standards. RFPs tend to come from the major users of cash management services and may request the bank to outsource the process for the corporate with the appropriate controls in place.

International cash management

Stage 6: International cash management services with more than one currency account

Key features:

- As Stage 5 with:
  - Accounts in more than one currency in more than one country;
  - Credit lines in more than one country;
  - FX credit limits;
  - Access to corporate desk or electronic FX real-time updates;
  - Derivatives;
  - Netting;
  - Pooling.

As soon as a company opens a bank account with a different currency it has moved into the world of international cash management. For the first time, the corporate has to consider ongoing foreign exchange, exposure management, netting, pooling, tax and regulatory environments. The level of cash management complexity has exploded and continues to accelerate the more international business the company adds.

Figure 1.7: International cash management

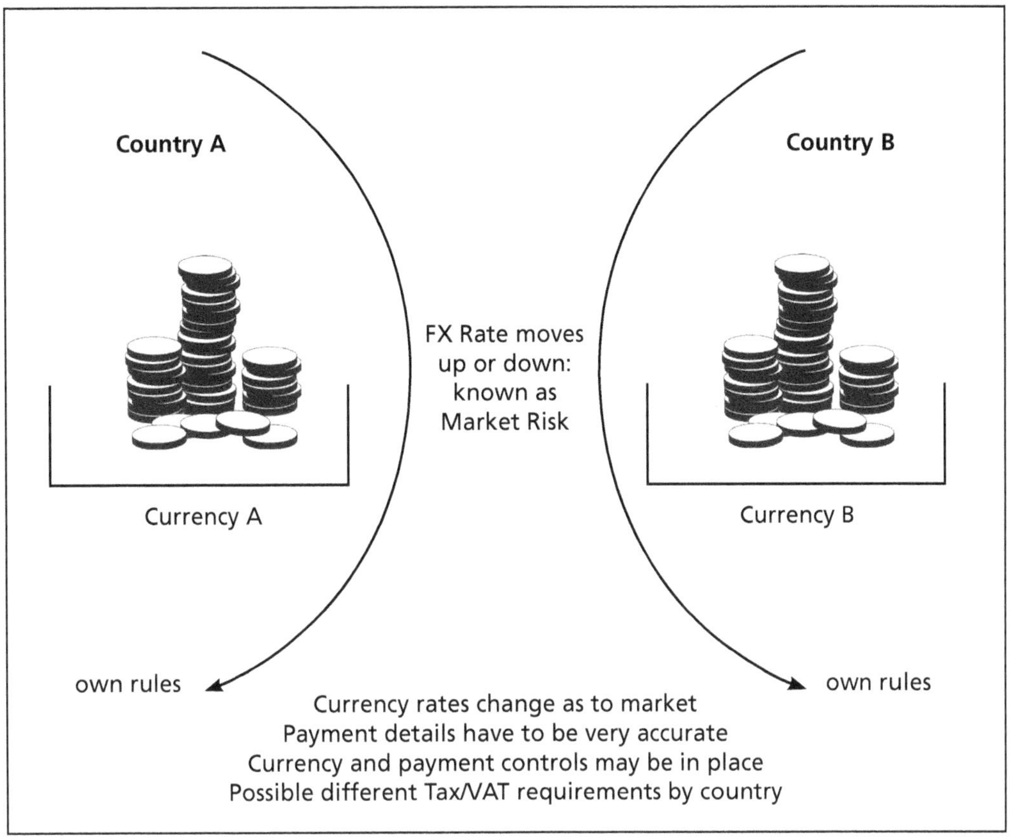

Source: IBS Publishing

Cash pooling to notional pooling

In their efforts to set up efficient liquidity solutions for the entire Group, many treasurers choose banks that have the widest geographical coverage and that are in a position to offer unified cash management structures throughout countries, among others a unified cash pool set-up. While this would be easy in a perfect environment, the reality usually turns out to be more complicated. Thus, understanding and addressing local requirements is the first step to take before implementing any cash pool solution. For example: "*... and we'd like to include our Polish subsidiaries into our cash pool set-up...*" is what corporate banks in Poland often hear from their international customers.

Expectations of companies (groups of companies) seeking to set up a cash pooling solution usually vary. Some of them consider improvement of the Group's net interest position being of highest importance. In this case, notional pooling might be a suitable tool.

Others want to improve the Group's net interest position, and, apart from that, to concentrate the Group's liquidity, to reduce its needs for external financing and to reduce its balance sheet. These companies will have to choose among different cash concentration techniques available on the market.

Figure 1.8 depicts various forms of cash pool available with notional pooling mirroring the information, but no movement of transactions are made until the end of the month. Here the bank credits the corporate with the agreed interest earned on the notional account.

Figure 1.8: Cash pool with notional pooling

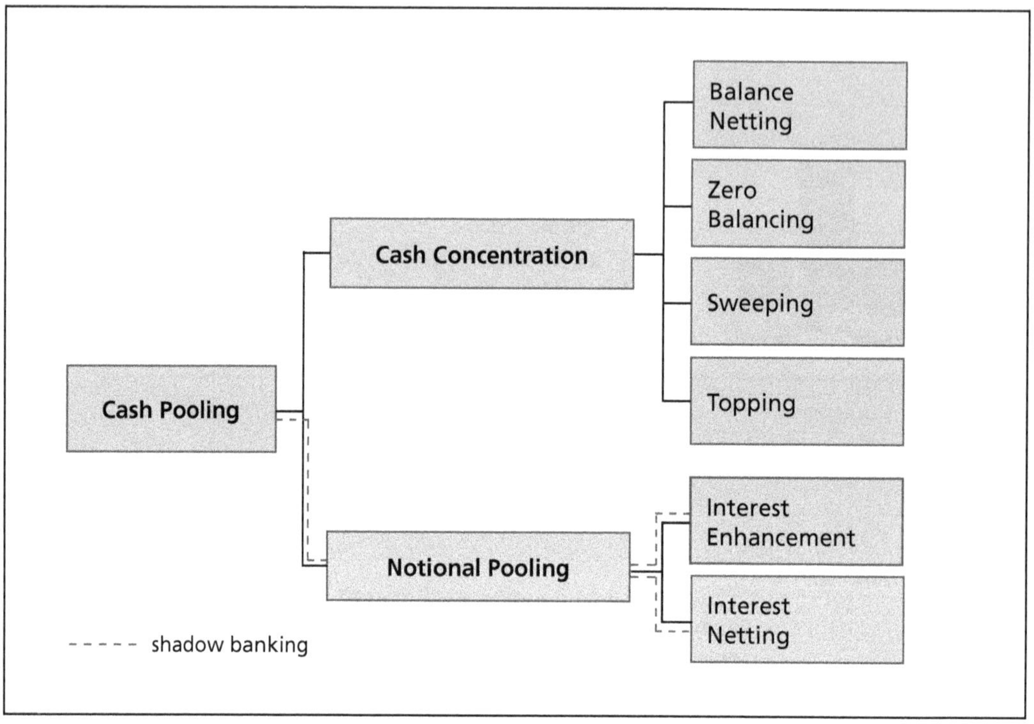

Source: Author

Independently of the form chosen, cash pooling helps to optimise the interest results within a group of companies or in the accounts of a multi-branch company. It greatly improves the group's result on interest when compared to separately investing surpluses and paying the costs of financing by individual account holders within the system.

From the banks' perspective, cash pool is rather a 'non-profit' product. One could even argue that pooling hurts banks' revenues, as it decreases the margins both on deposits and on loans. However, offering cash pool is a way to keep customers happy and should be seen as a part of a package deal between the bank and the customer.

Cash pooling considerations

The concept of cash pooling is often not mentioned in legislation. Banks offer different legal solutions, which potentially allow common liquidity management. However, there is still a considerable legal uncertainty. A number of legal and tax issues have to be taken into account when deciding upon a cash pool implementation. For example, for legal and tax regulations, common accounts owned by more than one legal entity may not exist. Consequently, cash pool solutions assuming that balances are concentrated on the group account/or top account/or master account are not permitted, and any form of pooling could result in transfers between accounts belonging to separate legal entities.

Transfer of funds between accounts participating in a cash pool structure can be regarded as inter-company lending, thus subject to tax (stamp duty, also called 'Tax on Civil Acts'). Clearly, the necessity to pay tax would undermine the whole economic sense of pooling.

Transfer pricing is another factor that needs to be considered. The way the benefits from the cash pool are allocated across participants can create a tax liability. To be able to treat the payments among cash pool participants as interest for tax purposes, companies will need to show that the transfers are made at arm's length pricing, i.e. in fact, the same which would have been charged directly by a bank.

Banks may be obliged to compute the mandatory provisions on the basis of the total amount of positive balances (deposits) of all customers. Balance decrease resulting from the usage of a cash pool means a decrease of the mandatory provisions computing basis. Thus, the cash pool structure to be implemented may need to be confirmed by the central bank.

The legal and tax obstacles described do not necessary mean that no form of cash pooling can be implemented. It means cash pooling popular in other European countries needs to be adjusted to the local legal landscape. For example, the usage of a cash concentration pooling can be achieved subject to establishing a legal basis for fund flows. This means that the cash pool structure has to be designed in a way to avoid the stamp duty liability.

Such a cash concentration technique can be based on assignments (and reassignments) of credit claims concluded daily between the bank and the cash pool participants. In order to enable effective pooling of balances, each cash pool participant shall have an account held with the same bank and a credit limit in current account overdraft that can be traded between the bank and cash pool participants (legal title for fund flows). In order to perform daily assignment and reassignment operations and any settlements connected on behalf of the company, those cash pool participants need to grant the bank an irrevocable power of attorney.

Notional pooling

Notional pooling is a mechanism for calculating interest on the combined credit and debit balances of accounts that a corporate group parent chooses to cluster together, without actually transferring any funds.

Banks recommend this solution (also in countries where the legal cash pool-related constraints have been solved), as traditional balance netting and zero-balancing cash pools appear to be rather inexpedient in terms of cross-border and cross-currency solutions. This applies to, for instance, the conversion of currency positions, differences in the possible reporting requirements of the various countries' central banks and cross-border intra-group loans.

The Interest Enhancement set-up gives a further compensation on the interest margins on a cross-currency as well as cross-country basis. Firstly, it does not result in any inter-company loans. Secondly, the interest compensation is distributed proportionally to the participants. Interests are booked on division account level or on the sub-accounts depending on the country.

Notional accounting

The use of notional accounting is still the preserve of the large corporate. Notional accounting allows the bank to reflect the worldwide banking activity to a corporate, and reward the corporate on the level of business done with them without incurring unnecessary transaction fees or tax liabilities. It is like a shadow banking record across the corporate and was first created by the study of international cash management.

These studies, often costing hundreds of thousands of dollars, help bring the treasury of the bank and corporate together. The level of treasury product development has grown rapidly in the last few years, especially alongside the growth of derivatives.

Services such as sweep accounts that were created for the largest multinational clients are now widespread through out banking, even down to individual accounts. The goal of the multinational of maximising their cash flow is the same common goal for banking customers.

Payment infrastructure

The addition of a second currency not only layers in a new set of services, but banks have historically earned considerably more on 'international' transactions. For example, international payments are often ten times more expensive than domestic ones, and these payments have to pass through another country's payment infrastructure. This infrastructure often requires additional information and a change in message format. International payments can take far longer, increasing the float to the banking system.

An excellent example of this is the European Union's SEPA initiative (the Single Euro Payments Area) to standardise payments across the eurozone. SEPA mandates to the banks a set of standard procedures to enable the euro to act like a domestic currency across country borders.

In parallel to the development of XML (see Chapter 4) is the banking sector movement towards agreeing standards. One of the biggest areas involving standards is SEPA. Europe continues to slowly to have a compatible payment process across the Europe Union. The banking network, SWIFT, is working with ISO to create XML messages that can be used worldwide. In the USA, the American Bankers Association (ABA), issues banks a 9-digit routing number. This allows the money to reach a specific bank account. In Europe there are now two codes, IBAN (International Bank Account Number) and the BIC (Bank Identifier Code). The IBAN, BIC and ABA numbers allow cross-border payments to automatically go from account to account.

On a separate front, the International Accounting Standards Board is establishing global accounting standards so a company from one country can see and understand the financial treatment of a similar company in another country.

As each country has its own existing and working payment settlement systems operating under each country's own regulation, the change needed to meet a global standard is massive and is slow to evolve.

One aspect of SEPA is the adoption of standards on a global basis, which can be seen by the increasing use of the IBAN and BIC numbers. Each bank has established its own BIC, which is SWIFT-compliant (SWIFT is a banking community-owned infrastructure). With the IBAN each company's bank account can be readily identified and payments directed from any account, anywhere.

This removes tremendous inefficiency from the international banking system, which is good for commerce and a mixed blessing for the banks. The banks want to remove the inefficiencies – repairing international payments, which is a small industry in itself, where the banks incur the expense – but removing the inefficiencies of the payment processes costs the banks money in reduced float.

To gain these efficiencies, corporates now needed to add BIC and IBAN numbers to their invoices to their clients. That is, more information is needed on the invoicing to international clients and suppliers. As BIC and IBAN are long streams of numbers, the chances of them being accurately transcribed manually are low. Hence corporates and banks are changing to provide information electronically.

On the international side, SWIFT provides data from other banks using a dedicated message type. Companies can receive their balances and transactions from multiple banks provided their bank offers it and, in turn, the company's international banks have installed the SWIFT functionality.

Global cash management

Stage 7: Global cash management

Key features:

- As Stage 6 with:
  - Notional accounting;
  - Full treasury participation, especially hedging;
  - Derivatives;
  - Asset management advice;
  - Cash management consulting.

The final development in cash management is to create the best blend of domestic and international cash management into global cash management. Global cash management is the province of the top 10,000 corporates. It is here the most sophisticated of cash management services are developed and applied.

Once these services are successful, these mostly new and often tailored activities are commoditised and moved back through the earlier steps of cash management.

Like corporates, banks also have bank accounts with other banks. These are called nostro (to receive money) and vostro (to send money to) accounts.

Reducing transaction volumes

Historically banks have processed payments as independent one-off transactions from one account to another. Banks have also, in the past, paid away one currency before receiving the second currency and still do today. Both of these legacy banking procedures are now being addressed, the first through payment netting, and the second through a banking-wide initiative known as Continual Linked Settlement (CLS).

- Netting – reduces the number of payments between accounts to one.
  - Bi-lateral netting is the simplest form of netting – see Figure 1.9.
  - Multi-lateral netting requires a lender of last resort, usually the Head Office of the company or the country's central bank – see Figures 1.10 and 1.11.
- CLS – the settling of foreign exchange transactions finally and irrevocably. Banks are starting to offer this service to their larger corporate clients.

CLS

Sixty financial institutions around the world were involved in creating the Continuous Linked Settlement (CLS) system. Initially designed to reduce the settlement risk between currencies, it also streamlines the foreign exchange transaction process between trading parties. Banks enable non-CLS settlement members to access the benefits of CLS.

CLS settlement services supports CLS participation, payments, and foreign exchange trade matching. This solution can be integrated with existing accounts at the bank. Enabling the execution of foreign exchange settlements on a 'payment versus payment' basis, CLS offers final and simultaneous settlement of all foreign exchange transactions. These services provide:

- Real-time access to CLS transaction and balance information;
- Integrated matching and reconciliation services;
- Reduced settlement risk.

Figure 1.9: Bi-lateral netting

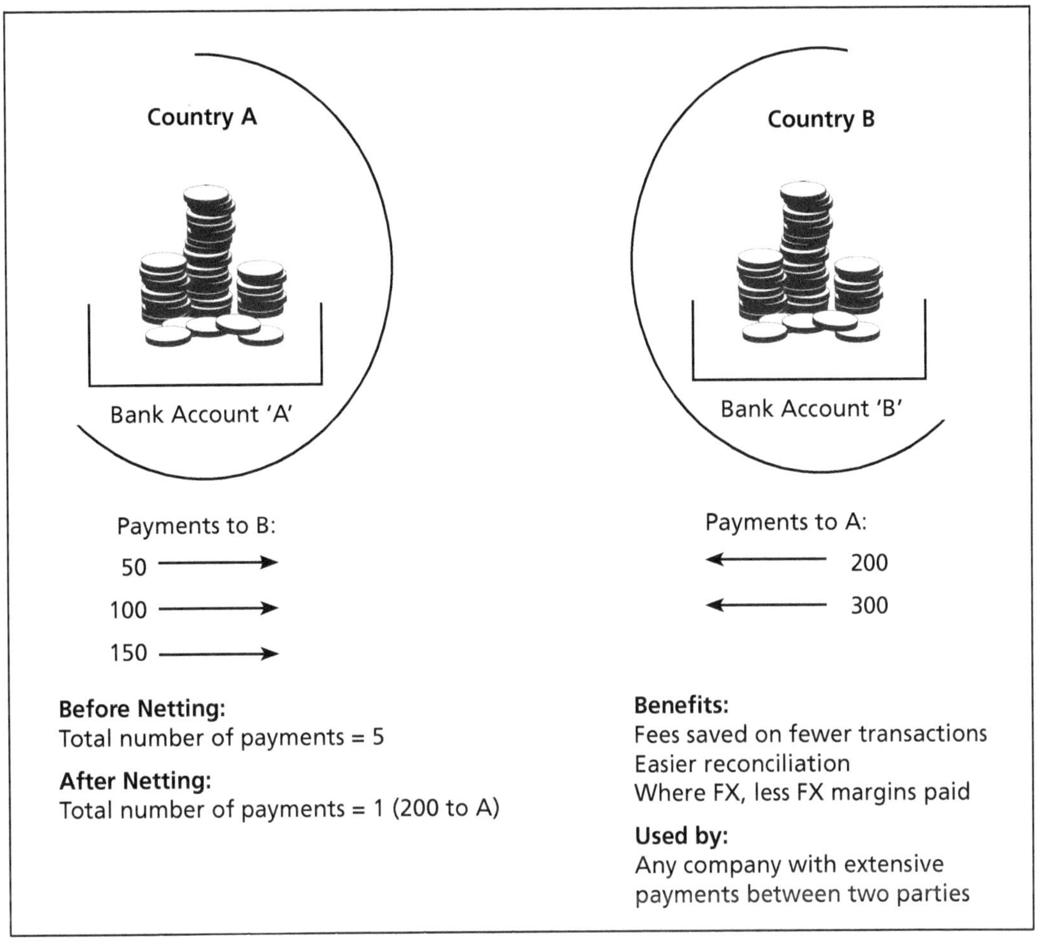

Source: IBS Publishing

Figure 1.10: Multi-lateral netting

	A	B	C	D	E
A		+50	-160	-10	+10
B	-50		-200	0	0
C	+160	+200		0	0
D	+10	0	0		+60
E	-10	0	0	-60	
End positions	+110	+250	-360	-70	+70

Transactions: A+B pays C, E pays D
Total transactions = 3

Benefits:
Fees saved on fewer transactions
Easier reconcilliation
Where FX, less FX margins paid

Much greater return over bi-lateral netting but need a 'lender of last resort', usually head office.

Used by large, multinational companies – highly sophisticated

Source: IBS Publishing

Figure 1.11: Bi-lateral and multi-lateral netting

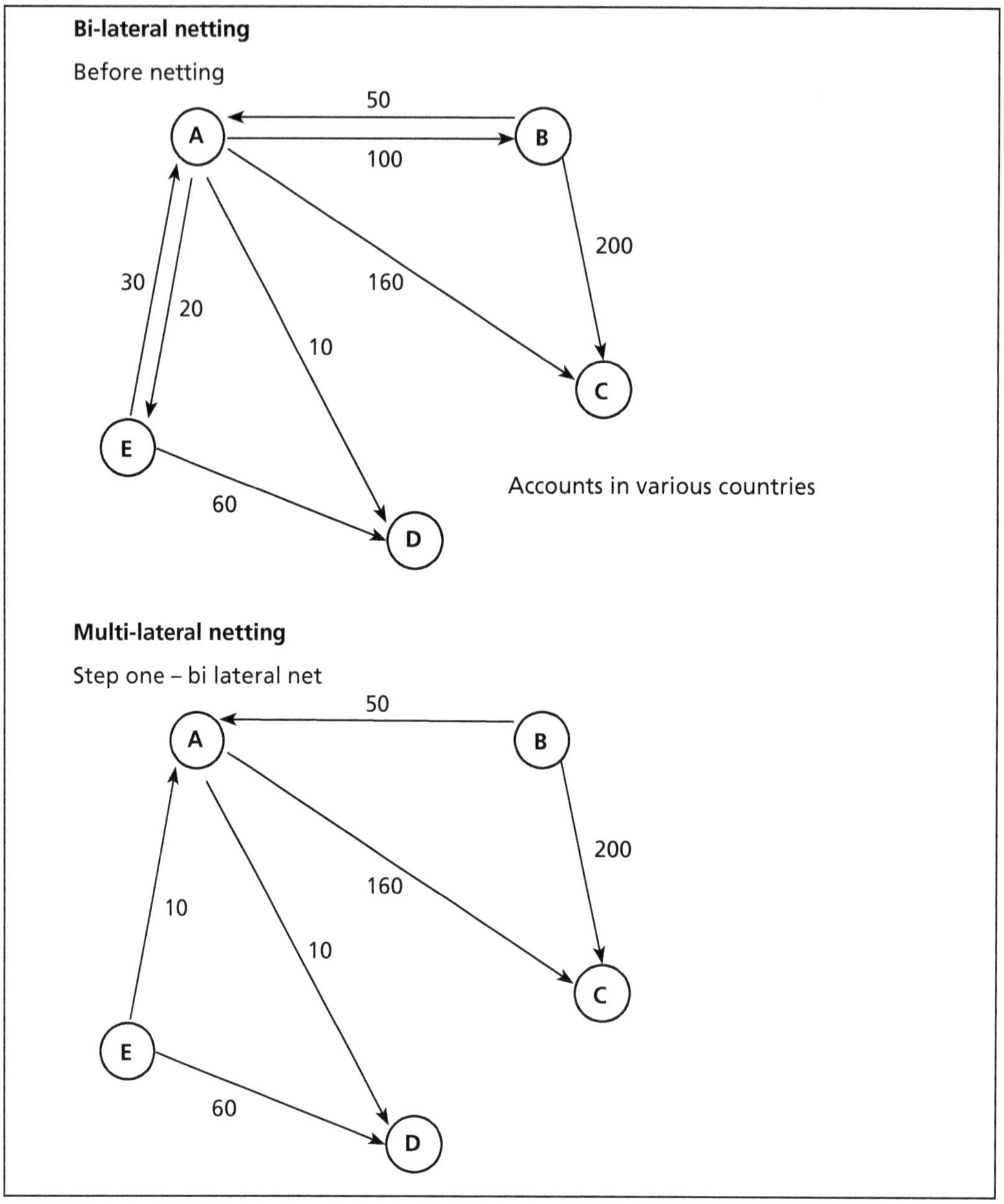

Source: IBS Publishing

The most sophisticated cash management applications for a corporate are required at this stage. These techniques are constantly evolving and often designed for a particular corporate. It is here that the largest and most advanced companies operate. It was the US companies that first started to push their banks in the 1970s to provide such services, which would help them manage their cash better. In the 1970s most banks thought a printed and mailed monthly bank account statement was sufficient. It was from the banks servicing the global companies that cash management consulting first began.

Cash management consulting is still part of many an international/global cash management's arsenal. These practices enabled many savings to be made on a worldwide basis and started the systematic automation of basic cash management. The pooling of accounts, zero balancing, and topping originated out of these studies. A further advance on these features, that are becoming quite common, is notional accounting.

Geographic approach

Nordic region vs eurozone

Compared to the solution with the rest of Europe, the Nordic setup is working more smoothly and effectively. Cash pooling has not become much easier because of the Euro. There are still a lot of barriers and the need to co-operate with several local banks, together with the European overlay bank, to make it work efficiently. With a single-bank set-up, the Nordic region, makes it seamless.

The set-up consists of local cash pools for the daily operations and a master cash pool for the concentration of liquidity. For example, in Norway, Denmark, and Sweden there are local cash pools in domestic currencies for the local Tele2 companies, with Tele2 Sverige AB acting as pool master.

In Sweden there is a multi-currency master cash pool in SEK, NOK and DKK. In the local cash pools in NOK and DKK the balances are brought to zero (target balancing) at 13:00 every banking day, through transfers to/from the master cash pool in Sweden.

Surplus balances in the local cash pools are swept to the master cash pool in Sweden via same-day-value transfers (either by intra-day or end-of-day sweeping). Deficits in the local cash pools are covered from the master cash pool in Sweden, using same-day-value transfers.

Rules on inter-company lending

Limited liability companies may or may not grant loans or issue guarantees in favour of a shareholder, director or managing director of the company or of another company in the same group of companies or to a company over which such a person has a decisive influence, unless the loan or guarantee is within the limits of the funds that are available for distribution of dividend and the loans or guarantees are adequately secured in favour of the lending/guaranteeing company.

The same applies to loan to/guarantees on behalf of any related person to the shareholder, director or managing director of the company.

Despite regulations on inter-company loans, a limited liability company may take part in a cash pool arrangement. Depending on the law, cash pooling may be allowed for any foreign parent company, as long as the parent company is a limited liability company and the amounts within the cash pool system are used for the purpose of the business of the group and not for distribution of dividends.

Any company considering loans or guarantees as described above or entering a pooling service is therefore strongly advised to consult its own legal and tax advisers, to make its own investigations and assessments of the legality and the tax consequences of this participation in the pooling service. The company should make sure that all regulations and laws are recognised and fulfilled to avoid, for example, unlawful loans, unlawful distribution of company assets and unexpected taxation, and to take into consideration, for example, transfer pricing issues.

Nordea recommends that all participating companies update such investigations and advice regularly

The technology that makes cash management work at banks

Figure 1.12 shows the complexity surrounding the bank. There are seven potential access points into the bank, from the branch through ATMs, and now the move into mobile banking. Most banks build their own core banking software platform and their own payment engine. Consequently, the ability to interface electronically with a particular bank requires a bespoke service, usually through the bank's own e-banking service. To access more than one bank often requires having each bank's own e-banking service and procedures.

The underlying technology for the majority of banks is the core banking system. These systems are often changed to meet the needs of the growing sophistication of the cash management stages. Many of the core systems are classified as legacy and need new functionality to support the supply chain. Many included the use of Excel spreadsheets to compete with other banks' cash management offerings. These spreadsheets are now seen as an operational risk and are being replaced. In many cases, spreadsheets have been banned, forcing the bank's business areas to work with the IT departments to provide an automated solution.

Figure 1.12: Payment and core banking landscape

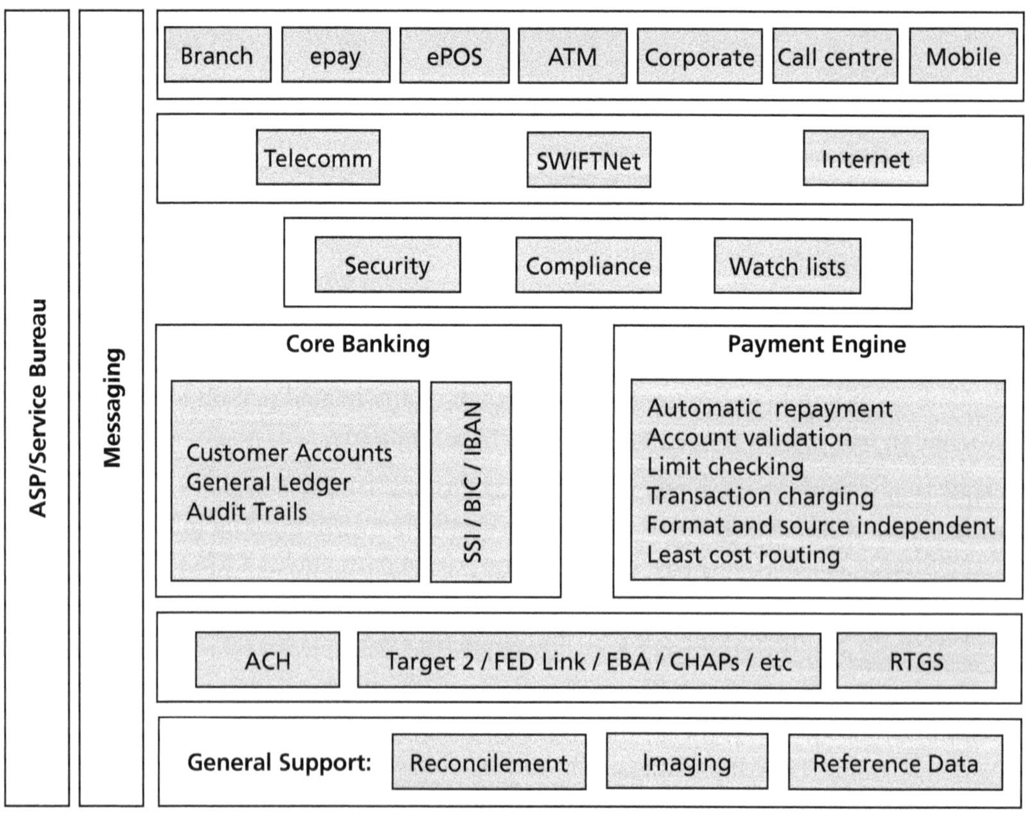

Source: Author

Figure 1.13: Core banking systems and payments landscape

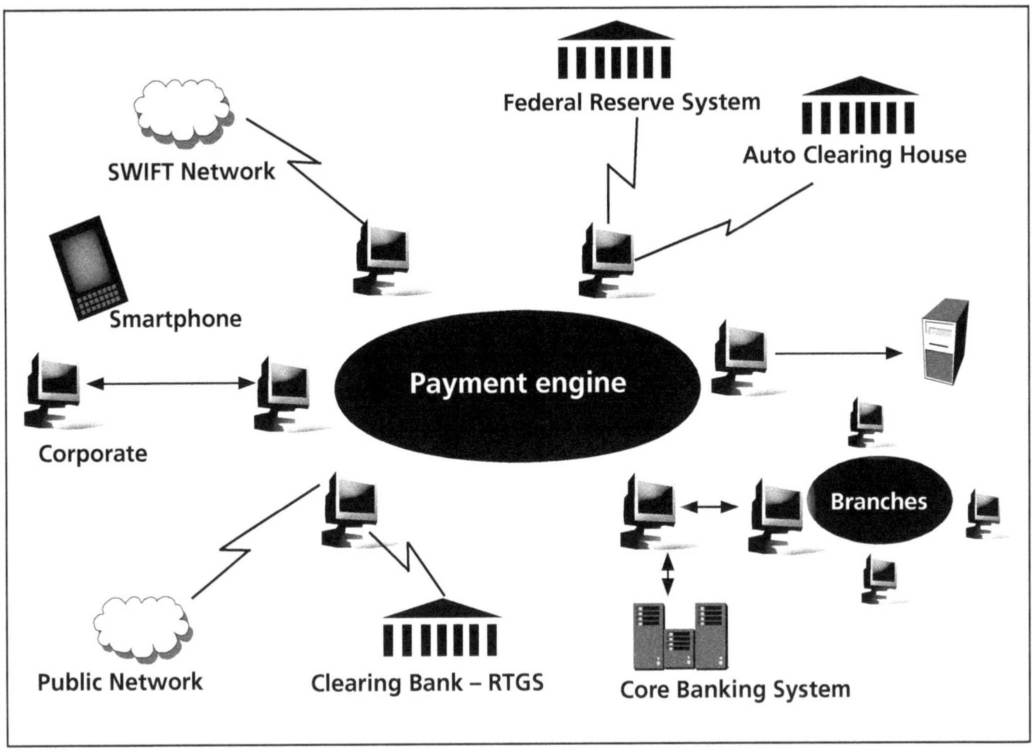

Source: Author

These changes, often requiring manual interfacing, can take the bank up to Stage 5. Beyond that, additional software is required which includes:

- Cash management modules for
  - Netting;
  - Pooling;
  - Notional accounting.
- FX systems
  - Real-time market rates;
  - Trade execution;
  - Spot, forward and options.
- E-banking
  - Internet systems;
  - Priority systems.
- Asset management systems.
- The start of cloud-based systems.

The future

Banks want to be in this market as it provides them fee-based services and an ongoing revenue stream. Each bank, depending on its market, will provide one or more of the steps and usually has a correspondent bank ready to assist in the process. The question has always been one of quality within the services offered. Unfortunately, banks thrive on inefficiencies and ineffectiveness when moving money.

Technology is starting to empower corporates as they can see how long the cash flow is taking and what fees are being extracted. Corporates are starting to take charge of the process and need to feed back poor practice to the banks. As they say, old habits die hard, and the banks, enjoying local regulations which makes opening a new bank very difficult, are like St. Augusta, who said: "Give me chastity and continence – but not yet".

CHAPTER 2

COMPLIANCE: NEW RULES AND REGULATIONS FOR BANK ACCOUNTS

Questions for the CFO, Treasurer or Cash Manager

Do I need to:

- Perform basic due diligence on my customers, suppliers and banks?
- Be aware of Anti Money Laundering (AML) procedures?
- Employ a compliance officer?

Key considerations

- State of compliance within European banks;
- AML checks and measures including Customer Due Diligence (CDD)/Know Your customer (KYC) and enhanced due diligence (EDD);
- Politically Exposed Persons (PEPS);
- US activities and their effect.

Compliance started in earnest in 2001

Since the terrorist attack on the New York World Trade Towers on 9/11 the US has led the world in trying to prevent the financing of terrorism. The initial legislation was focused in the Patriot Act, which defined regulations to prevent, detect and prosecute international money laundering and the financing of terrorism. The legislation included AML procedures and techniques that cover the banking, finance and investment communities.

Applying enhanced due diligence includes:

- Establishing an AML program –
  - Appointing a compliance officer;
  - Procedures that are kept up to date;
  - Ongoing training;
  - Audit by a third party;
- Reporting suspicious activities –
- Verification of customer identity –
  - CDD/KYC – usual passport and proof of address;
- Due diligence on the people who own/control companies with shareholdings in excess of 25%;
- Confirmation of the sender and receiver of amounts in excess of $10,000 in cash;
- Confirmation of the authorisers of foreign bank accounts.

Ongoing AML

Worldwide legislation covering AML and counter-terrorism financing (CTF) is forcing banks and other relevant financial institutions and companies to ensure appropriate measures are in place to verify the identity of customers, track and report on suspicious matters, keep appropriate records and maintain rigorous internal AML/CTF programs. The increasing complexity of the legislation and particularly the 'ongoing' nature of it means that only the very smallest are able to do this manually without falling foul of the regulators, incurring large fines and suffering the resultant reputation damage that ensues.

The US Patriot Act has been replicated in many countries around the world. The World Compliance organisation (www.worldcompliance.com) reports over 100 countries have tightened their AML laws and placed greater emphasis on cooperation between countries.

This has led to the banking community being regulated and measured against how they are performing under the various country regulatory authorities. In the UK, the Financial Services Authority (FSA) is due to be replaced by the Financial Conduct Authority for regulation in retail and wholesale markets for those firms not regulated by the Prudential Regulatory Authority (PRA), which will demerge from the FSA to be managed by the Bank of England. In the US, the regulators include the Federal

Reserve and the Controller of the Currency. In addition, the US has passed two major pieces of regulation in the form of Sarbanes-Oxley (SOX) and Dodd-Frank, which have been designed to add protection and transparency to financial activities across companies and banks in the US. It is these regulators that decide who are fit and proper people to manage the banks and the penalties for non-compliance.

The Association of Financial Markets in Europe reported in October 2011 that:

- 50% of the banks performed inadequate EDD;
- 33% have ineffective procedures to indentify PEPS (see below);
- 33% have inadequate CDD;
- 33% have very high profits from areas where 'unacceptable' risk arises.

In fairness to the banking community, prior to the world going global, the opening of bank accounts required little research, as most of the people were local and known to the banking community. Similarly, companies were locally based. Less than 30 years ago the actual information kept at the bank on a bank account was often minimal. Usually, just enough information was available to identify the owner of the account. For example, in New York, there was a legal state statute that required any bank account with money in it that had been inactive for many years to have the money in it turned over to the state. The reason was that the account was probably dormant due to the fact that person opening the account had probably moved away or died and the money was just left there. All the banks operating under this legislation would try to contact the owners through various methods, including advertisements in the local papers.

Politically Exposed Persons

PEPS, their families and close associates are considered high risk and can be:

- A senior official in a country's administration, military or political party;
- A senior executive in a foreign government-owned company;
- A substantial owner of a company tied to a particular country;
- Any family members or known close personal or professional associates of the above.

The goal is to ensure funds going to and being sent by a PEP are above the law. World Compliance has created a database of 900,000 profiles of PEPs and average 25,000 new profiles and 5,000 updated profiles per month.

Due diligence by the corporate

The onus on compliance with the various regulations lies with the financial institutions. However, it is necessary for the corporate to know with whom they are dealing, not only from a compliance viewpoint but also from a credit point of view. Most companies provide and expect services and products to be paid for within 30 days. A company with a poor credit record or one which, when applying the bank's due diligence, flags up PEPs or connected directors to other companies which have had a record of poor business practice, may be one to keep a close watch on. It is wise to maintain an ongoing due diligence program.

Ongoing due diligence would include tracking the payments due against the relative strength of that particular customer. If the payments are getting later by the month and the company's credit record is deteriorating, then the necessary actions can be taken to ensure the potential damage is controllable. Similarly, if key directors who sign off the various activities change or are reported to or investigated by the authorities, then care needs to taken to protect the company's position.

Awareness of AML is needed especially if requests to pay away to third parties are made instead of to the company itself. Companies can contra payments and often do so when the customer is also a supplier. The payment owed is contra'd against the payment due (contra is Latin for 'against'). Again, contra against a third party needs to be considered carefully to ensure compliance in terms of AML and good corporate governance.

Enhanced due diligence on customers is a good practice. It helps understand the customer better and can prevent unexpected surprises.

The determination of whether or not a compliance officer is needed depends on the offering of the company. If the company is involved in the provision of financial services, a compliance office is needed. In the majority of instances, a compliance officer will not be required.

Due diligence by the bank

Basic due diligence is information about the customer and the business relationship sought. The bank should have a clear idea of what the company is providing and what the business is about. Often, this is covered in the contacts between the bank and the company. Banks are obliged to verify the accuracy of the customer's explanation on the object and purpose of the company in order to establish the credibility and accuracy of the information.

Figure 2.1: Ongoing due diligence

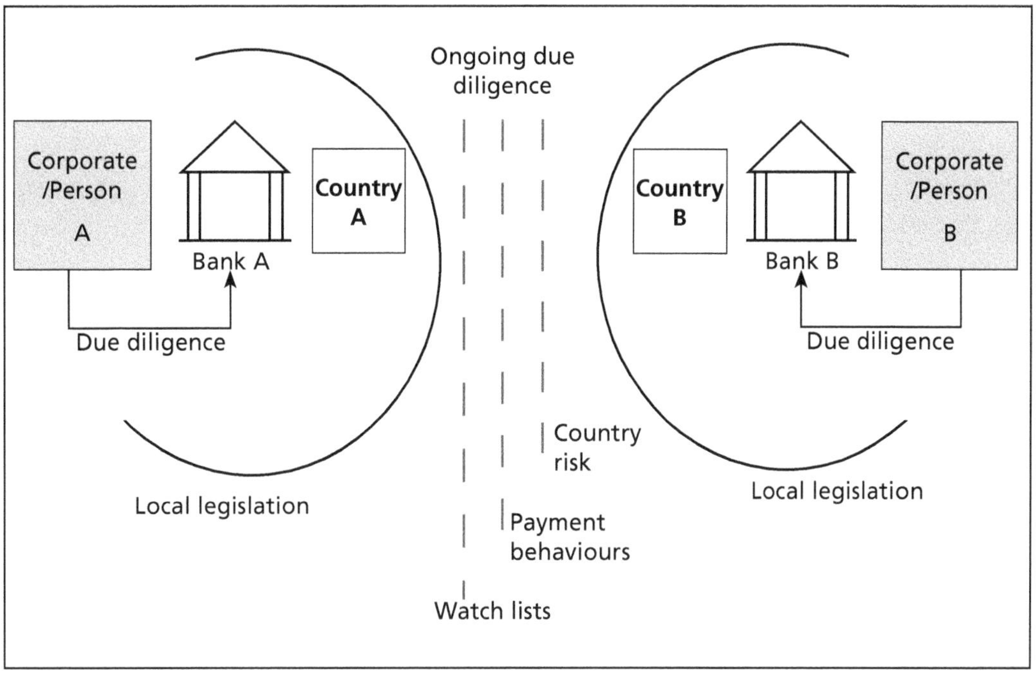

Source: Author

High risk criteria

The following circumstances should be considered high risk criteria:

- When data on the customer's identity is insufficient or not deemed to be reliable or accurate;
- When ambiguities for basic due diligence remain;
- When suspicions of money laundering or terrorism financing exist;
- When the business relationship includes transactions, services or products that may favour anonymity (e.g. use of cash);
- When the client is domiciled in, or transactions are carried out in, a country with a known record of encouraging terrorism.

In addition, extra due care is needed with a PEP who is resident abroad.

Documentation

The banks have found the easiest and quickest way to obtain information about the customer's identity and ownership structure is to ask the customer for the required information and documentation. The documents routinely requested are:

- A certified copy of registration certificate not older than three months;
- A certified copy of the share register – majority owners to undergo CDD/KYC – see below;
- A copy of the adopted business plan;

- A copy of adopted budget;
- The number of persons employed;
- All authorised signatures need to prove their ID and address (passport and utility bill).

The documents are checked for authenticity. The business plans are reviewed for logic, with heavy emphasis on cash flow. The people involved are checked against watch lists (see below) and their credit records reviewed.

Customer Due Diligence/Know Your Customer

CDD/KYC is legally required by the banking community and is tracked by:

- Document management – the definition, scanning, management and tracking of customer documentation, and reporting of any deviations;
- Account monitoring – the tracking of movements over account(s) looking for deviations outside of a pre-determined profile;
- Watch list checking – watch lists are names of companies and individuals wanted by various governments. Enter a name and the system will check to see if the name, or like sounding names, appear on any of the watch lists (e.g. Office of Foreign Assets Control (OFAC), Bank of England and others). There is control over the granularity of the name checking so as not to create too many false alerts. Messages that fail watch list checking are put in a quarantine queue for manual intervention;
- Message monitoring to check all inbound and outbound messages, irrespective of format, to see whether any field (normally the ordering customer and beneficiary) appears on one of the watch lists;
- Full audit trails of all checks and actions taken.

Anti Money Laundering

To establish a new bank account, the company needs to go through AML in addition to the bank's KYC requirements. These new requirements, coupled with Sarbanes-Oxley and Dodd-Frank in the US (financial and accounting disclosures), mean face-to-face meetings with the bank are often required. In addition, payments going out or coming into an account are screened against watch lists, as above. By law, the bank has to continually review payment transactions.

Under money laundering legislation there are essentially three obligations:

- To identify and verify customers (due diligence);
- To review transactions that could reasonably be expected to constitute or be aimed at money laundering;
- To report suspected cases of money laundering.

The purpose of the policy and the instructions are to ensure that the company's anti-money laundering and terrorist financing and other serious crime prevention measures are always adequate, appropriate and in accordance with current standards.

Banks and credit companies are subject to the criminal liability provisions of the law when they participate in certain financial transactions for a client. The new legislation provides for changes in a number of respects, including those relating to customer due diligence, providing information, compliance and enforcement. Money laundering legislation is important and difficult to apply as most legacy systems are not are designed to handle large amounts of data. Consequently, at many financial institutions procedures are layered across the existing infrastructure, often in an electronic/manual way. The legal requirements must be observed by all concerned with or working with customers and money transactions for a company's business. To this end there has to be a constant awareness and ongoing checks to ensure payments being made are legitimate.

The Financial Action Task Force, FATF (Financial Action Task Force Against Money Laundering), was formed in 1989 by the G7 countries and is active. FATF currently has a mandate to continue its operations in 2012. The organisation publishes on its website information on money laundering and its activities (www.fatf-gafi.org). There are 40 recommendations forming the basis for much of the regulation concerning measures against money laundering, as well as updates to the lists of non-cooperative countries and territories (NCCT).

The money laundering schematic

Money laundering refers to measures taken to conceal or convert the proceeds of a crime, i.e. it is about action to 'launder black money white'. There is thus a prerequisite to ensure that money or other assets are not laundered profits from criminal activity.

Money laundering is usually schematically described as a process consisting of three stages:

1. Placement stage – the placement of money in a bank or a financial product;
2. Outline stage – transactions in order to break or hinder the links with the criminal origin;
3. Integration stage – money (or what has come in its place) is integrated into the legal economy.

Terrorist financing is usually considered as 'reverse money laundering', whereby profits from crime or other illegal actions are used to fund terrorist activities This means not only to make direct contributions to terrorism, but also to collect, provide or receive money or other assets to finance terrorism. The International Working Group on Financial Action Task Force (FATF) in October 2001 expanded its activities to include combating terrorist financing.

Risk-based assessment

Customer due diligence can be achieved by a risk-based assessment, the so-called 'risk-based' approach, which means that resources should be where they are most needed, i.e. in situations where the money laundering risk is greatest. Risk-based assessment is needed of factors such as who the customer is and what activities he engaged in, which kind of service / product the customer requires, the customer's residence and the countries in which transactions are carried out – some countries carry a much higher risk weighting than others.

Enhanced due diligence is required on transactions amounting to a sum equivalent to €15,000 or more.

Customer screening

Banks need to maintain an internal database of names that is automatically populated from publicly available lists such as OFAC, UN, EU, HM Treasury, DFAT and others. Many also maintain a 'bank's own approved list'. This list has been refined from previous instances of the system reporting a potential AML suspect being genuine. This is termed a false positive – that is, it looked like a positive hit on the watch list, only to find it was a like-sounding name. The bank list ensures that next time that client's payment passes straight through. For the purposes of automatic PEP list checking, interfaces with third party lists such World Compliance, Dow-Jones and others can be made.

Changes to the publicly available lists are automatically downloaded at a frequency defined by the user (normally daily). The changes will automatically update the bank's database and, if being used in an integrated manner, a complete sweep of the customer data repository will automatically be undertaken.

This ongoing sweeping (often termed EDD), say monthly, can help insure the integrity of the bank's customer base towards the established regulations. The established banks with millions of accounts have an enormous task in screening their older clients. Here many banks tend to be reactive to the customer when they request changes or additional services. At that request, the bank checks to see if the due diligence requirements are in place. If not then additional paperwork is requested. Often the expiry dates of passports are now tracked and upon expiry a new copy is requested.

Single view of the customer business within the bank (CRM)

Banks often struggle to maintain a single customer view of what products that customer has with them. The reason is a historic one. There are often many IT systems and business silos within a bank. Core banking systems (usually where the General Ledger is held) are often at least 10 years old. Updating of the modules tends to be a patchwork arrangement as replacing the core banking engine is both expensive and risky. Consequently, many banks' IT looks like solar systems, with information held based on the service needs rather than that of the customer.

Over the last few years many banks have installed Customer Relationship Management (CRM) systems, which collect data from the many systems. The information concerning a customer is then maintained only once, no matter how many branches the customer has a business relationship with. Similarly from a compliance view, a director or beneficial owner can be viewed, no matter how many service offerings they have taken.

The amount of information that is now required, and continually is asked for by the regulators, is extensive. The data structure of older software needs to be revised, replaced or supplemented.

Account monitoring

Banks are continuously tracking customer accounts and linking multiple accounts from multiple host systems in a variety of combinations as follows:

- Aggregated, where many accounts in multiple host systems are pointed to one account and automatically analysed against a series of rules;
- One-to-one accounts are analysed against a series of rules;
- Mixed, where the user analyses host system accounts using a combination of aggregated and one-to-one accounts.

Bank applies compliance testing to bank accounts

To ensure compliance, banks have developed a series of tests that try to assess the chances of non-compliance taking place. These tests are often termed Business Intelligence (BI) rules. These sets of rules track the bank account across three main categories:

- Turnover;
- Transactions;
- Behaviour.

Turnover rules are designed to monitor and flag abnormal changes concerning daily, monthly, rolling monthly and annual activities across value, type and number of transactions.

Transactional rules are where the bank defines the transaction types that are permitted and monitored over the account. For each transaction type, the bank can establish daily, monthly, rolling monthly and annual rules in respect of the value, number, type of transaction and geography.

Behaviour rules looks for sudden and arbitrary changes in the managing of the account. For example, the account suddenly goes from dormant to active. There are three basic activities that govern behaviour over an account:

- Entry point, which looks at the type and number of transactions conducted at more than one channel (branch, ATM, telephone, etc) within a given time period;
- Distribution, that looks at the type of transaction credited to an account and how the funds are dispersed over a user-defined time period;
- Dormancy rules, where the account is marked as dormant after a user-defined period of inactivity and reports it should the account become reactivated.

Bank applies compliance to payment messages

Banks are monitoring SWIFT and clearing payment requests using the screening tools on both inward and outward messages to check that the ordering customer, beneficiary bank, beneficiary customer or country are not on any sanction list stored in the database. Messages that are deemed suspicious are quarantined pending manual intervention.

Workflows ensure that, as a minimum, two people are involved in the releasing or suspending of a message in the quarantined area. The reasons for the action taken on a message are recorded and held with the message. In the event that two clerical officers cannot agree an on how to process a message, it may be passed to a third person for final approval. Santander puts such quarantine messages in a 'hold' queue; the hold reasons are investigated and resolved.

Additional regulation

The US and the EU are leading in producing new regulations to provide transparency across the financial chain. One such regulation, which is starting to overlap both jurisdictions, is Foreign Account Tax Compliance Act (FATCA). FATCA is aimed at US persons avoiding tax through the use of offshore accounts. Any US person who has money invested outside the US needs to report and comply with the Act.

The Act includes penalties for non-compliance. Starting July 2013 any financial institution with US customers will suffer 30% withholding on US income and capital payments unless the institution has established an agreement with the US tax authorities.

Heavy fines are levied against non-compliance by financial institutions by the in-country regulators. In the UK for example, FSA fines in 2011 totalled £66 million.

The future

Banks are having to cope with an avalanche of new regulation to ensure that their clients are who they say they are, make certain that the clients are not funding terromism or crime, keep a check on payment behaviour and notify the authorities of any suspicions. This is a mammoth task, given most core banking systems are at least eight years old (source: IBS Publishing). The penalties for not complying will only grow. Most banks shrug off small fines as mere inconveniences or misunderstandings and address the situation only reluctantly. Regulators will continue to ensure best practices and compliance will not go back to the old days.

Corporates will also be assessed to who their customers are, and naivety will not be a defence. The leveller here is the Web. While it is full of both right and wrong information and needs to be checked when something out of character occurs, it is also best to check to see if any negative information is correct. It shows everyone that the company is switched on and cares.

CHAPTER 3

BANK ACCOUNT STRUCTURES

Questions for the CFO, Treasurer or Cash Manager

- Will your money be returned to you if the bank fails?
- Do you have a single view of your bank accounts?
- Can you run a central or decentralised account structure internally effectively and efficiently?

Key considerations

- Bank account safety;
- Different bank account structures that may help you:
  - eBAM (Electronic Bank Account Management);
  - Third party cash management for internal and external handling of cash.

How safe is your bank balance?

Many countries offer deposit protection schemes, which pay out should the bank default. In Europe this tends to be about €100,000 per account per entity. Consequently, having more than €100,000 in an account carries the risk, should the bank default, that difference will be lost. Sweden, for example, has seen many of its banks disappear and many people there make certain that their money is spread across many banks.

In the US there is the Federal Deposit Insurance Corporation (FDIC), a government entity that guarantees the safety of deposits in member banks; each depositor is insured up to $250,000 per member bank. In 2006, The Federal Deposit Insurance Reform Act of 2005 (the Reform Act) was signed into law. The Reform Act merged the Bank Insurance Fund (BIF) and the Saving Association Insurance Fund (SAIF) into a new fund called the Deposit Insurance Fund (DIF). This change was made effective in 2006. In 2010, the Dodd-Frank Wall Street Reform and Consumer Protection Act (Dodd-Frank Act) was signed into law. The Dodd-Frank Act established a minimum designated reserve ratio (DRR) of 1.35% of estimated insured deposits, mandates that the FDIC adopt a restoration plan should the fund balance fall below 1.35%, and provides dividends to the industry should the fund balance exceed 1.50%.

According to JPMorgan Chase, the cost of the FDIC program is running at approximately 40 basis points per year. The FDIC has close to 1,000 banks on the watch list in terms of financial health. These banks are being monitored closely and often encouraged to merge to produce a fiscally stronger institution.

While bank accounts are often covered by insurance protection programs in case of bank default, usually up to $100,000 per account depending what money is in the account at the point of default, Credit Default Swaps (CDS) provide a payout equal to that which the CDS was prepared. Terms are usually in the $10–$20 million range and from 1 to 10 years, with five years being the average. The underlying documentation is provided by ISDA (International Swaps and Derivatives Association). A CDS is a credit instrument between two parties, which can be sold on in the market by either party.

Table 3.1: Deposit protection schemes

Country	Savings limit	Coverage
Belgium	EUR 100,000	100%
Bulgaria	EUR 100,000	100%
Czech Republic	EUR 100,000	100%
	Ordinary deposit guarantee scheme applies after September 30, 2010, covers up to DKK750, 000	
Denmark		100%
Finland	EUR 100,000	100%
France	EUR 100,000	100%
Germany	EUR 100,000	100%
Greece	EUR 100,000	100%
Hungary		
Ireland	Unlimited	
Italy	EUR 100,000	100%
Netherlands	EUR 100,000	100%
Poland	EUR 100,000	100%
Portugal	EUR 100,000	100%
Slovakia	Unlimited	100%
Slovenia	EUR 100,000	100%
Spain	EUR 100,000	100%
Sweden	EUR 100,000	100%
United Kingdom	GBP 85,000	100%

Stability ratings and stress tests

The FDIC assigns each financial institution into five categories. Composite ratings of 1 or 2 mean the institution is financially sound with only minor weaknesses. A rating of 3 means that if the weakness highlighted are not corrected, then serious financial distress could occur. A rating of 4 or 5 means substantial probability of potential loss.

The European Central Bank reported a financial stability review of the euro in December 2011 – a stress test on the eurozone financial system. The report highlighted several key issues:

- Contagion and negative feedback;
- Funding strains;
- Weakening local economies – credit risks for banks and a second round of funding needed;
- Imbalance of global economies.

The first point is a universal one. Once there is a common perception that the company, individual or country needs money, the more difficult it is to obtain it. It is important that perception does not overshadow reality, so communication is key in times of fiscal trouble. It is a question of confidence, so any stress testing results, if negative, should first be addressed in-house with a plan to correct the situation; then, if needed or legally required, the plan should be explained rationally to the media.

Bank account fees

Each bank has its own policies and charges surrounding the bank account. Many charge a monthly fee plus transaction charges. The fees become complex as they are often broken down by payment channel – cheque, ACH, wire transfers, cash – and charges added for incorrect usage of the account, e.g. payments being made with no funds in the bank. If there is no money or not enough money present when funds are requested, then no movement occurs and the bank reserves the right to charge for that failed transaction. Phrases like 'insufficient funds' are used and the fees associated for rejecting items can be high. It is not unusual in the UK to be charged a £20 fee. In addition, for a direct debit to be returned, the beneficiary of the DD can also charge a fee, which too can be £20. These charges can be avoided by monitoring the cash flow though the account. Some banks offer a texting service, which shows their clients when the account is running low of funds.

Late payment fees are also high in the UK and there has been political pressure to lower them. Banks and credit card companies have responded that the fees tend to be £10–15 per item, as opposed to the £20–40 per item price range.

In addition, when a transaction has failed it is often reported to the credit bureaux. This in turn can lead to higher cost of credit or a decline in credit by banks as delinquencies result in poor credit scores. Once banks have declined credit, then those industries that specialise in higher risk situations come into play. Here credit may be obtained, but the cost of it could be much higher than the bank.

In addition to fees, a bank may have policies regarding the handling of payments. The biggest one globally is the time allowed for crediting one account from another. Here it is in a bank's interest to make that time as long as possible. In Europe, SEPA aims to formalise the time banks hold the money by suggesting a three working day standard. The UK, for example, has a three-day ACH standard, with cheques returnable within 10 days. It is up to each country to set their standards and here value dating comes into effect (see below).

Electronic Bank Account Management (eBAM)

Bank account management related to the opening, closing and maintaining of bank accounts is a manual, labour-intensive and often very slow process. It frequently involves paper-based transactions completed by visits to the bank with follow-ups by email, telephone, fax and mail.

Corporations are challenged by a lack of process standardisation from country to country, and even bank to bank, throughout the bank opening procedures. The bank account structure within a company can be extensive and complex. Bank accounts can exist throughout a corporate, especially one that has under gone acquisitions. Corporate bank accounts reside in subsidiaries. Subsidiaries can report to subsidiaries and to head office. Pools of cash may lie within in some subsidiaries, while others have no cash and have had to use external credit lines to meet obligations. Many companies lack a centralised repository for all bank accounts held. These factors can contribute to high transactional and operational costs, inefficiencies, and a greater potential for fraud and exposure to risk.

eBAM is designed to remove the extensive paperwork required when opening and changing accounts at the bank. The process has been approved by the banking industry and is made up of 15 different eBAM XML ISO 20022 standard messages.

The eBAM solution is designed for existing customers only. It is for a customer that has an established relationship with the bank, or a new legal entity for a known customer. KYC requirements are not captured in the solution, as they should have been completed at time of the original bank opening. If any additional KYC activities are required they are handled as parallel and separate activities to eBAM.

The benefits of eBAM are:

- Single view of bank accounts;
- Bank-neutral solution;
- Reduces risk;
- Increases efficiency;
- Reduces operational costs;
- Achieves compliance.

Extensible Markup Language (XML)

To support eBAM the bank and the corporate have to be able to use Extensible Markup Language (XML) messaging. XML is designed to transport and store data. The file structure within XML can be used to provide more accurate, comprehensive, flexible and adaptive data. The use of XML allows instantaneous transforming of data from one format to another format. For example, .xls is a file extension used on computers running Microsoft Windows to identify files created in Microsoft Excel. A file extension is a set of two to four characters after the last period in a file name. The benefit is by double-clicking on the file it will open up in Excel regardless of the release version.

To illustrate how the 15 eBAM XML messages may be combined, we give here below three examples of business scenarios.

Figure 3.1: eBAM - opening a bank account

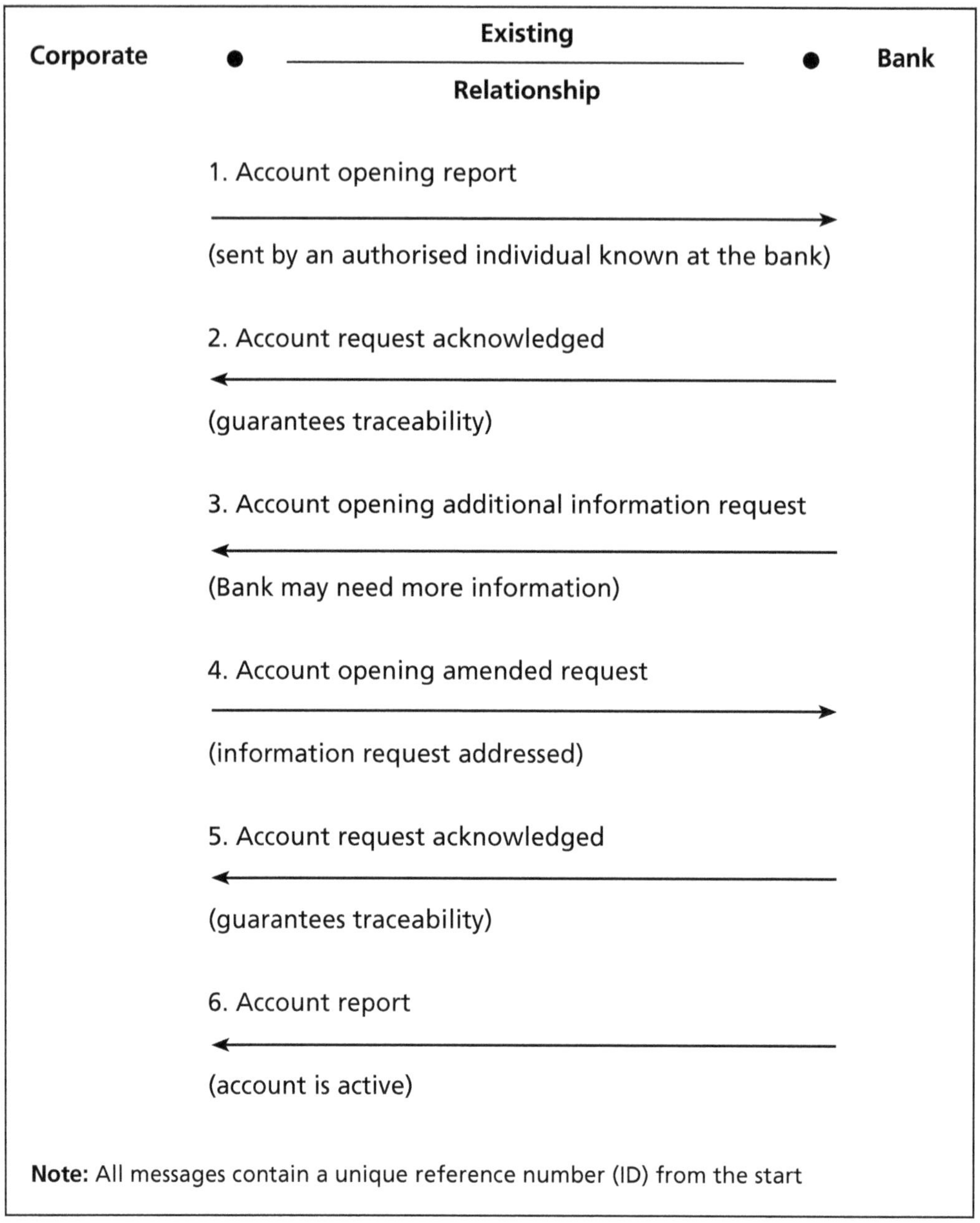

Source: Author

Figure 3.2: eBAM – account maintenance

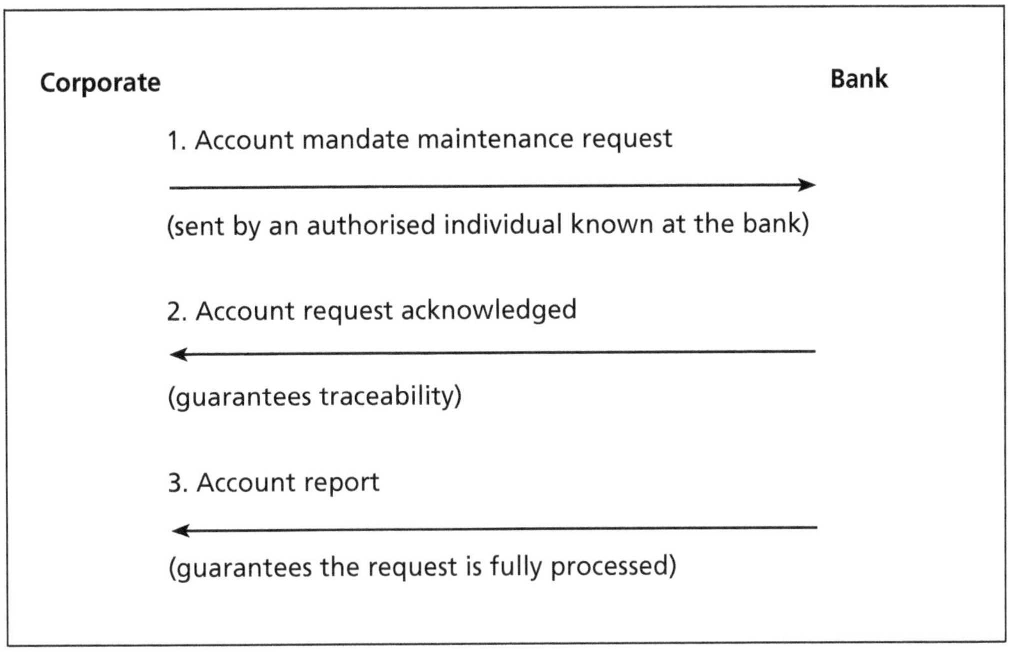

Source: Author

Figure 3.3: eBAM – account closure

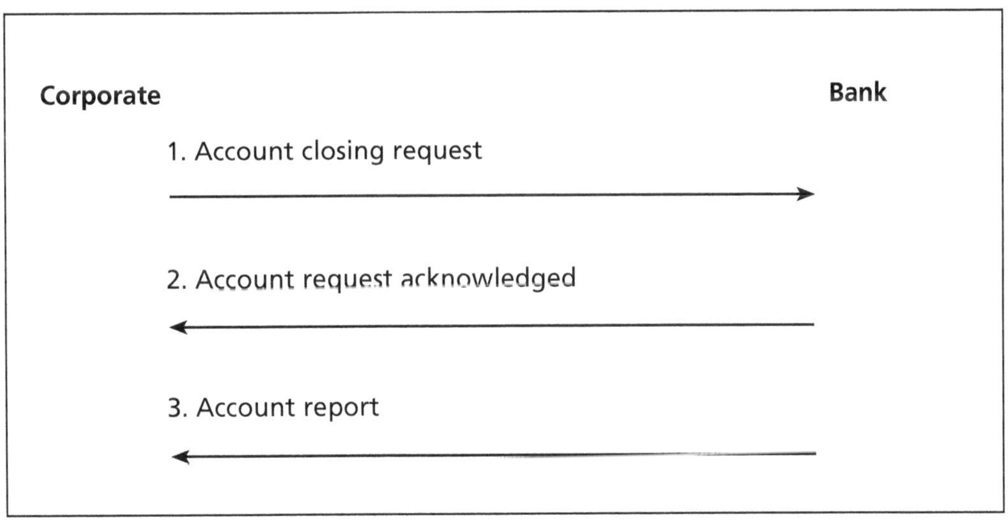

Source: Author

The other major changes that are happening alongside the internet are the increasing advance of XML, the formation of global standards for banking transactions and the ongoing advance in internet security.

XML was designed to moving information-rich documents across the internet in large volumes. It addresses the format of the document itself. With XML, information is structured and can be added to a document through tags and relationships. There can be no pre-defines and XML documents can be defined by applications or style sheets, and importantly, processed at either end by computers. It is this ability to create messages from documents that can be reviewed, amended, approved, verified and distributed electronically that is most exciting. Any document, regardless of initial structure, can be delivered to a bank and be processed electronically.

Banking mandates

Managing bank accounts involves the exchange of information on individuals authorised to perform financial transactions from the designated bank account(s). This information – commonly known as bank mandates – includes:

- Name;
- Function;
- Financial limits up to which one individual is authorised to order transactions;
- Financial limits up to which two individuals can authorise;
- Actual (physical) signature(s) of the individual on file.

Currently, this information is captured on paper on a 'signature card' and held at the bank. With the eBAM solution, the signature card is often not needed because the related information is within the XML message.

In addition, although the developed XML messages capture the core of the information needed to manage bank accounts, it is virtually impossible to replace the entire set of paper documents that is used today, due to the lack of harmonisation between/within banking groups; the lack of harmonisation between countries/regions; and legal constraints based on each country's laws.

As a result, banks and corporates can complement the XML messages with these paper documents in electronic format. This data is attached as a file. In such cases these documents may often have to be digitally signed to comply with security requirements. Three business needs requiring digital signature at individual level have been identified:

1. Signatures of authorised individuals (e.g. CFO, Treasurer, Cash Manager);
2. Digital signature of the XML message containing the information on authorised individuals. This signature can replace/complement the signature on the main mandate (the signature is that of the individual at corporate level);
3. Digital signature of an attachment to the XML message containing the non-standardised information and paper documents.

Message delivery can be sent over SWIFT. SWIFT's FileAct messaging service allows for electronic transportation of different items under different formats (XML + attachments in non- XML format) over SWIFTNet. Specific rules have been defined for the FileAct header info fields to enable transportation of eBAM-related information – XML and/or attachments.

Value dating

This is the time when a credit to the account can actually be used. The credit may be posted to the account, and seen on the account, but the actual use of funds is only available once the 'credit' instrument has cleared. The use of value dating helps protect the bank from monies not arriving from the other bank should the transaction be returned unpaid from the other bank.

Figure 3.4: Value dating

Bank Account	Today	Day 1	Day 2	Day 3	Day 4
Balance in Account	1000	-	-	-	-
Value dated transactions (2 days)	500	500	500	-	-
Available for use	1000	1000	1500	2000	2500
Balance	1500	2000	2500	2500	2500

Note:
Funds available for use lags balances.
If payments are made when the balance is there but the funds are not available for use, fees are often charged.

Source: IBS Publishing

Value dating is used heavily with paper-based items and foreign currency payments. To place value dating within some parameters, for cross-border payments the European Union requires banks to make payments within an agreed timeframe (five working days), after which a bank's customer can ask for compensation. Especially around foreign drafts (paper payment orders), banks often give a three-week estimate and point out that the fees involved to process a foreign cheque may be substantial. The bank handling the paper in the country upon which the cheque or draft is drawn may also add an additional fee. Any cheque or draft from one country to another for less than $25 is probably going to be worth very little after going through the collection process, which involves administration charges.

Often a bank sees the transactions that are value dated and allows transactions through based on the relationship with the customer.

Figure 3.5: Value dated transactions

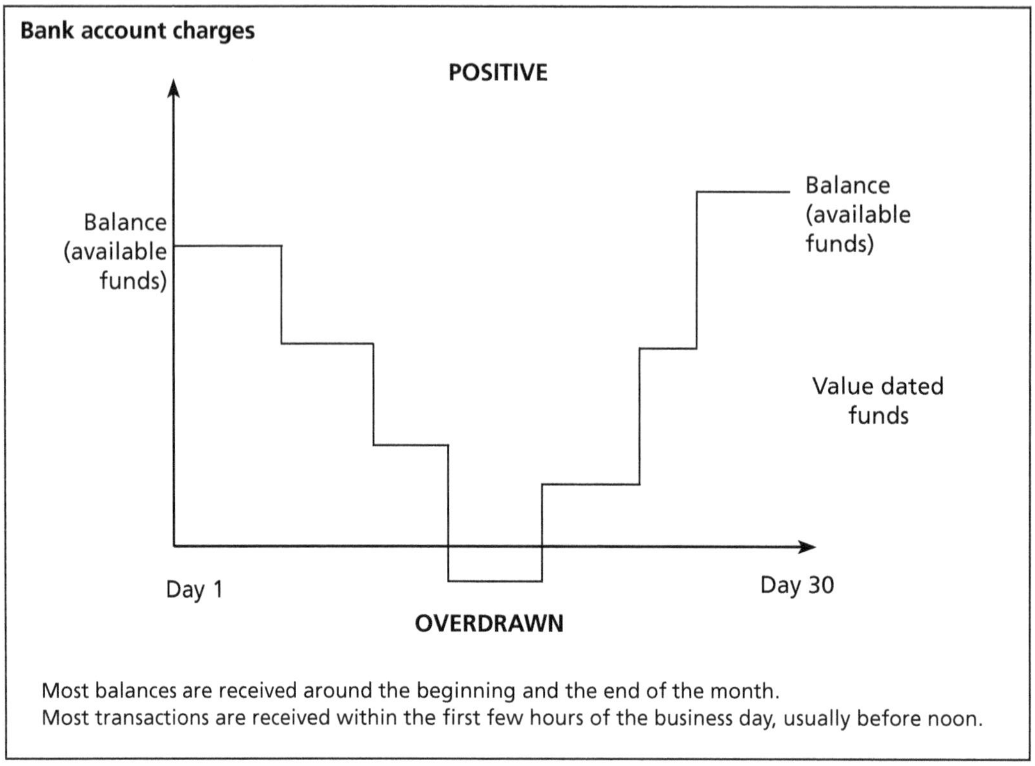

Source: IBS Publishing

Credit attached to the bank account

It is becoming common for a bank to attach an unsecured revolving line of credit to the bank account, which is called an overdraft. The bank sets the level of overdraft, known as a credit line, based on creditworthiness. However, many banks now issue a small line – usually up to $500 to cover requests for money when the account is low. In many cases the cost of returning that request is often more than the request itself. A normal charge for an overdraft in the UK is 12–15% per annum. The charges are calculated and taken out of the account by the bank at the end of the month. If the amount being accepted by the bank exceeds the overdraft limit, then an unauthorised fee is charged. These fees are charged at a premium rate for the amount of time the account has been in overdraft. These charges can also be a factor of the country's base rate. For example, in the UK, an unauthorised overdraft can be many times the standard central bank rate, e.g. 30% against 0.5%. Authorised overdrafts in terms of revolving credit limit, interest rate levels and set-up and maintenance fees, are often negotiated between the bank and its client.

Branch foreign exchange rates

Most banks in Stage 1 can make international payments for their corporate customers. The process is often manual, with forms to be filled out explaining why and to whom the payment is going. There can be a charge for the foreign exchange transaction along with the foreign rate at which the amount is to be exchanged. Most branches are issued with a 'branch rate sheet' and a limit up to which to go before a call is needed to a foreign exchange dealing centre.

Figure 3.6: Branch foreign exchange rates

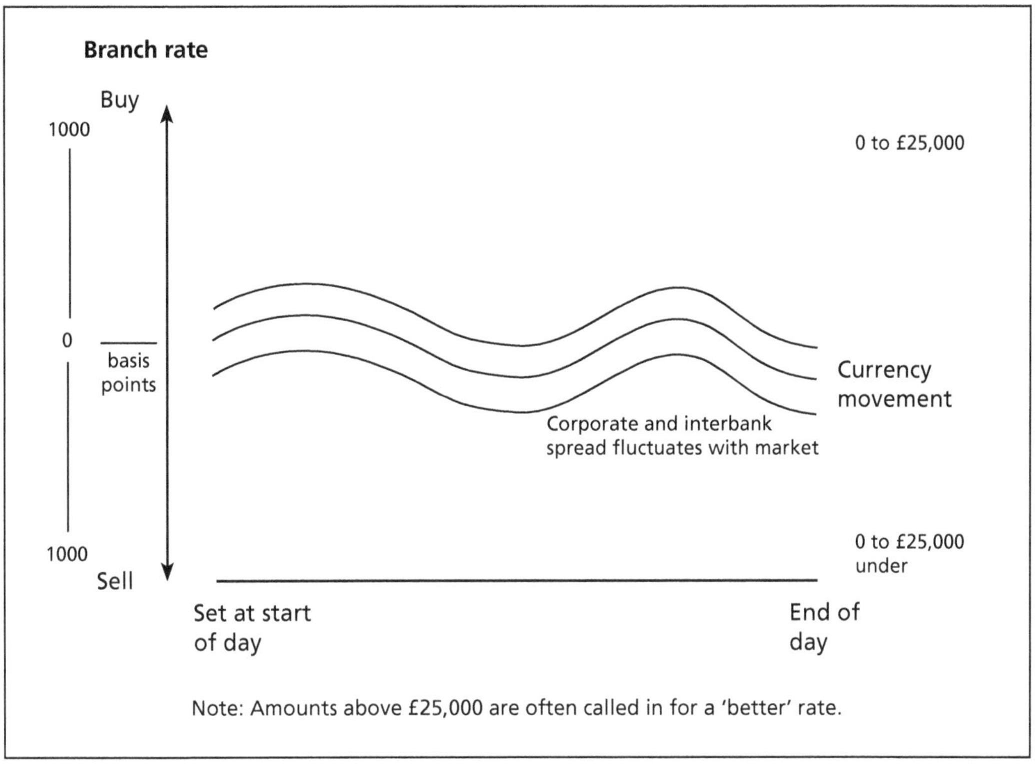

Source: IBS Publishing

The branch rate usually good up to $25,000 and the foreign exchange rate used is often the 'tourist rate' for individuals. These rates are shown as 'buys or sells' and the difference between the two is called the spread. In the dealing room a spread on USD and EUR currencies is normally 5 basis points (0.05%) as the currency amounts being traded are so large. The average interbank transaction is called in numbers of millions. The average corporate payment is usually under $100,000 and the average branch rate amount is under $1,000. Consequently the branch rate for an USD/EUR rate spread can be 300 to 500 basis points (0.003% to 0.005%). The spread on $10,000 is $5 for the interbank market and up to $500 for the branch. Therefore the smaller the foreign exchange transaction, the more expensive it becomes. The cost for the bank does not change with the amount, so small trades cost the same as larger trades.

Bank accounts for third party cash administrators

The client cash account is centred on the 'other parties looking after your money' concept. The money has been transferred into an account, and only an authorised person, not the person who the money belongs to, can approve payments. These authorisers – both individuals and companies – are called third party cash managers. Often found in many different corporate sector verticals, they may include insurers, solicitors, local authorities, rent collection agencies, pension administrators, trustees, internal banking for corporations, asset management, and broking.

The process is as follows. The third party operates like a bank, with the actual money staying in the bank. Cash receivables are collected from the individual or corporate into one account. This account is reflected at the bank. The cash is then moved to accounts that can be set up instantly for cash to be paid out (accounts payable). The account holders can request payments and the administrator authorises the payment.

The need for third party cash management goes beyond the traditional commercial transaction-based activities. Increasingly, social factors are creating new groups of people who are generating burgeoning demand. One such group comprises the people suffering from dementia. Dementia UK noted in a report to the Alzheimer's Society in 2007 that there were then 700,000 people with dementia in the UK; this figure is expected to rise to over 1 million by 2025. Clearly, people suffering with dementia are likely to need third parties to handle their money. Another group comprises people who have a difficult time handling debt, which until the crisis was freely available and plentiful.

Another group comprises those individuals who would like some trusted persons to look after their money. Bankers used to be one of the most trusted professions after doctors and the clergy, but the financial crisis has taken its toll. In 2011 the Chicago Booth/Kellogg School Financial Trust Index noted only 23% of those surveyed said they trusted the US's financial systems, down from 25% in June 2011. A poll by Ipsos Mori for the BBC in the UK showed 70% of people had yet to restore their faith in banks now they had returned to profit. This leaves a very low level of confidence in the banks today.

The trusted third party can organise the cash flows by taking money at source – accounts receivable – then setting aside money to cover the regular commitments, and then paying away. Access to the account can be given to both parties so that they can see what has been paid and what is outstanding.

Client cash structure: today and tomorrow

Figure 3.7 provides an insight into the client cash relationships between the bank, the customer and the end clients. For each end client, the customer will have a ledger account opened on behalf of the end client. This is the conventional structure today for banks handling client cash using only a ledger-based solution.

Figure 3.7: Virtual account model

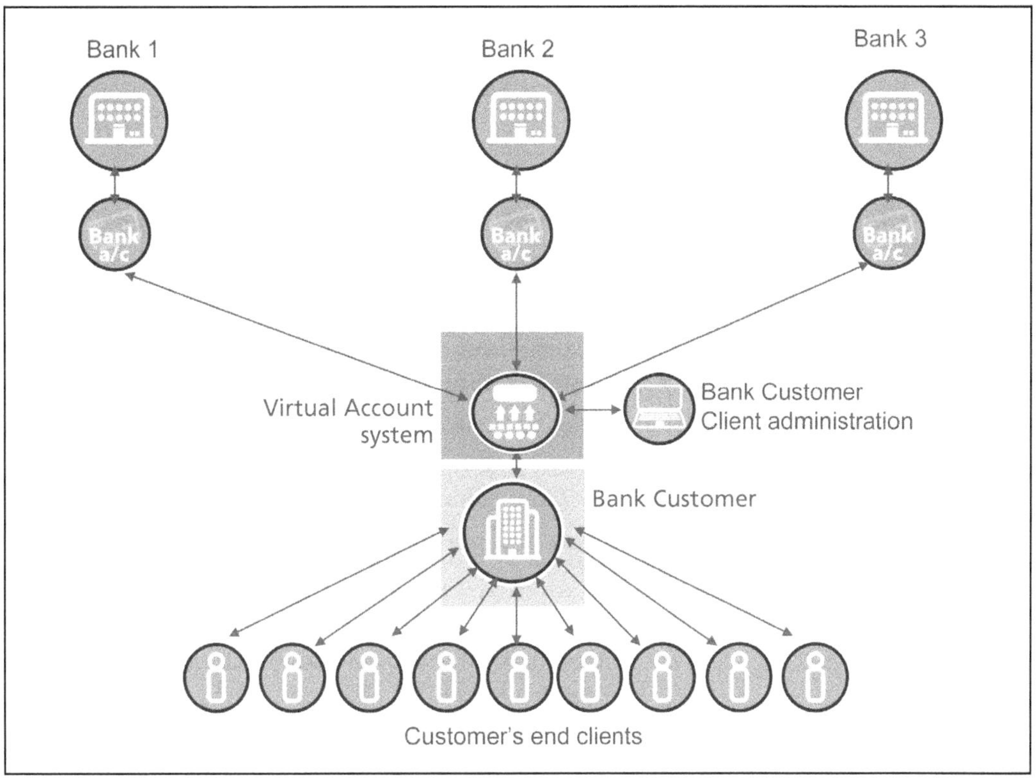

Source: Author

Figure 3.7 shows the same relationship under a virtual account model. The customer holds a single pooled account with the bank, which is an aggregate balance of the customer's client cash deposits with the bank. The end client's accounts are opened as virtual accounts and the total nets out with the total of the pooled account.

The virtual account model substantially reduces the number of bank ledger accounts and bank administrative resources required to operate a client cash service, whilst offering significant downstream customer benefits.

Benefits of client cash

The nature of the third party cash management business creates an extend chain of customers. Client cash offers a range of benefits for each of the customers in the extended customer value chain.

	Bank	• New business exploits scale economies of virtual accounts with minimal additional back office investment • Enhancement of capital adequacy positions (FSA and the Federal Reserve allows client cash to be counted as retail deposits) • Ability to offer different interest rates tied to certain accounts and the third party manager • Application of charges at account level • Bank branding
	Bank's customer	• Customer-friendly online access and control of virtual account structure • Near real-time client cash visibility across all accounts • Service efficiencies and administration cost savings requiring smaller back office • Customer's branding can be applied
	Bank customer's end client	• Access to near real-time information on individual accounts • Beneficiary of improved client service from reduced delay in the customer chain.

To illustrate the benefit, take the example of a conveyancing solicitor who is completing a house purchase for a client. With a ledger-based system banking system, a 'real' account is opened and managed by the bank on instructions from the solicitor (customer) on behalf of the house purchaser. Payments and receipts to the account are applied on the bank system with advice/confirmation by telephone and statements generated at the end of day. This convoluted situation is at its most acute when the home purchaser is awaiting confirmation of transfer of funds to the vendor to complete the property transaction. The customer experience is particularly poor, as multiple calls between the customer value chains are required, exponentially increasing the opportunity fees incurred by all parties.

Many of the global banks have developed bespoke solutions to service their client cash market. In essence, this top-tier group is able to take a long-term view of the market and so often will invest in developing a solution to meet their major clients' requirements.

The cost of in-house management of the multiple bank accounts held in the bank by the third party manager on behalf of their clients can be substantially reduced. For example, one of the largest UK property companies employs 10 people to simply reconcile the receipts and payments for rent, rates, insurance, cleaning and other services across their portfolio of properties.

The client cash market for customer deposits is growing. The reasons include the move out of more risky stocks and shares to that of a cash position. Many investors use the maxim of selling once a level of loss has been released – 10 to 15% – and then keeping that money until the market settles down. In the UK a popular line was to sell in May and buy in September as the markets historically hit a summer dip in share price.

Consequently, stockbroker funds, the legal and other professions are holding greater levels of cash as clients become more liquid as seen in the Bank of England statistics.

Figure 3.8 provides an indication of the total market size, showing deposits to MFIs by non-financial and other financial sectors had grown from £1,169 billion in 2005 to £2,394 billion by the end of 2010, and that third party deposits grew at a compounded rate of 18% per annum over the three years from March 2007 to March 2010.

Figure 3.8: Deposits to MFI by non-financial and other financial sectors

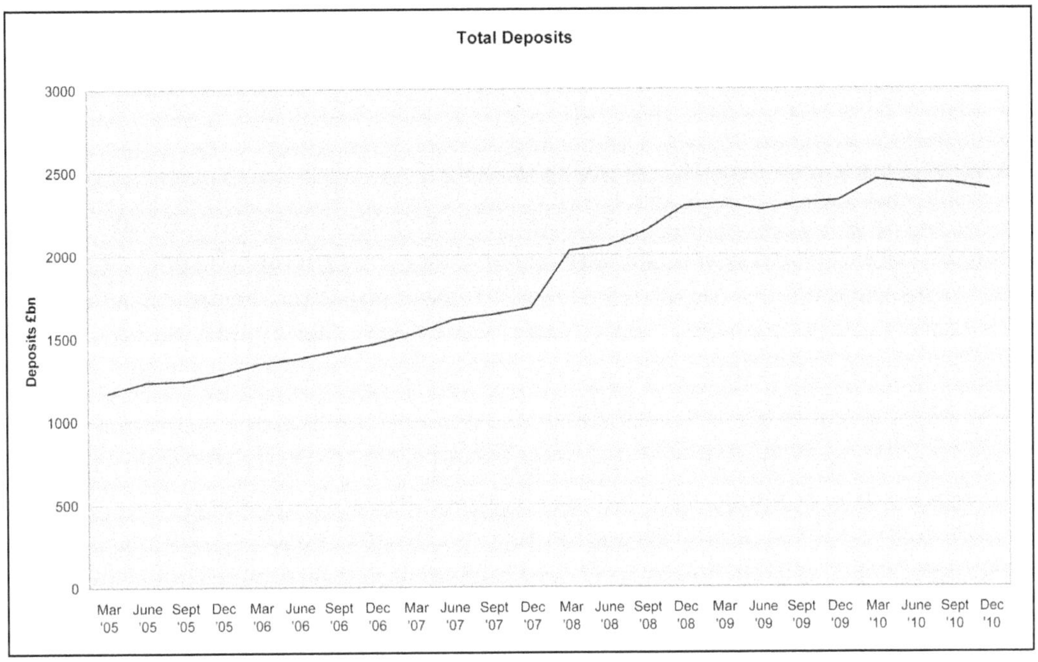

Source: BoE statistics 2010

Bank – today (with little automation)

The bank has the third party cash manager (intermediary) open up many bank accounts for their clients under the intermediary's name. Usually, one account is opened per client. However, depending on circumstances, two or more accounts may be opened for the same client, for example when cash-generative assets have to be kept, or family members have active trust accounts. The bank takes on the administration of the banking activity and often mails or emails the statements to the intermediary for them to reconcile. The bank awaits the telephone call to make the necessary adjustments, often a month later.

Bank with third party accounts (full automation, complete STP)

The bank only opens one account for the intermediary – the pooled account. The responsibility for reconciling the account remains with the third party cash manager; however, there is only one account at the bank. (An intermediary is often one with 10 or more accounts at the bank). One UK clearer estimates the cost of opening one account instead of 10 saves £630 per annum across the core banking infrastructure.

Intermediary – today

The intermediary has to provide administration to open and manage the client accounts at the bank. Each month the printed statements are matched against the companies' own records, with any changes involving a time-consuming procedure.

Intermediary with virtual accounts

The intermediary can open many accounts for a single client immediately. The pooled account with the bank is matched against the client accounts automatically each day. The mismatches are highlighted and ready to be resolved. Each account is assigned a unique reference number.

Corporate employing third party accounts

Corporates can become third party managers for their own companies. The above structure can be layered across the existing bank account structure. The bank accounts feed the information into the third party's centralised structure. The central is then able to see where the money is located, and from the centralised pool (no actual money has moved), the third party manager can authorise transactions, resulting in subsidiaries receiving the cash as agreed.

The bank sees a reduction in bank accounts, often from at least 10 per third party to one. This saves on administration within the bank. One UK bank estimates it costs £80 per year to provide the infrastructure and support for a bank account. They also see a build-up of deposits as the money is pooled into one account from many, both within the bank and from other institutions.

The cost of a third party looking after other people's money is about the same as a packaged bank account, i.e. from £10 to £20 per month for active accounts, with inactive accounts often at a much lower level. The chief benefit from the payment side is that only payment instructions will be executed provided there are sufficient funds in the account.

The future

Most banks will continue to offer bank accounts and will not explicitly inform the holder if the account exceeds the insurance level. Others may notify you, although regulations for companies operating with other people's money are responsible for the money's safety. The chances are high that companies with client money under management will see a neutral third party holding the money and await their instructions. With today's technology the money can be moved almost instantly and it does take away the temptation of another Lehman or GF Global using client's money for their own use.

Corporates will map their activities more closely to the information on the money themselves and make virtually instant payments. The tracking of the money will be in safe accounts with known fees and conditions and changing as the business evolves.

CHAPTER 4

LIQUIDITY MANAGEMENT AND CASH CUSHIONS

Questions for the CFO, Treasurer or Cash Manager

- How big is your cash cushion in terms of operating expenses, months and amounts?
- Are your cash forecasts within 10% of the actual cash for the quarter?
- How liquid is the organisation in terms of percentage of assets and within asset group?
- What is the trend in the liquidity over the last 18 months?

Key considerations

- Liquidity is paramount;
- Banks' new capital requirements will affect us all;
- Cash is king in times of economic uncertainty and stress;
- There are different degrees of liquidity – not all assets are comparably liquid;
- Cash cushions should be factored in and used as a fall-back when needed.

Liquidity management

The need to stay liquid is paramount. During these financially difficult times, banks are selling non-core assets to meet their regulatory obligations. Banks also need to manage intraday liquidity as they are receiving and paying out large amounts of money throughout the day.

A report by SWIFT in 2011 showed the priority requirements for banks today were:

- A view on intraday cash positions (93%);
- Ready-made liquidity risk analytics and business intelligence (91%);
- Advanced interactive cash and collateral management functions within payment infrastructures (88%);
- Ability to build predictive positions (88%).

While the trading floor often knows its actual cash position across assets within seconds, because of their size and complexity, banks often do not know. The best example of this was the Board of Royal Bank of Scotland, which when asked what its capital position was, noted that it ranged from 4% to 8% – a spread of billions of dollars, reflecting the complex nature of the business and a lack of internal coordination resulting in the inability to give an accurate figure to which it could be professional managed.

Figure 4.1: Liquidity management for a bank

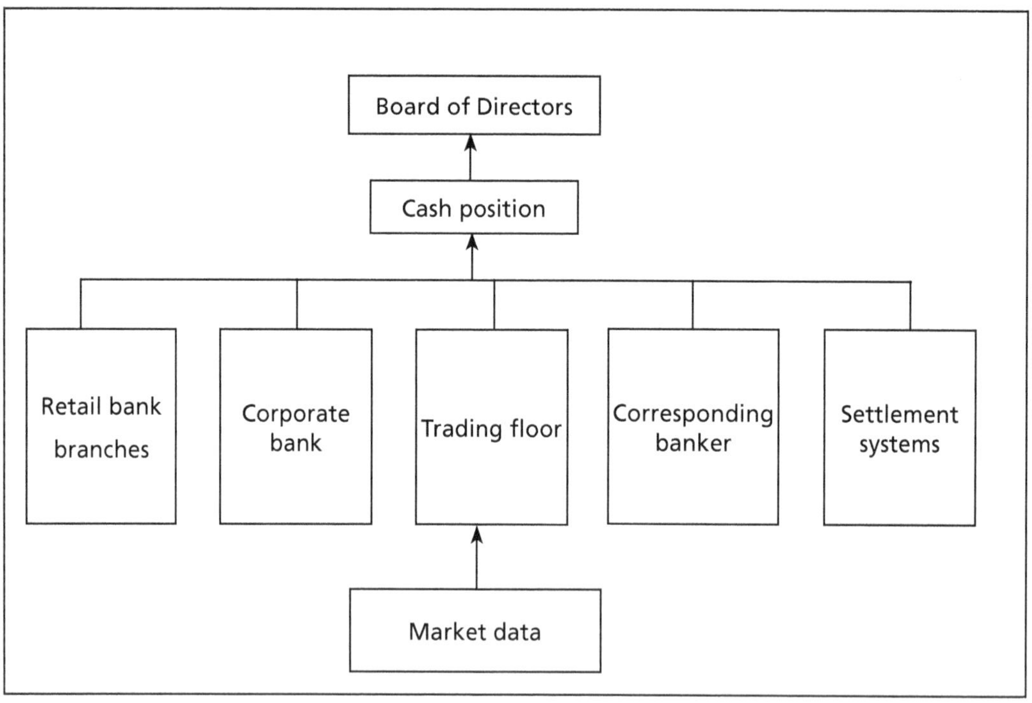

Source: Author

Liquidity management is the ability to pay bills when they become due over an acceptable time horizon, usually 12 months. Often companies have a three-month time detailed cash horizon and then a 12-month rolling average. Liquidity is now a main concern for everyone. Many check the balance on their bank account on a daily basis. This is becoming easier with e-banking and m-banking. Companies, up to and including Board members, are now requesting liquidity reports.

Intraday liquidity in clearing and settlement

Liquidity in real-time services is needed in a country's wire transfer systems. These systems are under the watch of the central bank. The systems in the UK and US are called CHAPS and CHIPS respectively and are managed by the Bank of England and the Federal Reserve. The reason is that the central bank is the lender of last resort should one of the Bank's default on payment. Without liquidity, the system would become gridlocked and stop. This almost happened during the fiscal crisis in 2007 when banks would not extend credit to other banks in the same country. The central bank was the only bank the others would trust.

Deutsche Bank has been monitoring the cost of the central bank extending credit – this is on top of the overdraft charges being charged by the central banks of the US, Canada, Japan and Switzerland – over the last six years. The costs increase during times of crisis, as can be seen in 2007 and 2008 during the sub-prime crisis and 2011 during the euro bond crisis.

Year	2006	2007	2008	2009	2010	2011
Cost of intraday credit	22	90	190	12	25	70
(Basis points)						

As central banks' systems cannot become gridlocked, the more modern systems, such as the one used by the Estonia Central Bank operate on the principal that each participant needs to deposit money into the system at the start of day. Should that deposit be paid away, no more payments are made until more money has arrived in the participant's account. This can happen in two way: credits are received during the day, and/or the participant bank adds more deposits.

Timing, measurement and collateral to cover shortfalls is now part of the intraday process. High quality liquid assets are needed for collateral. This needs to be monitored to ensure it can be mobilised quickly to cover any shortages.

Pricing intraday liquidity

Banks are regulated individually, so the price of liquidity will vary by bank. The Bank of England's view is:

- Defaulters pay – Need to know credit risk;
- Tiered participation – DVP (Delivery vs. Payment), RTGS, central bank money;
- Resolution – Living will – just in case a bank suffers failure the payment system participation continues through the insolvency process.

Few banks price intraday liquidity at this time. However, there is a growing sense that intraday pricing will start. One approach is to reward payments made at the start of day and charge them at the end of the day. This method of pricing may be used across corporates and financial institution clients to get them to transfer money without leaving gaps in liquidity that result in unwanted float. The kind of intraday pricing could well be like train fares during the business day, which rise and fall dependent on demand. The highest intraday pricing will be geared towards the end of day. At the end of day, if the payment is made and there is no credit to cover it, then collateral is used. The bank then pays the cost of the collateral and would need to amend its terms and conditions to pass the costs incurred onto the 'last minute' clients. Figure 4.2 shows the hierarchy of credit cover as Bank A makes three payments throughout the day without receiving payments or changing the deposit position. The end result is the central bank covering the position or not making the payment. Bank A needs a loan from the central bank to cover its position. In 1985, the Bank of New York had to borrow $23.6 billion overnight from the Fed due to a software fault. The bank was worth much less than that at the time, and paid $5 million in overnight interest.

Figure 4.2: Intraday money flows

Scenario

Three payments into the system by Bank A and none received
First payment uses up deposit
Second payment uses some of the collateral
Third payment uses more collateral and may be rejected or credit extended by central bank

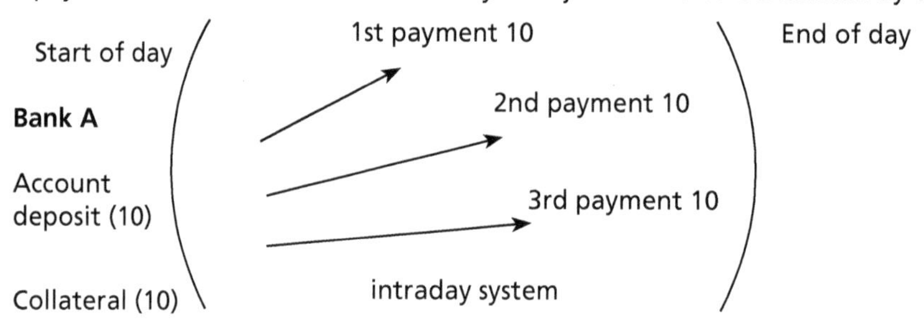

Central Bank

		1st payment	2nd payment	3rd payment
Intraday position	10	0	0	0
Collateral	10	10	0	0
Central Bank credit	0	0	0	-10

Source: Author

Delivery versus payment (DVP) is a technique borrowed from the security market. The delivery of the security (in paper or electronic form) is instantaneously paid for with irrevocable funds. Today, the banking industry can use this technique with large payments by matching them by amount to the buyer and seller before releasing the funds to both parties.

Reduction in bank lending capacity

The banks have been particular squeezed in this area over the last few years. The regulators are requiring banks to have more liquid assets (capital adequacy) to cover unexpected events. The term liquidity covers cash and cash-like financial instruments offered in the money markets, such as commercial papers (basically IOUs) and repos (a sale and repurchase agreement). Unfortunately, the credit crunch has seen a 'retreat to quality', making issuance for many banks at an acceptable rate of interest difficult.

The proposed Basel III is recommending a 15% capital adequacy ratio, as compared to Basel I, which was 8% for the smaller banks. Banks are allowed to lend money up to the level of the capital held back to cover unexpected events. Under Basel I the bank could lend a 12.5 multiple of the amount on deposit. By 2019, the multiplier will drop to 9.5, a reduction of close to 25% in lending terms. Also, the types of collateral that can be used is now greatly scrutinised and has to meet the 'Cash Outflows over 30-Day Stress Test', reducing the assets available for liquid collateral. Wells Fargo estimates that under the new Basel III proposals they will need to add 26% more capital under the new rules just to maintain the equivalent of their current Tier 1 capital of 9.35%.

Figure 4.3: 30-day cash outflows

Cash outflows over 30 days			
Retail deposits	0% term	5% stable	10% less stable
Unsecured SME deposits		5% stable	10% less stable
Wholesale deposits for operations			25%
Unsecured wholesale funding		75% Government Corporate	100% others
Secured funding backed by collateral	0% level 1	15% level 2	25% Government
Margins used above calculated by asset class			

Source: Author

To offset this reduction in lending capacity, banks have become very prudent concerning whom to lend to and often review their lending book to reduce exposure to sectors they believe require greater risk management. Consequently, the flow of credit funds has been reduced and the cost of these funds has increased. In addition, administration costs have risen as the level of due diligence has increased, both through new regulations and in terms of KYC and AML (see Chapter 3).

Credit scoring

The main methodology of assessing credit is the use of credit scoring, and each bank scores credit in its own way. On the consumer side, outside agencies often score out of 1,000 points based on the use and repayment of credit. In the corporate market, credit reports show the company's history, with many giving an indication of creditworthiness at that point in time. These reports are only used as a guideline for banks in their own assessment of credit risk. The key to a good credit report is making payments on time, consistently. In addition, the most recent three months are of intense interest and any missed payments are regarded as very serious. Any blemishes in this period will overshadow the previous few years of credit history.

Degrees of liquidity

Assets held by a company should be graded by degrees of liquidity – i.e., the time it takes for the assets to be sold and converted to cash. Ownership of various items needs to be listed and an estimate made of the time to convert to cash, forming a 'liquidity pyramid'. The same pyramid can be used with cash forming the base and non-liquid asset at the top. Every asset has a value and a time it would take to sell, either in part or whole. Owners of property can sell it completely, or take out some of the equity, or, if a company, sell and rent back the property. Each of these events causes cash to be raised. The timeframe can be six months to a year.

The higher up the assets are in the pyramid, the less liquid the company is. The loss of liquidity results in less flexibility being available to make decisions and take action. This is often referred to as 'mortgaging the future'. Control over highly illiquid assets is often lost and market forces tend to take over.

Cash and the flight to safety

The level of interest rate rises with the level of risk of the proposed investment. It is a balance between earning better interest rates and the chances of the return of the cash being extended. The bank is often prepared to pay more interest based on time and certainty of the money not being taken back. Consequently, the level of interest rises the longer the money is set aside. Also, terms and conditions surrounding longer-term money can result in bonuses and fines based on time. The bonus can be kept if the money is held another three months after term and an extra amount of interest is received. The fines are applied if the money is taken out before the term, where normally no interest is paid. But the significant factor is: will the money be returned?

"Cash is king", as the saying goes, and as reported in CFO.com in December 2011, the latest report from REL Research shows public companies in the US continue to hold cash at record levels, with 1,000 of the largest companies holding $850 billion in cash. A further $800 billion is unnecessarily tied up in receivables, payables, and inventory. Corporate filings through June of 2011 show that as revenues have increased over the past year, so has cash on hand, with companies now holding 11% more cash than they did in Q2 of 2010.

Total debt also increased by 7% during the period, indicating that companies are taking advantage of low-cost borrowing opportunities to increase their cash on hand. Companies are beginning to incrementally increase the amount of cash they are putting to use for purposes such as paying dividends, making capital expenditures, and share buy-backs. Companies are now taking 2% longer to collect from customers, and are holding nearly 2.5% more in inventory. Companies actually improved payables performance slightly, offsetting some of the losses in other areas.

It is a perpetual balance for a company between collecting the money in before having to pay it out. Most want the luxury of being paid immediately and then enjoy as much time as possible before paying out. In a zero-interest environment there is little to be gained by this practice, except the good feeling of having money in the account. It also provides a good track record to show the bank when going for credit. While some or all of it is required elsewhere, it does provide a sense of comfort, and often a false sense of confidence – beware!

The working capital numbers in the research clearly show that, while companies managed to right-size their working capital in late 2009 in response to economic challenges, they lost focus once revenue growth returned, and the improvements made were not sustained. Companies become less efficient as accounts receivables grow, and they hold more inventory.

Cash cushions

Having cash in an account that is waiting to be paid away is not the same as a cash cushion. A cash cushion is designed to be able to handle events, both positive and negative, which demand immediate cash. The phrase 'saving for a rainy day' covers this behaviour. In the proposed Basel III regulations, a cushion of up to 2.5% is being promoted. Hence, in the event of an adverse change of business, the first 2.5% can be absorbed as business as normal.

The financial crisis has seen a change in behaviour towards money. Companies are holding cash, with cash positions well above the 2007 levels. Going forward, the identification of a cash cushion should be determined. This way companies can see what they have as a fall-back position should difficulties arise.

Cash cushions should be considered a permanent feature and reviewed on a regular basis, say every six months. The level of 2.5% as for banking should be considered as a measurement level for companies. Each company should clarify what that means financially. This analysis is often called stress-testing.

Stress testing

Stress testing supposes abnormal events that are plausible and compares this against the status quo. For example, how would a drop of 20% in revenue affect the ongoing solvency of the company? Similarly, how would a call from the bank to return 20% of the credit extended affect the future?

The future

Banks will end up capitalised to the requirements of Basel III by 2019. Many countries will insist on a higher capitalisation. In the UK, the Vickers Report is ring-fencing the banks' retail businesses from their investment and trading activities. The report recommends a capital ratio of 10% in risk-weighted assets (RWA) and a further 7–10% cushion to absorb any unexpected losses. That means that the UK retail bank will be capitalised at 17–20%.

Like the banks, corporates will begin to report cash cushions. The availability of such reserves brings a level of confidence to shareholders, stock exchanges and regulatory bodies, as companies with cash cushions are showing prudence.

CHAPTER 5
PUTTING CASH TO WORK

Questions for the CFO, Treasurer or Cash Manager

- Is any money in the company earning any interest?
- How predictable is the stable money in the bank accounts?
- How can we get more certainty into our cash flow?
- Do you do stress testing on the cash flow?

Key considerations

- How to put cash to work effectively;
- Islamic banking;
- Interest rate forecasts;
- Taking advantage of stable balances.

Earning interest

Most banks recognise the need to provide a return on the balances in an account. The birth of the NOW account in the US recognised this need and banks offered accounts with perpetual interest being applied to any balances. Interest is dependent on the country; for example, France does not permit interest to be earned on certain bank accounts. Islamic banks do not permit interest at all.

Islamic banking

The Institute of Islamic Banking and Insurance (www.islamic-banking.com) states: "Islamic banking refers to a system of banking or banking activity that is consistent with the principles of the Shari'ah (Islamic rulings) and its practical application through the development of Islamic economics". The principles, which emphasise moral and ethical values in all dealings, have wide universal appeal. Shari'ah prohibits the payment or acceptance of interest charges (riba) for the lending and accepting of money, as well as carrying out trade and other activities that provide goods or services considered contrary to its principles. While these principles were used as the basis for a flourishing economy in earlier times, it is only in the late 20th century that a number of Islamic banks were formed to provide an alternative basis to Muslims although Islamic banking is not restricted to Muslims.

Islamic banking has the same purpose as conventional banking except that it operates in accordance with the rules of Shari'ah, known as Fiqh al-Muamalat (Islamic rules on transactions). Islamic banking activities must be practiced consistent with the Shari'ah and its practical application through the development of Islamic economics. Many of these principles upon which Islamic banking is based have been commonly accepted all over the world, for centuries rather than decades. These principles are not new, but arguably, their original state has been altered over the centuries.

The principle source of the Shari'ah is the Qur'an, followed by the recorded sayings and actions of Prophet Muhammad (pbuh) – the Hadith. Where solutions to problems cannot be found in these two sources, rulings are made based on the consensus of a community of learned scholars, so long as such rulings to not deviate from the fundamental teachings in the Qur'an.

Islamic banking does allow fees to be charged. This is transparent when buying and selling goods for cash and Islamic banking works well. The fee for activities for which interest is used needs to be redefined as a fee, which meets the needs of an Islamic customer. Here new Islamic methods of finance have been developed which were approved by a recognised Islamic scholar. Cash management is as important in the Islamic world as it is elsewhere.

The ability to move cash instantly removes a number of barriers for Islamic banking. For example, having same-day FX removes the need to fund the two-day wait for one of the currency pairs to arrive. Both currency payments occur at the same time, meeting Islamic requirements on completing a commercial obligation there and then.

Linking the savings module to the bank account

The most common is the linking of a savings module to the bank account. The two accounts often have different numbers and are kept separate from each other. The company can manage the funds in either account by instructing the bank to move the money between the two. Often, should the bank account go overdrawn, the savings account remains as is unless the bank has an automated system and agreement with the corporate to move the money between the separate accounts. Overdraft charges tend to sharply overshadow the level of interest the bank is prepared to pay on a savings account.

Figure 5.1: Bank account with savings account

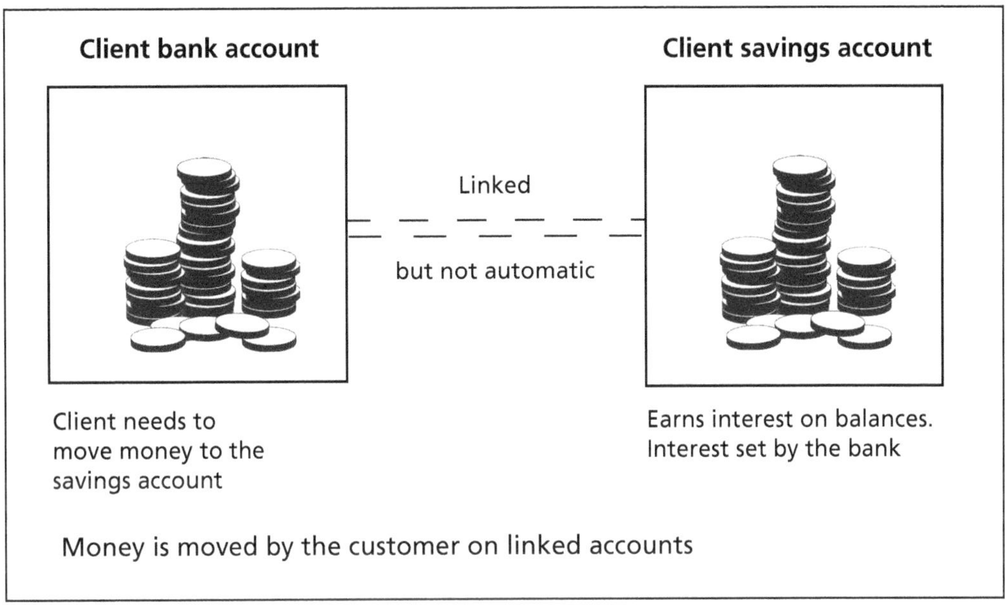

Source: IBS Publishing

Outside investments

As the balances in the main account grow, some banks have the option to move money into higher interest paying accounts outside the bank offerings. To take advantage of these accounts, the minimum amounts being moved start at $25,000 increments. Depending on the bank, the number of outside investments can be high, with a wide variety of risk available. The level of risk is clearly indicated and the corporate is advised of its nature. These outside-the-bank investments have lead to many corporates having an investment policy on the level of risk being undertaken. There is a hierarchy of risk levels, especially in bonds, which start with ratings by the major agencies from A+ downwards. Outside of bonds, money market and commercial paper, few corporates invest elsewhere, with virtually none in equities.

Figure 5.2: Outside investments

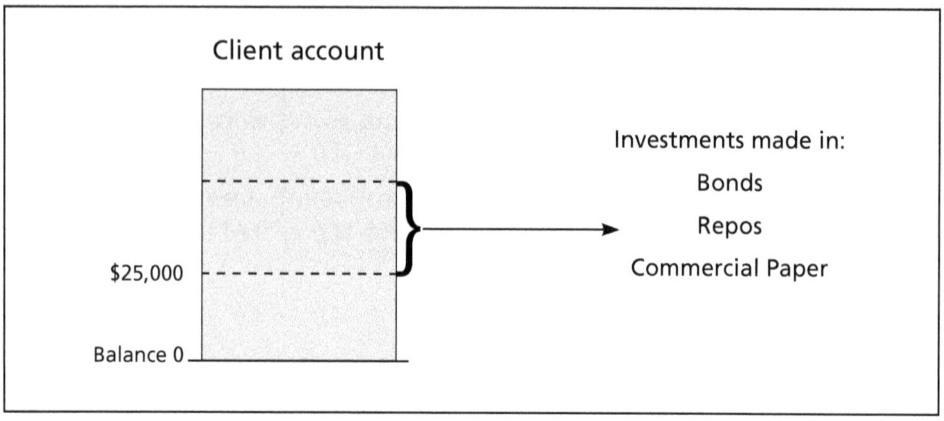

Source: Author

Forecasting cash flows

Over time the pattern of money flowing into the bank account becomes predictable. Often a company has peaks and ebbs in its accounts. The account can be reviewed to see which monies can be invested for a longer period. Banks often pay more interest on monies put on deposit for longer times. Hence, corporates with established balances can earn more money by moving day-to-day savings into longer-term commitment – seven or 30 days or three or six months.

Figure 5.3: Company balance over time

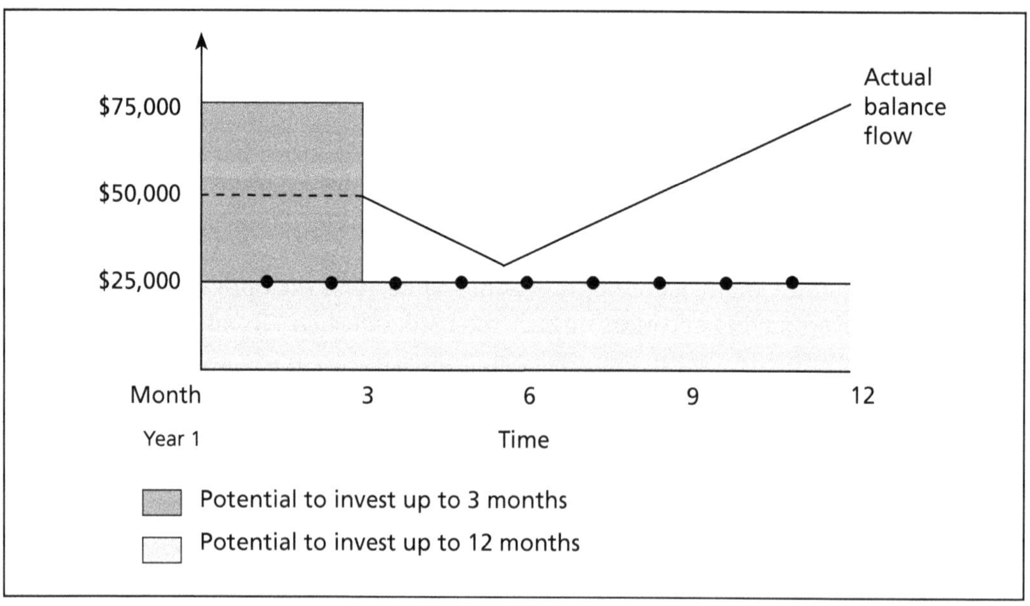

Source: Author

The area of forecasting money both into and out of the account has received little attention to date. Most banks do not offer any services around this area of cash management. Corporates are also guilty of not forecasting cash flow for accuracy.

The entire need for forecasting the future financial health of the company is changing. In the US in particular, the Sarbanes-Oxley (SOX) legislation asks directors for comment on the future. The Australian Stock Exchange also requires companies with a negative cash position to file accounts showing estimated cash flows over the next quarter. The goal for regulators is to create an early warning system to help prevent major corporate disasters such as Enron and Worldcorp and financial institutions such as Lehman Brothers and MF Global. The forecasting discipline being demanded by the regulators can also be helpful to banks and corporates.

Predicting revenue and expenses

The keys for generating a cash forecast are revenue and expenses. The expenses side tends to be the easier of the two to predict. Most companies' costs lie in people. Given many countries' employment laws, these costs, depending on the length of service the people have with the firm, should be considered with a minimum of three months' break. In most cases, when layoffs are required there is money set aside to meet the financial redundancy needs. However, the payroll should be forecast as it is today for the next 12 months, adjusting each quarter to the changes in the company head count.

Revenue is the most unpredictable, as is the cash arriving into the bank account. It is common to see company financials on a quarterly basis compared with the same time period 12 months prior. While proceeding through the financial year, the half year should be compared to the half year 12 months prior, and, similarly, the 3rd quarter compared to its prior year's counterpart. Similar cash flows should be forecasted. In this way, the next quarter's cash and 12-month rolling forecast can be reviewed and actions made to improve the cash collection and to make determinations on the cash distribution. In addition, the business can foresee potential shortages or excesses

The revenue component can be split into two – recurring revenue and all other. Recurring revenue is common in many sectors, for example insurance and software. Here clients have agreed to pay monthly or quarterly revenues tied to signed contracts. (The best contracts are those that exceed three years or more as they can be securitised and used as collateral should additional funds be required). Most companies have a combination of the two. The next step is to turn this into predictable cash. The best way to do this is to sign up a direct debit (DD). Not only does this make the cash 95% predictable, it also guarantees the cash will arrive on a certain date.

A few banks are starting to work with corporates in assisting them in forecasting the cash needed over the next four quarters. This is initially being done with the larger or more visionary institutes. Forecasting does change the relationship, with one Japanese bank pointing out their intention of a joint plan so as to become more intimate with their clients. The IBM Institution of Banking for Business Values in Banking report 'Fit, focused and ready to fight' echoed the Japanese view that 'customer intimacy will generate client loyalty'.

Figure 5.4: Forecasting company balances going forward (1)

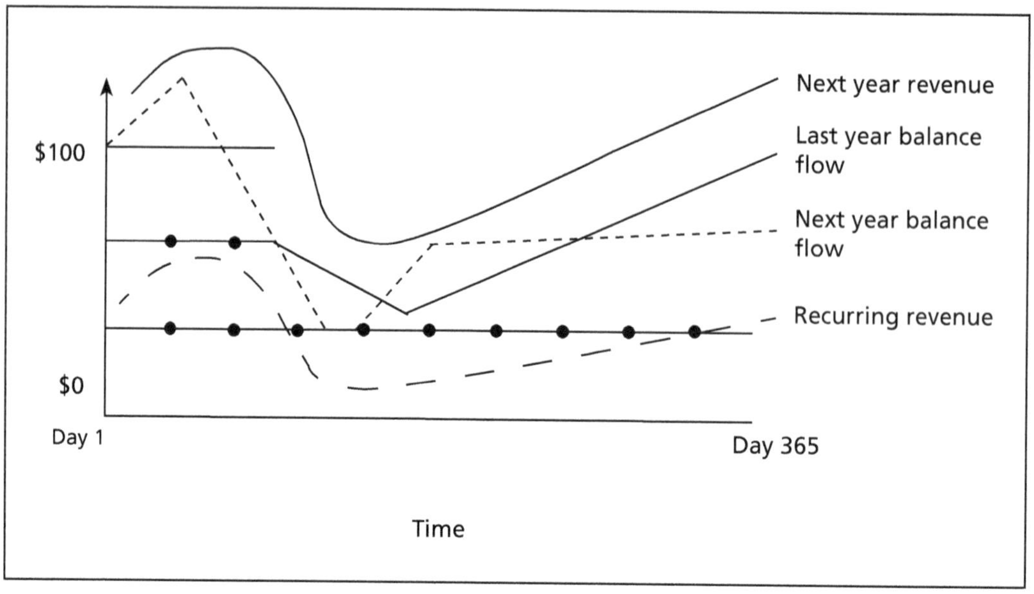

Source: Author

Figure 5.5: Forecasting company balances going forward (2)

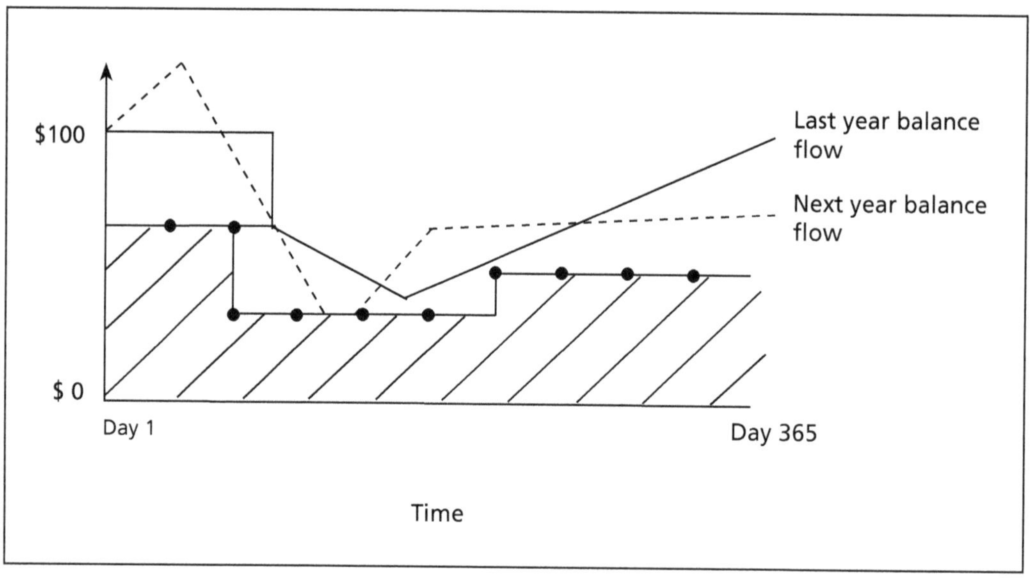

Source: Author

Making money on the money

The worldwide environment for interest is based on the level of risk of the instrument taking the money. The safest investment in which the principal is guaranteed to be returned is offered by the banks themselves, with insurance protection programs. The rates the banks are offering are very low and could stay that way for the next few years. Most economic forecasts are similar to the Wells Fargo economic forecast 2011 in Table 5.1.

Table 5.1: Wells Fargo economic forecast 2011

Country		GDP	
	2011	2012	2013
Global	3.50%	3.20%	3.70%
Advanced Economies	1.50%	1.50%	2.10%
Developing Economies	5.90%	5.30%	5.70%
USA	1.70%	1.50%	2.10%
Eurozone	1.50%	2.00%	1.90%
UK	0.90%	0.80%	1.70%
China	9.20%	8.20%	8.60%
India	7.30%	7.10%	7.70%
		3 Month LIBOR	
Interest rates	**2011**	**2012**	**2013**
US	0.50%	0.50%	0.45%
Japan	0.20%	0.20%	0.20%
UK	1.00%	0.70%	0.70%
Eurozone	1.20%	0.70%	0.70%
		10 Year Bonds	
Interest rates	**2011**	**2012**	**2013**
US	2.10%	2.50%	2.60%
Japan	1.05%	1.15%	1.16%
UK	2.40%	2.70%	3.00%
Eurozone	2.20%	2.60%	2.80%

As central bank interest rates have fallen to the lowest level in recorded history (for example, the Bank of England rate is currently 0.5%), to help prevent an economic depression the interest rates offered by the banks themselves have also fallen. Historically, banks are the first to drop interest rates when the central bank lowers its banking rate, but often lag when the interest rate rises. An increase in the bank interest rate gives the commercial banks a window of opportunity (usually four to six weeks) to increase the spread between the cost of the money to the bank (interest paid out) and the money they earn on loans.

The central bank rate is the basis of rates charged to those banks borrowing from them. Each country has its own central bank looking after that country's currency.

Given the current global economic situation, the GDP of the advanced economies is expected to grow 1.5–2%, while the developing economies' estimated growth is 5–6%. In other words, the developing countries are expected to grow three times faster than the advanced ones, as is made clearly evident by the rise of the economies of China and India.

The interest rates now being offered by banks for immediate use of money is extremely low, often 0.01%. These rates climb based on agreements involving the length of time money is put into the market (for example time deposits) and amount. See Figure 5.6.

Figure 5.6: Interest rates vs. time (UK, December 2011)

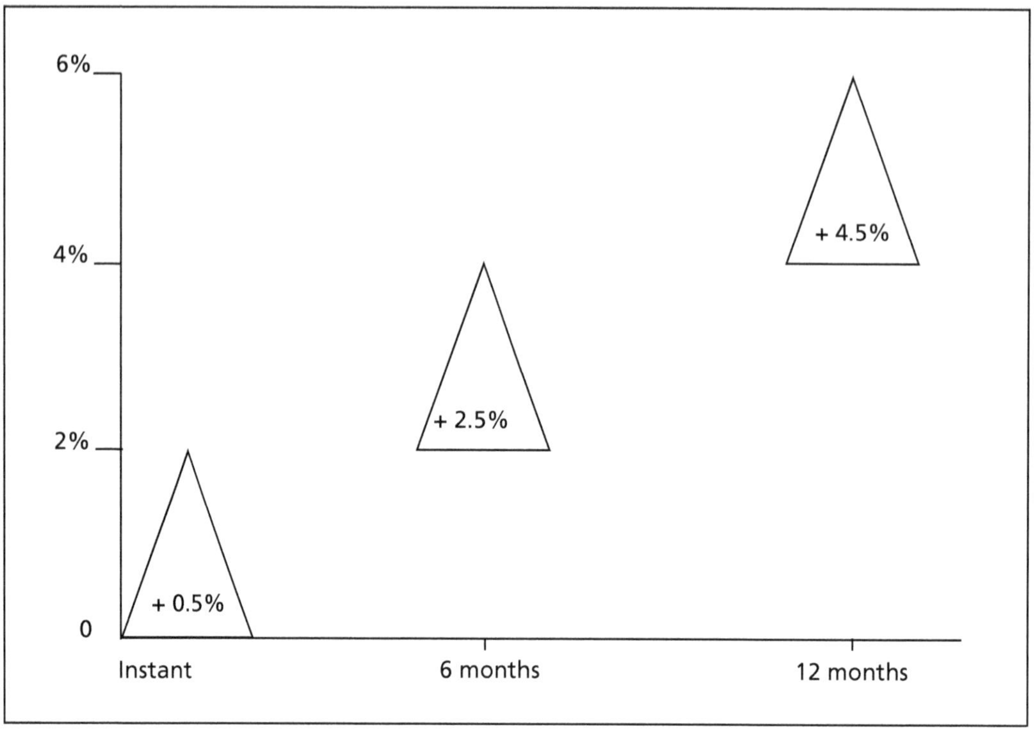

Source: Author

The future

It is highly likely that interest rates will remain low for a while so cash has to work hard to earn any money. The banks are highly unlikely to offer anywhere near market rates, especially to existing customers. The phrase 'for new customers only' reflects greater returns to new rather than existing clients. For a bank, the cost of the interest reduces their margins.

Corporates need to continually review where the best interest rates are being offered. These rates may not be from banks, so security and confidence in getting back 100% of the money is needed. For Islamic corporates with surplus cash, interest is forbidden. Holding that surplus in a strong currency may appreciate the cash without interest.

CHAPTER 6

RISK AND INTEREST STRUCTURES

Questions for the CFO, Treasurer or Cash Manager

- Should keeping surplus cash in a stronger currency than the home currency be considered?
- Is there an investment strategy for cash over the short and medium term?
- Is gold with a stop-loss as an investment worth considering?

Key considerations

- Understanding risk levels of investment from safe to speculative;
- Using currency and gold as an appreciating cash asset with stop-losses;
- Gold trends.

The investment risk pyramid

The level of interest being paid for cash is proportional to the risk of the instrument and the issuing organisation. The instruments are often rated by the agencies, as they are seen in the market as being unbiased. The investment pyramid that follows shows the base as being 100% safe, rising to highly speculative. Most Cash Managers invest the cash-in-hand at the base level. It is convenient and safe, but barely keeps up with inflation in most countries.

Base level investments – no risk to principal and highly liquid

This is a set of ultra-safe investments that, as a result of these financially depressed times, paying minimal interest rates (e.g. in the UK less than 3%):

- Cash deposits in the bank account – 100% liquidity and money available within three days. Accounts secured up to €100,000 in case of default;
- Bank may offer greater interest on the account by increasing amount size;
- Cash sent out to money market funds (money is returned after an agreed timeframe – 30, 60, 90, 120 days – usually with minimum amounts of £25,000);
- Repo agreements (minimum amount of £25,000);
- Commercial paper (minimum amount of $100,000).

Appreciating cash investments – up to 15% market risk and highly liquid

As there is little money to earn on base level Instruments, companies can hold assets which are highly liquid and can appreciate above a level of potential forecasted loss. By taking a known and approved risk (for example a stop-loss at 15% below the market price at purchase), strong gains can be realised over the short to medium term.

A stop-loss order is an instruction to sell the currency (or any security, including gold and bonds) when the market price falls below the purchase price. For example £10,000 is converted from GBP to USD. The conversion rate is 1.58, so $15,800 is the amount held in dollars. The level of risk taken is based on a company's own assessment. The maximum loss suggested is 15%. A stop-loss is requested such that when the price of the dollar reached 1.85 then the currency is sold. At 1.85 the amount of pounds being repatriated is £8,540. The loss has occurred because the USD has weakened against the GBP. Consequently more dollars are needed to buy pounds. This is true for all market-traded securities, currencies and commodities.

These investments are as follows.

A strong currency

The cash is deposited in a particular currency other than the one the company is currently operating in. The currencies have to be monitored and a level of loss attached to the investment. For example, the currency normally is GBP and the cash is parked in Chinese Renminbi (RMB). Should the RMB to GBP exchange rate drop by 15% (or the level of loss agreed), then the Chinese currency is converted back into pounds. In the last two years the RMB has appreciated 16% against the euro. The cash in the adopted currency can use the same base level investments as above, with the exception of agreed timeframes. The timeframes restrict the movement of the currency and open it up to market risk. Liquidity into cash can be quick, with payment being made usually within three days.

Gold

The cash is deposited into gold. Gold has appreciated consistently over the last five years. In 2011, gold rose 12% year-on-year. Again, a level of market risk has to be assigned and the gold price tracked, with a stop-loss of less than 15% of the price purchased. While there are no interest rate opportunities for the gold, it can be used for collateral for securing credit. Using gold as collateral can reduce the speed of liquidity, thus exposing it to more market risk than agreed. Liquidity into cash is fast, with payments made usually within three days. See further below.

The commissions for buying and selling the currencies and gold should be factored into the risk level before moving into appreciating cash investments. The longer-term cash cushion could be invested into these alternative cash funds.

Speculation – up to 50% market risk

Derivatives are in this category as they can be used for hedging and high-risk investment. In this category spread betting can be added, along with options, futures, warrants, swaps and contracts for difference (CFDs).

Speculative investments using derivatives can:

- Make a greater gain or loss from the same price movement that would result in actually buying the underlying asset in the first place;
- Make a gain from a fall in the price of the underlying asset.

Figure 6.1: The investment pyramid

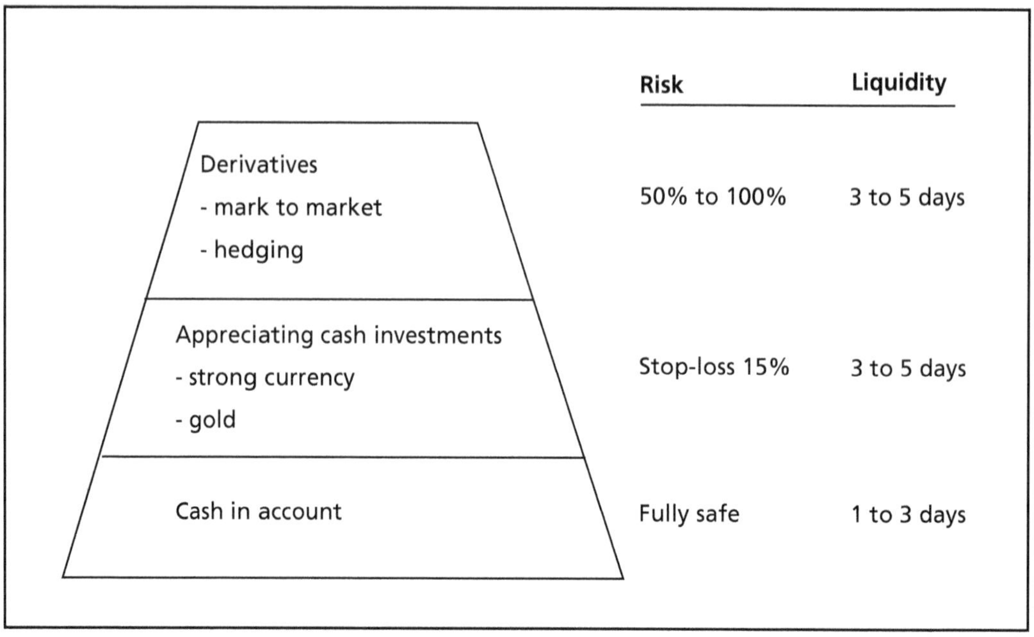

Source: Author

Gold – the universal currency

Gold can be described as a universal currency. It is often held by central banks, and in 2009 the Indian central bank bought 200 tonnes from the IMF (International Monetary Fund).

Gold used to play a central role in the international monetary system until the ending of the Bretton Woods system of fixed exchange rates in 1973. Since then, the role of gold has reduced, although it is still an important asset in the reserves held in by many countries. The IMF is one of the largest holders of gold in the world. As of 31 August 2011, the IMF's gold was worth $164 billion.

Gold is a finite resource and used in many applications as it does not rust. Most gold comes from South Africa; since 1910 75% of all gold ever produced has been extracted there.

Similar to FX, the price of gold is readily available and relatively easy to convert into cash. The price of gold is fixed twice a day and this forms the basis of the price of gold offered in the market. Gold is priced in USD per troy ounce (31.1 grams; one ounce equals 24 carats). The price of gold is pro-rated to the number of carats used in its make-up. The popular amounts are 22, 14 and 9 carat gold.

As gold is priced in USD, a UK entity would have seen the value of gold increase consistently over the last five years. Since 2008, the price of gold in sterling terms has increased 34%, 13% and 31% in 2010. In 2011 it rose 12%.

When buying gold bullion the price is based on the amount being bought. For example, buying one-ounce gold coins can carry a 10% spread over the fixed rate at that time. By buying 100 coins the price drops to around a 7% spread.

Figure 6.2: Gold – London PM fix 2000-2011

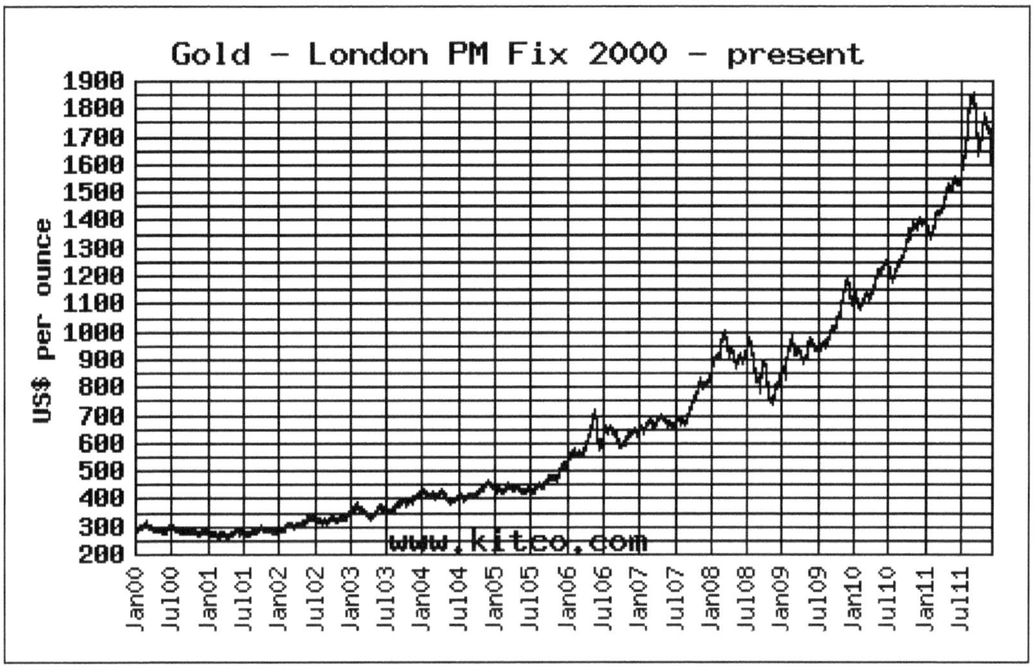

Source: www.kitco.com

The future

Banks have become increasingly risk-averse, and due to the need to rebuild their capital bases, are offering below-market rates of interest for passive clients. This will continue unless the clients become active or the regulator steps in. Historically, banks are fast to drop interest rates when the central bank rate goes down, and slow to drop the lending rates. Similarly, if the rates go up, the banks are quick to increase the lending rates and slow to increase the savings rates.

The corporate should be actively managing its cash and reporting to the Board the best rates and opportunities available with acceptable levels of risk. The cash may be at the bank or in the market.

CHAPTER 7
THE CREDIT LADDER

Questions for the CFO, Treasurer or Cash Manager

- What is your average cost of credit today and how does that compare to last year?
- Do you have access to credit at a good interest rate, should you need it?
- Who is managing the credit rating displayed by outside agencies?
- Has anyone provided personal guarantees?
- Are intraday overdrafts occurring?

Key consideratlons

- Watch out for credit facilities charges;
- Credit agencies are monitoring trading activities;
- Be careful of intraday overdrafts;
- Credit Default Swaps are a guide to the level of risk.

Charges for credit facilities

Both corporates and SMEs are finding it difficult to access credit from banks at this time and the cost of borrowing has increased. The spreads – interest rates – offered by banks and specialised lenders have grown dramatically. The key is the annual percentage rate (APR); the greater the figure, the more interest is being charged and the more money is needed to pay back the credit. In addition, there could well be additional fees for setting up the credit, including administration charges as well as penalties for paying back early.

Table 7.1: Charges for credit facilities

Type of credit facility	Term	Collateral	APR
Corporate loan	3–5 years	Sometimes required	5–10%
Account overdraft	Ongoing	No	10–18%
Credit cards	Ongoing	No	10–35%
Invoice financing	4–6 weeks	Yes	18–36%
Unauthorised account overdraft	Ongoing	No	18–36%

Source: Author

The cost of credit is determined by:

- The organisation's credit rating – the higher the score the better;
- Relationship – how long with the bank and how familiar it is with the business;
- Timing and amount – the amount of money and how quickly it is needed; the credit process can take six weeks, especially if Credit Approval Committee agreement is needed.

Table 7.2: The credit ladder

Interest rate	Type of credit	Term	Collateralised
0 to 10%	Corporate loan	3 to 5 years	No
	Leases	3 to 5 years	Yes
10% to 20%	Revolving credit - overdraft on accounts - credit cards	Ongoing	No
20% to 30%	Invoice financing	4 to 6 weeks	Yes
	Authorised overdraft	Ongoing	No

Source: Author

Credit rating agencies

On the country and corporate front there are three main credit agencies: Fitch, Moody's and S&P (Standard and Poor's). Their mission is to establish the likelihood of a default on monies being advanced. While they have different credit analysis techniques, the end-result of a league table from AAA to Ca rating is similar. The greater the chances of being repaid, the higher up the table the country or company is positioned. Here, for Fitch and S&P, AAA is the highest credit rating that can be achieved, while Aaa is the Moody's equivalent. These ratings are regarded as 'Prime'.

For a Prime rating, a borrower would see very low rates of interest that are readily available, as the chances of default are minimal. The term 'flight to quality' covers the movement of money out of lower rated credit instruments to those of a higher quality, especially Prime. In difficult financial times the cost of money for Prime customers can actually go down, such is the demand. Hence the economic and prestige value of being Prime is very attractive.

The price and availability of credit below AAA is dependent on the market. In times of crisis, credit availability dries up and what is available commands high prices and shorter durations.

Table 7.3: Credit rating agencies ratings guide

Credit category	Fitch/S&P	Moody's
Prime	AAA	Aaa
High Grade	AA+	Aa1
	AA-	Aa3
Upper Medium Grade	A	A1
	A-	A3
Lower Medium Grade	BBB+	Baa1
	BBB-	Baa3
Non-investment Grade	BB+	Ba1
	BB	Ba2
Substantial Risks	CCC	Caa
Extremely speculative	CC	Ca

Source: Author

The grade of BB+ and below is regarded as 'junk' in the market. The lower the grade, the less chance there is of 100% of the principle being returned. If a client is rated as junk, it often results in a proposed 'haircut' to help keep the client solvent. A haircut is the establishment of a price that is below the original valuation of the asset. The euro crisis has seen Greece being downgraded to between CCC and Ca by the three rating agencies, and many owners of Greece's debt have taken a 50% haircut. That means that, if they had put £100 million into Greece's sovereign debt, then only £50 million will be returned.

Initially, the feeling in the market was that the euro could be credit rated as a whole rather than by individual country. The early ratings were as a group and market sentiment backed that view. This was similar to Citibank's view that countries do not go bankrupt (held before the Latin American debt crisis). Now each EU country is judged on its own fiscal resources. To return to group ratings, the European Central Bank would have to be the lender of the last resort for all of the European debt. This is difficult, as the amount of debt is in trillions and politically there needs to be a way of preventing excesses across the group. The European banks themselves have taken €489 billion in loans in 2011. This followed €300 billion of loans in 2009. In 2012, the European banks need to refinance €700 billion as existing contracts mature. The interest rate on the €489 billion was 1%.

Banks and financial institutions' scoring techniques

Banks and financial institutions have their own scoring techniques. These are developed to reflect the level of risk they feel comfortable with at the time. These scores can be moved up or down depending on the credit appetite of the institution. Credit appetite is a measurement and desire that refers to the amount of credit that financial institutions want to extend to a particular market segment or group of companies or type of loan. In times of crisis, the appetite is often reduced and as such, the higher credit scorers are approached first for any approval. In the UK, for example, the level of property investments made by banks in the past now severely restricts new bank money being allocated and approved for this sector.

Most banks offer 'corporate lending' facilities through the in-house 'Credit Committee'. The committee constitutes bankers with 'Credit Initials', often called 'Sanctioners'. A Credit Initial is related to the person making the credit approval and reflects the level of credit that person can approve. The larger the amount required, the greater is the due diligence needed to approve the loan. The size of the loan, given the risk the bank sees, may need to be well be collateralised.

The whole process is referred to as commercial lending and many of the larger loans are customised for the corporate borrower to provide the security and payment schedules the bank feels most comfortable with. The cost of providing a fully customised service is both expensive and time-consuming; hence the immortal banking phrase: 'If you want a quick decision it has to be no". Large commercial loans are often collateralised with a company's assets. In other words, the bank takes a secured position in the company's hierarchy of payment. The bank is amongst the first paid out in a failed situation.

Intraday overdrafts

In 1994, the Federal Reserve introduced daylight overdraft fees. This move helped correct a market situation in which large credits were kept open to the end of day. Banks were not covering their intraday exposure as and when it happened.

This move also signified a change for the Federal Reserve from simply processing payments to managing intraday risk. Credit by the Federal Reserve before 1994 was unlimited. This was highlighted by a computer hitch at the Bank of New York, where the daylight overdraft turned into an overnight credit that was bigger than the value of the Bank of New York. The Bank of New York had to borrow $23.6 billion from the Fed overnight due to a software fault and paid $5 million in overnight interest.

Real-time processing is now more common and the timely money movement encouraged by the fees involved in intraday overdrafts which have reduced the levels of daylight exposure. Batch entries still occur throughout the banking system and these can cause intraday exposures. Batch entries are an accumulation of payment instructions that have prepared and then released into the system, for example, paying of interest at set times.

Large value payments

The issue today, not only for the Federal Reserve but for all banks, is the size of the large value payments. A $1 billion trade is now a common daily event. To handle such trades between banks without payment delays or returns, a system of credit lines are established between banks which are often collateralised. The collateral used is such that it can be liquidated quickly with minimum market risk. The large trades are often held in each bank system until there is enough credit to process them.

Before the financial crisis, banks often left credit with other banks; now they tend to keep it with the central bank. This consolidation of credit to the lender of last resort has left many banking systems short of credit flexibility. This in turn slows the financial system down and makes it more cautious.

Other credit techniques

Outside of commercial lending and the revolving loan area, a number of credit techniques have been created that include:

- Asset based financing;
- Loans against equity;
- Inventory financing;
- Government return financing;
- Financing via other collateral; and
- Credit default swaps.

Asset based financing

In its simplest form, a company can pledge some of its assets for a loan. These can include balance sheet items such as accounts receivable, short-term investments, inventory, equipment and assets that can be turned into cash. This can occur in three forms:

- An outright sale, such as banks selling off non-core items;
- A sale and leaseback; or
- An asset such as a precious metal being pledged for a duration of time off-site.

Sale and leaseback

Sale and leaseback often occurs in real estate when the company owns the building in which it resides. The building is acquired and a lease is drawn up for the company to continue in the premises. These transactions take time, three to six months on average, but once completed, cash is released from the premises and the monthly lease cost of the floor space becomes the ongoing cost of doing business.

Leasing other assets

Leases can be written for most things, with equipment being the most common. The lease itself can contain many clauses. The size of the lease is determined by the value at the equipment at the start of the process and its retained value after three years.

When money is raised on a particular asset, the institute releasing the money usually holds that asset. For example, the asset can be leased. Leasing can cover any asset that has a value and the leasing agreement can last over three years. For example, most computer equipment is set over three years, with the residue value after the third year set at zero.

The person providing the money is called the Lessor and the person with the now leased asset the Lessee. The Lessor agrees to lease to the Lessee and the Lessee thereby agrees to take on lease from the Lessor the asset (equipment) on the terms and conditions of the Master Lease and any additional terms set out in the Equipment Schedule.

The agreement is in the form of a Master Lease complete with an Equipment Schedule.

The Master Lease remains effective as long as any Equipment Schedule is in effect. The term of each lease is set in months or years. Extension of the Initial Term can be agreed as long as the proposed period is at least three months prior to its initial expiration date.

Before extending any equipment lease, renegotiate the price of the term, as the Lessor has had the money for the equipment and any going forward is often a bonus. That is, older the lease, the higher the chances for the Lessor making close to 100% margin.

The Lessee pays the monthly lease payments usually by direct debit in the UK and acknowledges that such lease payments are made without notice or invoice. The Lessor will make reasonable efforts to supply invoices to the Lessee but lack thereof does not alleviate the Lessee's obligation to pay.

Leases are normally calculated on a 30-day basis. Any lease payments or other sums payable not paid on the due date can be subject to a late charge. These charges can be 2% per month.

Lease payments may be varied at the sole discretion of the Lessor. For example, a common clause states that at any time, if the reference rate has altered by 0.5%, the lease payment would be pro-rated by any such change. if applied. So read the lease document carefully.

Many companies offer leasing. The actual manufacturer often provides the funding' for example, General Motors and General Electric have extensive leasing operations. Refinancing existing assets, provided they have a value, is one way to add liquidity in the form of a lump sum, which is based on equipment leased over three years. The cost of leasing today is from 8–15% based on the availability of funds and thecreditworthiness of the Lessor.

Non-payment of the lease results in the equipment being taken back by the leasing company and sold. The leasing company would then pursue any shortfall between the money due and the money being made through the sale of the asset. The chances are very high that there will be a difference, and usually a large one. It is at this point that any guarantees taken out during the leasing process are enforced.

Loans against equity

Banks follow the liquidity of equity before making a loan using the share as collateral. Banks can extend credit on shares, but usually with large margins taken against the collateral – 50% is not unusual. The bank wants the shares to cover the credit position and will often write into the contract that they have the right to sell should the equity value look endangered. This usually means the top 100 shares have collateral that meets the bank's criteria, albeit with healthy safety margins. Other equity positions are at the bank's discretion. Directors of a company whose shares have been placed have to notify the authorities.

Inventory financing

Inventory financing can be used by manufacturers making products, e.g. cars where inventory tends to form a significant percentage of assets. A loan can be made to a manufacturer using its inventory as collateral.

Where companies deal in products which have a market value, e.g., wine, then banks can to grant credit against the inventory. The credit amount is often at a sharp discount to the wholesale price, with the bank becoming the owner of the goods should something happen to the company

Government return financing

Where a company has an obligation from a government body, e.g. a tax rebate, provided it has the right paperwork, a bank can issue the company a credit against the forthcoming rebate.

Financing via other collateral

Contracts signed with credit worthy parties can be used as collateral provided the length of contract exceeds three years. Often a group of contracts can be put together and pledged against the extension of credit. Margins are high, and provided the bank is comfortable with the credit risk, credit is extended. Collateralisation is used extensively in the money market to guarantee bonds. This methodology has created bonds backed by everything from credit card receivables, through David Bowie's music royalties, to mortgage-backed guarantees and, of course, sub-prime bonds.

Credit default swaps

CDS are a form of insurance protection. The seller of a CDS is prepared to compensate the buyer should the loan default for the principal (face value) of the loan. In the event of the default the loan documents moves from the buyer to the seller in exchange for the cash for the defaulted loan. The interest due is often forfeited.

CDS themselves are priced in basis points. The higher the basis points, the more likely the market believes the chances of getting the principal back 100% diminishes. Figure 7.1 shows the market's view on sovereign debt across Europe. In November 2011 Greece had to pay a premium of 8.1% – i.e. for every $1 million of loan principal $810,00 per year is needed before any interest payments costs are made.

Figure 7.1: Sovereign credit default swaps January 2010– November 2011

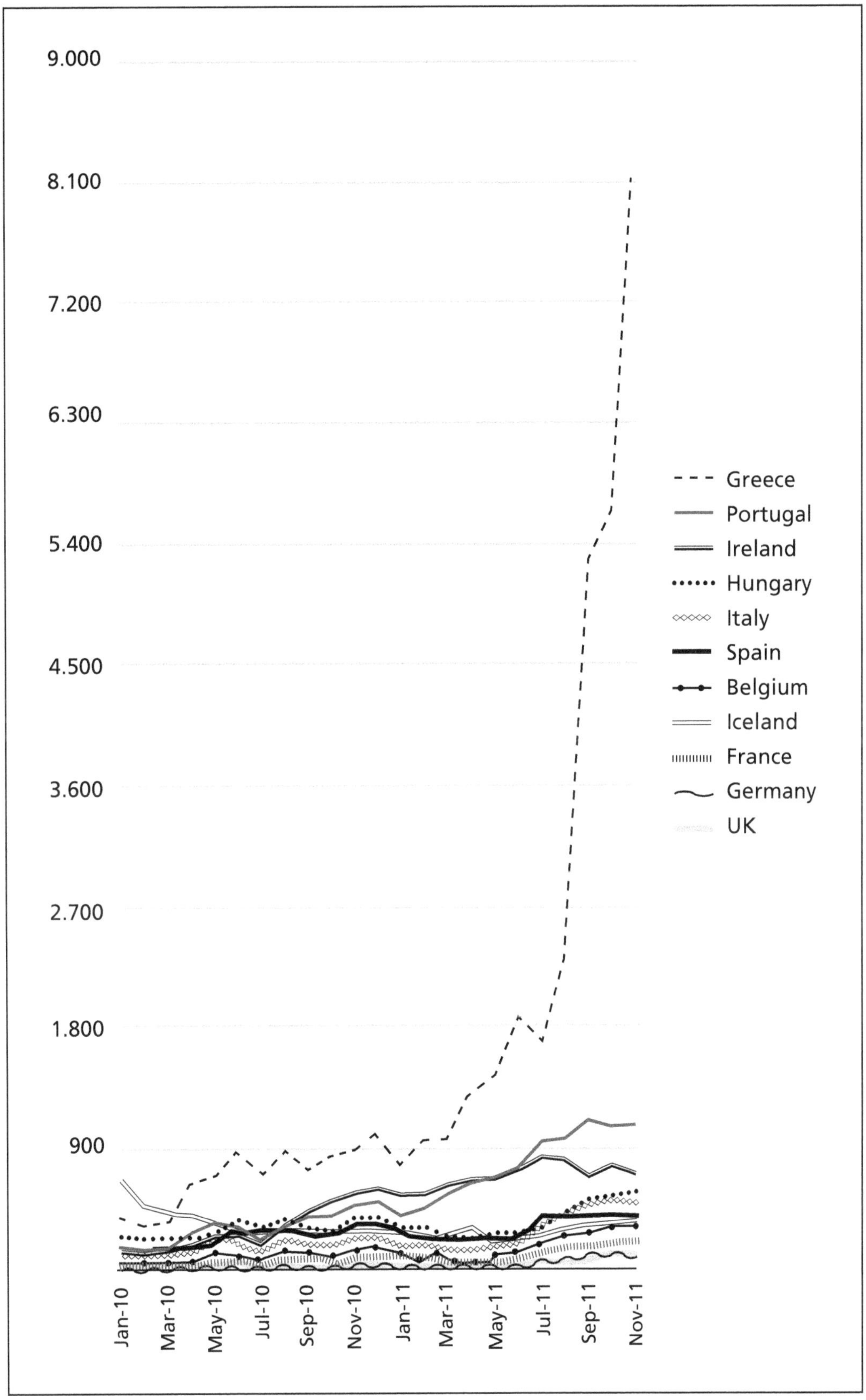

Source: Bloomberg

The future

The banks' appetite for credit is defined by capital equity, which from 2019 will be a 6.7 multiple of that capital. This is about 25% less than it is today. Consequently, credit is becoming a scarce resource. As such, the price and levels of credit approval will rise. In addition, more decisions will be made centrally with information collected from a number of sources, including credit bureaux.

Corporates' need for cash to grow will continue and banks will be only one resource open to them. The use of asset finance techniques will facilitate the raising of cash. The credit report will be central to any assessment, so the Board will need to be advised of its stature.

CHAPTER 8
THE INVESTMENT PYRAMID VERSUS THE CREDIT LADDER

Questions for the CFO, Treasurer or Cash Manager

- What is your net interest income between the interest generated by the cash and the cost of the credit being used?
- When comparing your company's investment pyramid to the credit ladder, what makes you feel comfortable and/or uncomfortable?

Key considerations

- Managing the Net Interest Income,
- Comparing investment against credit.

Net Interest Income (NII)

The difference between the revenues generated from interest on the loan and the cost of the money to provide that loan is called the Net Interest Income. For banks this is a key measurement because it indicates the interest spreads between its loans and its deposits. Banks have a wide range of loan rates based on time span and risk profile. To support the loan business banks use their clients' deposits, deposits from other financial institutions, and the money markets. The use of the money markets was rampant especially in the early part of this century, but since the credit market correction in 2007 due to sub-prime loans, access to the money market is difficult. Extensive regulations have also been enacted to help prevent a repeat of the credit crisis.

To gain a wide NII, the bank seeks to pay the lowest amount allowable for its deposits and charge the highest amount possible for its loans. In the US, many of the smaller banks have a policy of a minimum of 5% spread on top of the base bank rate for new loans. Historically, loans to companies with good credit ratings were often made at 1–2% above base. Blue chip companies often have a better credit rating than their banks and could command interest rates at less than 1% over base.

Similarly in cash management, the company receives interest on deposits and is charged interest on any loans or overdrafts. The difference between the two is often dramatic and not in the favour of the company. Money held in the bank account should be put to work. The banks are often tempered by their positions on the deposit side as compared to its loans. If, for example, the bank is deposit-rich, the need to pay interest on its deposit base is reduced, resulting in rates slightly above 0% for immediate access to the cash.

When banks need deposits (and this is currently a major priority for many banks, especially in the US and Europe), then the chances of offering better interest rates are more common. Deposits for banks come with the added criteria that they have to be stable and that the money should not leave as quickly as it arrives. Often termed 'hot money', this type of cash needs incentives to stay.

Comparing the pyramid with the ladder

Comparison of the investment pyramid with the credit ladder is an indicator of how the cash situation is poised. Having a great investment pyramid with few credit facilities suggests a cash-rich company. An investment pyramid in which the credit ladder is on balance suggests an ongoing working company. At the point where the credit ladder starts to exceed the investment pyramid, then cash flow issues are likely. The more these issues persist, the greater the need for cash and the greater the chance of the credit facility becoming expensive. As this expense grows, the ladder starts to pull the pyramid towards a negative situation.

Figure 8.1: The investment pyramid vs the credit ladder (1)

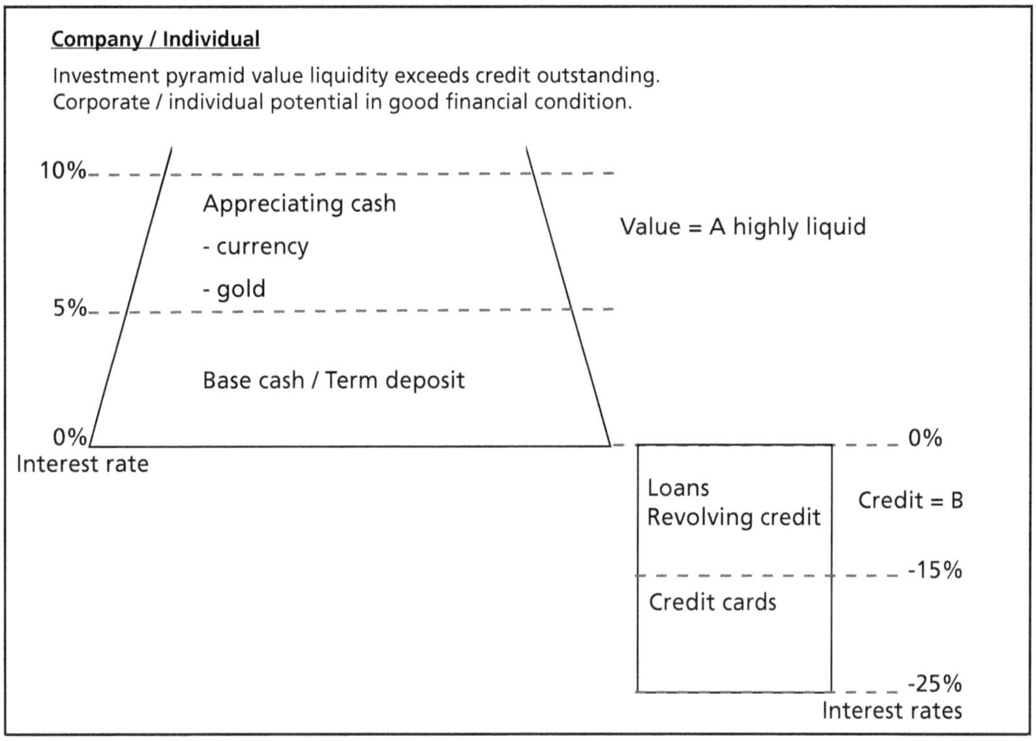

Source: Author

Figure 8.2: The investment pyramid vs the credit ladder (2)

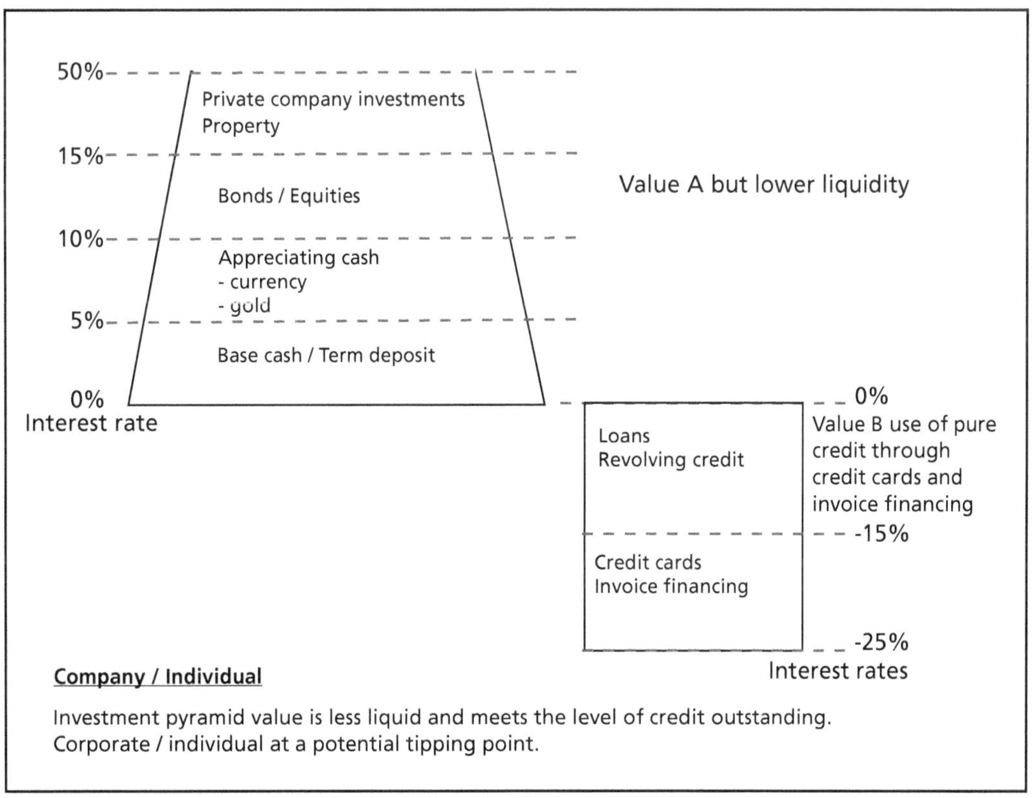

Source: Author

Figure 8.3: The investment pyramid vs the credit ladder (3)

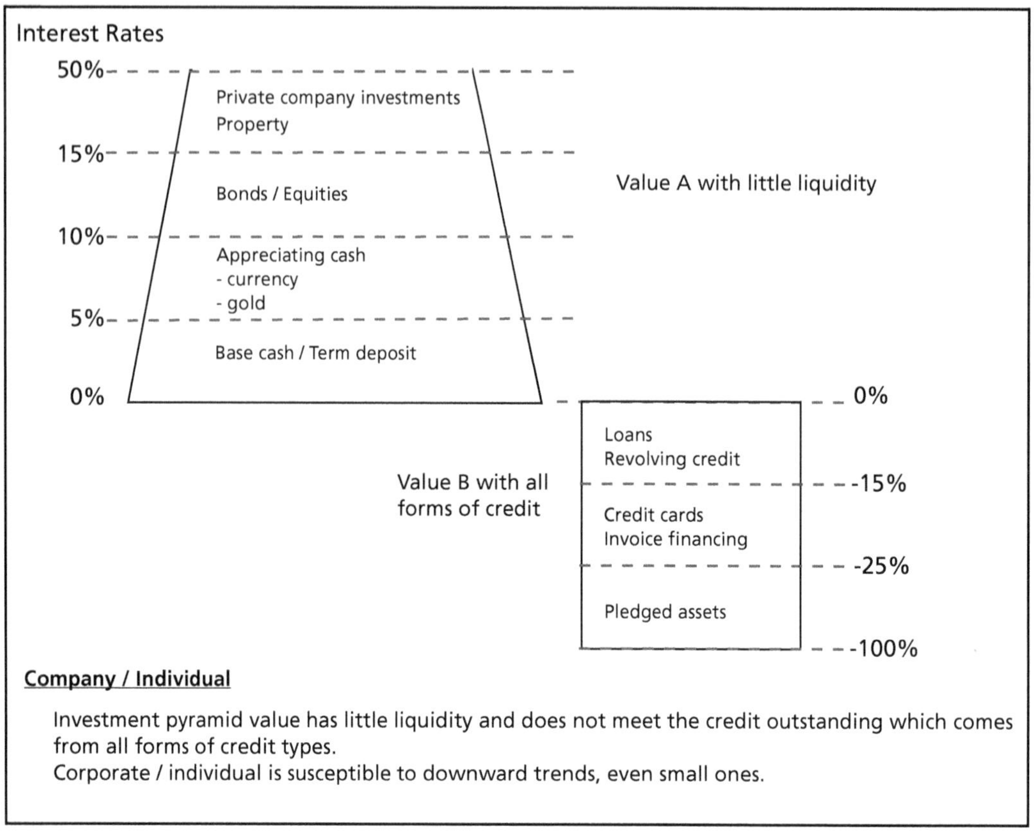

Source: Author

The future

Getting the balance between investment and credit right is an age-old issue. The days of easy and cheap credit appear numbered. To get credit, a credit report is needed and to get a good rating it has to show credits being taken and repaid. So credit is a part of the financial make-up.

Investments need to be biased towards liquidity. The spectacular gains are just that – something that happens a few times in a decade. The need for liquidity is to provide flexibility to take opportunities as they arise.

The least risky positioning is towards the bottom of the pyramid and towards the top of the ladder.

For banks, this positioning is part of their governance and monitored by the Assets and Liabilities Committee. Rarely do assets and liabilities balance exactly. Each bank will have its own view on the mix, although it is now biased towards greater liquidity.

Corporates will need to focus more on their collections of assets and liabilities and on putting them to greater use. Going forward, collateralisation of credit is on the rise and an exit or liquidity route is required. Banks have the right to call in credit, usually at any time, and did so often during the crisis, regardless of the corporate payment history. Liquidity is therefore the key at such events.

CHAPTER 9
PAYMENTS

Questions for the CFO, Treasurer or Cash Manager

- What percentage of our payments are received and paid by direct debit?
- If have we been paying by direct debit for a while, are all the direct debits still valid, as some are often for services not required, e.g. telephones?
- Is our bank account reconciled automatically and daily?
- What is our payments volume and can we reduce the price?

Key considerations

- Use of immediate payments over being paid by common forms of payment, both bank and non bank;
- Management of payment timelines standards;
- If in two or more European countries, use Single European Payment Area (SEPA);
- Management of payment fees.

Creating harmonised payments

The payment landscape is changing. No more cheques in the post or checks in the mail. Immediate payment is now available through 'Faster Payments' in the UK and worldwide through warehouse accounts suppliers such as PayPal.

Each country has evolved its own payment and clearing systems. Each also has its specific rules surrounding corporate governance. The central banks historically had a lock on their own unique payment clearing rules and regulations. These rules are becoming synchronised with each other as the world is becoming more interconnected. The level of commerce over the internet, especially when buying and selling in multiple countries, is growing rapidly.

In Asia, payments cover a broad spectrum of requirements, with varying payment formats and systems. In some countries, paper instruments are more commonly accepted and in others, electronic payments are the norm. Domestic payments infrastructure is developed in some countries while still evolving in others.

With the creation of the euro, the EU set out to harmonise the money being moved between the EU countries. Studies made prior to the establishment of the euro showed that fees for international rather than local payments often cost often 10 times as much as the domestic charge. Since 2001 a directive (2560/2001) limited bank fees on cross-border transactions to a similar level to domestic charges.

Float and timeframes

In 2006, the EU published the Single Euro Payment Area (SEPA) scheme book which outlawed float. It is in the banking community's self-interest to keep money in the system, unallocated to any account for as long as possible. This is called float. Float is the money earned by banks on money in transit between accounts. Banks invest this 'free' money into interest or fee earning instruments (investment vehicles) and retain the money they generate. As the money is free, i.e. the bank does not have to pay interest on the money, the bank's margin on float is 100%.

Float has to be balanced between customer service and any associated laws, based on the timeframe. The EU defines this timeframe as five working days for the eurozone. After that timeframe, claims for compensation against the originating bank are permitted. Otherwise, the time between an account being credited after one that has been debited can become unacceptably long. Before the EU regulation, a cross-border payment could take as long as a month. The length of time a bank can keep funds in transit often becomes a political issue in many countries.

In the UK, for example, the banks use BACS, an Automated Clearing House (ACH), which moves money after three business days. This timeframe was taken as a standard because it matched the same amount of time it would take a cheque to clear, prior to automation. Technically, payments can be done instantaneously; the UK now offers instant payments termed Faster Payments through the bank-owned VocaLink company.

Faster Payments can be used to move money in less than 15 minutes, provided the bank sending the money and the bank receiving it have installed the required software and procedures into their IT environment. If they have not, the payments follow the BACS route. Faster payments can go up to any amount and from 1 January 2012, most banks will send up to £100,000. The European Payment Services Directive also became law on the same day and euro payments must be completed in D+1. That is, payments need to be paid by the bank within two working days anywhere in the euro zone.

Same/next day funds transfers – urgent payments

Increasing global complexities and industry competitiveness demand maximum convenience, flexibility and cost-effectiveness in managing internal payments.

When a corporate needs to disburse funds for immediate delivery or needs to accommodate suppliers who want funds credited directly to their accounts, the capability to provide the credit for payment to the beneficiary bank account for same-day payment regardless of currency depends upon:

- Meeting applicable cut-off times;
- The ability of beneficiary bank to receive electronic funds transfers;
- Intervening holidays and non-business days in country of currency;
- Funds transfer instructions requiring a repair may be delayed;
- Complete counterpart account and bank details.

Other payment methods

Cheques

The use of a cheque for payment peaked in the UK in 1990 with 11 million cheques issued. In 2010, 3.1 million cheques were issued and throughout 2011 a decline of 12% was evident. In many countries, for example Scandinavia, cheques virtually do not exist. The USA is the world's biggest user of cheques, but in the 10 years from 2001 to 2010, cheques have gone from being the dominant form of payment to 22% of all payments. The cheque trend is one of continued global decline. Globally, in 2005 22% of non-cash payments were made by cheque and by 2009 the figure had dropped to 16%.

The UK operates on a '2-4-6' time system for cheque clearing. That is, the cheque is presented to the bank on day 0; after day 2 the bank would pay interest, if applicable. On day 4 the bank can allow money to be withdrawn and by day 6 the money has been cleared and settled.

Figure 9.1: Cheque (paper) payment flow

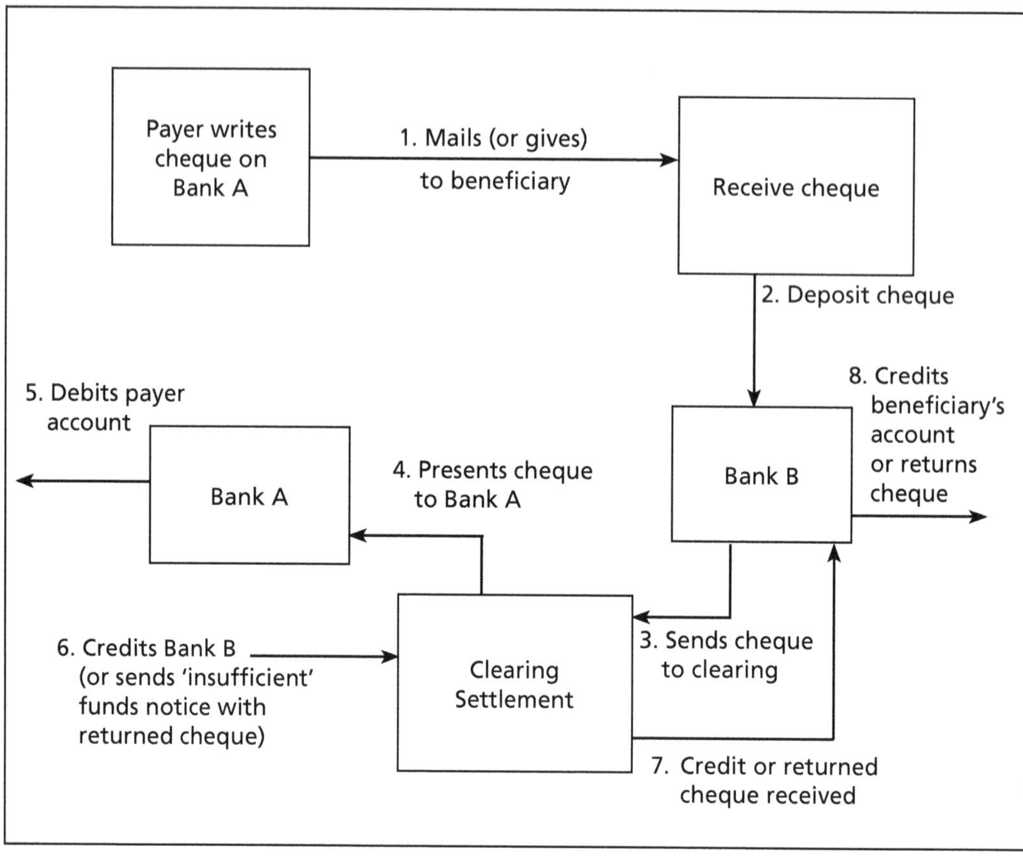

Source: Author

Automated Clearing House (ACH) payments

As cheques have declined in use, electronic payments have increased. In the UK in 2011, 59% of all payments processed by BACS were direct debits (DD), 39% were direct credits, and 2% standing orders. The average value of a DD was £313 in Q3 2011. Over 80% of adults in the UK have at least one DD and they are used by over 100,000 business and organisations.

In the US, the ACH network is a batch processing, store and forward system, governed by the NACHA Operating Rule Book. (NACHA is the US electronic payment association). The ACH connects financial institutions which batch the transactions as they are received and then forward them at predetermined periods into the network. The number of transactions in the first half of 2011 exceeded 8 billion and grew 2.7% in the 2nd quarter as compared to the previous year. The average transaction amount is $2,100. The schedule of fees for 2012 for a Depositary Financial Institution, e.g. a bank, is $0.000145 per item plus an annual fee of $144.

Figure 9.2: ACH payment

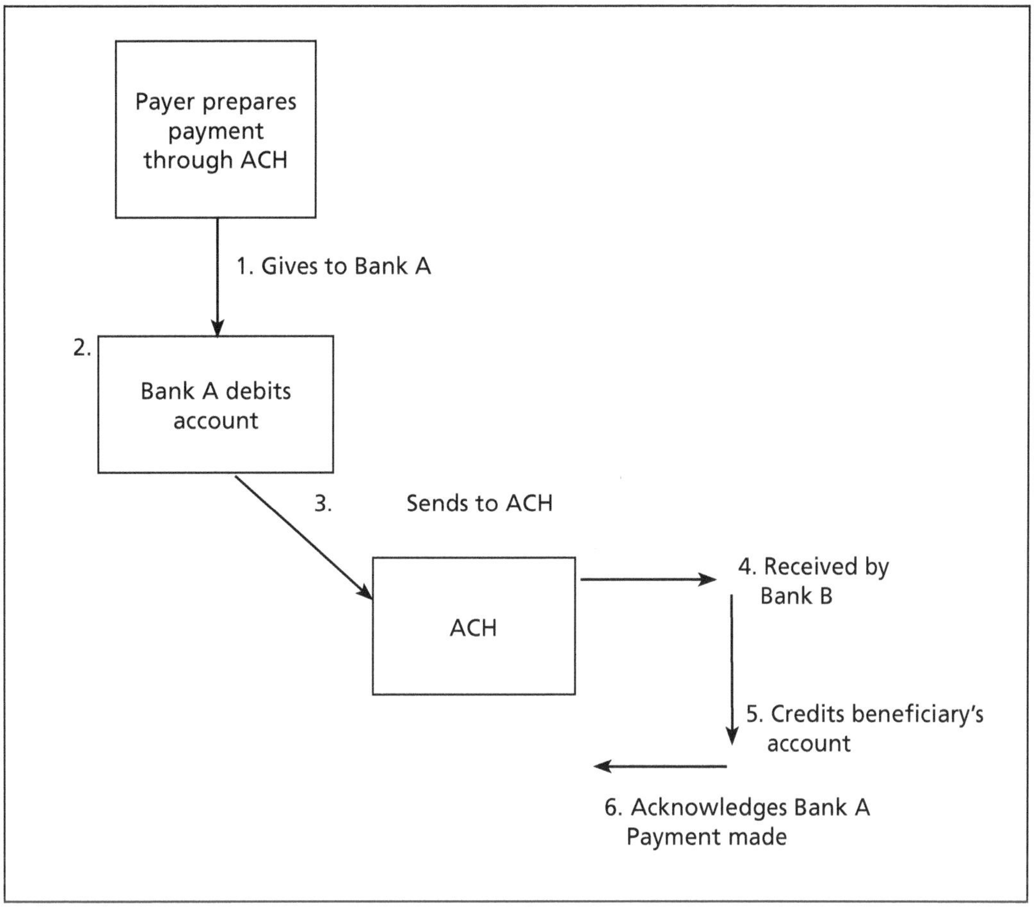

Source: Author

ACH for non-urgent payments

Electronic payments are processed through local country clearing systems rather than through the traditional funds transfers that clear through regional clearings systems such as CHIPS or EBA. ACH payments are traditionally low-value, non-urgent payments processed with value dates of two to five days depending on the clearing country. For example, the EU is setting the standard across its member countries of three working days for SEPA (Single European Payment Area). The actual size of the payment is irrelevant provided it is non-urgent.

The standard requirement for processing ACH payments is maintenance of a clearing account in each country where the company makes payments. The benefits include:

- No administration or cost of having international bank accounts to process local electronic payments;
- A single point of entry to process multiple payment types to multiple countries in multiple currencies;
- Full audit trails and management reports.

Direct debit

A direct debit is an extension of a single ACH payment. A DD is an instrument originated by a customer authorising the bank to pay a beneficiary by collecting monies from the customer's account. A DD allows for the amount collected to be processed provided the customer has been informed in advance. Should a DD bounce (note the cheque process reference), then as long as the customer is informed, the DD can be reinstated and the money taken provided there are funds in the account.

In the US, this type of payment is often referred to as pull service. That is, the money is taken out of the account (pulled) on agreed terms.

Figure 9.3: Direct debit payment

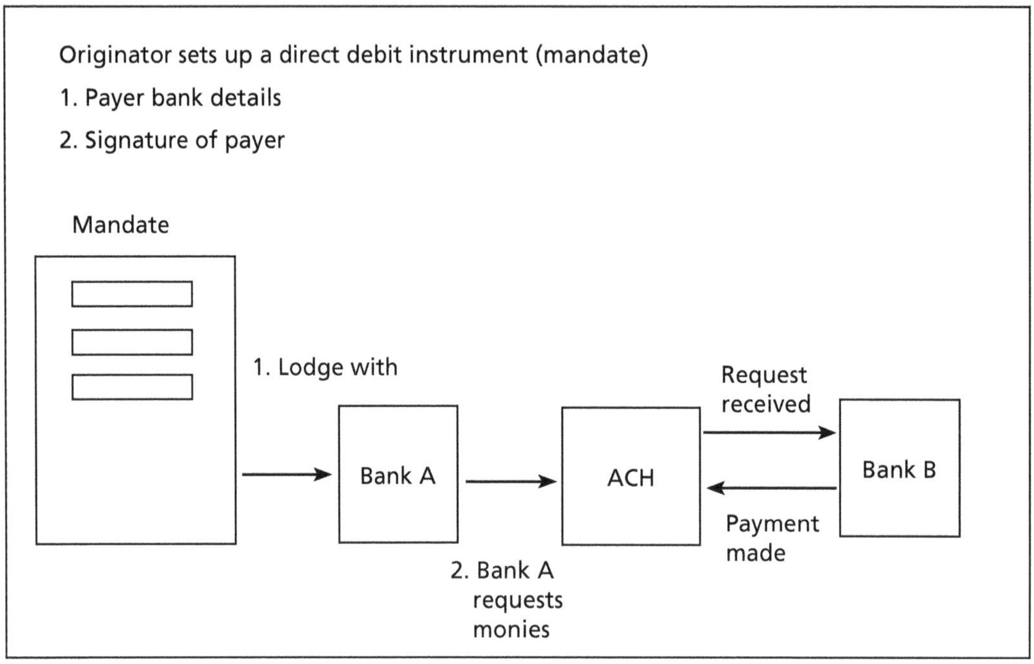

Source: Author

SEPA Direct Debit (SDD)

The SEPA Core Direct Debit Scheme – like any other direct debit scheme – is based on the following concept: "I request money from someone else, with their preapproval, and credit it to myself".

The SEPA mandate is an authorisation from a debtor (a customer purchasing goods or services) to the creditor (a retailer or service provider) to collect payments automatically from their bank account. This is called SEPA Direct Debit and has the following characteristics:

- Mandate forms to be completed by customers are usually provided by creditors themselves;
- The EPC now offers guidance to creditors on the creation of streamlined, easy-to-use SEPA mandates;
- In addition, the EPC provides translations of the mandate text as specified in the SEPA Core Direct Debit Scheme Rulebook into the SEPA languages;

- 16 to 18 million businesses in the euro area and all public administrations collecting payments in SEPA are now in a position to create the user-friendly SEPA mandate forms which best meets their needs.

The SEPA Core Direct Debit (SDD) Scheme Rulebook defines the rules for the content of SEPA mandates (section 4.7.2 – The Mandate). Customers who complete and sign such forms will eventually provide virtually the same information on a SEPA mandate as in any mandate issued under most legacy direct debit schemes today.

The EBA (European Banking Association) reported a volume of 6.5 million transactions per day in the 4th quarter 2011, which is double the volume for the 1st quarter 2011.

Table 9.1: Payment systems comparison

Payment method performance	Time
Domestic	
Cheque Automatic Clearing House	Minimum 5 days
One-off payment	24 hours
Direct Debit	3 days
Faster Payments (UK)	15 minutes
International	
Bank-to-bank	24 hours
SWIFT – transporter, not payment	15 minutes
PayPal	same day
Cheque (UK)	minimum 10 days
Check (US) – 21 Act allows a physical check to be replaced by a digital one	Dependent on bank – some allow credit same day and reverse out if money is not forthcoming
SEPA Direct Debits (SDD)	3 days (Europe only)

Local direct debit schemes vs. SEPA

In many SEPA countries, mandates that were issued by a debtor under existing national direct debit schemes do not conform to the SEPA Mandate. To facilitate the changeover to the SEPA Direct Debit Scheme, however, it is imperative that the millions of mandates in place today can indeed be used under the SEPA Scheme, at least for a transition period. EU Member States must, where necessary, create legislative solutions to ensure the continued legal validity of existing mandates under the SEPA Direct Debit Scheme. The principles are:

- The SEPA Direct Debit aims to make every DD scheme in Europe identical so payments can flow through the eurozone efficiently. It is based on the same principle as the local DD programs which permit the request of money from someone else with their prior approval and a credit to the requestor.
- The payer and the biller must each hold an account with a payment service provider (PSP) located within SEPA.
- The account maybe in euros or any other SEPA currency; however, the transfer between the payer's bank and the biller's bank always takes place in euros.

- SDD allows a biller to collect from a payer's account provided a signed Mandate has been given to the payer by the biller. The Mandate is different from the local DD and legally, often an existing Mandate can not be novated (depends on the law in each country) into a SDD without a new Mandate being signed.
- The new Mandates require additional information, including IBAN (International Bank Account Number) and BIC (Bank Identifier Code – often called the SWIFT number).

It is estimated that up to 10% of the existing Mandates are for services and products are now not currently required by the payer. Any new Mandate will probably provoke the need to examine the need to continue the service. The payer will look anew at what has been paid previously and may request a refund. Hence the holders of legacy mandates want the move to SDD from DD to be as seamless as possible, and if available simply novate the DD into SDD. Each country has different novation laws so the legacy mandates will either be completed without a new signed agreement, or a new agreement must be signed. All new DD mandates are converted to SDD mandates once SEPA becomes legally binding. The standardised messages can include up to seven reasons for a rejection. On 15 February 2012, the European Parliament agreed the SEPA end-date, making it legally binding for banks to offer SEPA payment processes from 1 February 2014.

To offer SDDs as a main, volume-based service banks need to make the interfaces as seamless as possible. The EBA document (Interfaces Specification for Multi-purpose Pan European Direct Debit Processing Service – a 115-page document) shows the scale of this activity. Most banks' legacy systems have yet to move over to XML and ISO 20022 standards to really accommodate SDD in volume.

Table 9.2: Multipurpose Pan-European Direct Debit

Business Level Message	File Type	XML Message Used	XML Message Description
Debit request	Input	S2SDDpacs.003	FI to FI Customer
Request for Cancellation	Debit File (IDF)	S2SDDpacs.006	Direct Debit
Reject		S2SDDpacs.002	Request for Cancellation
Refusal		S2SDDpacs.002	Payment Status Report
Return		S2SDDpacs.004	Payment Status Report
Request for Refund		S2SDDpacs.004	Payment Return
Reversal		S2SDDpacs.007	Payment Reversal

Source: Author

Finland is one of the forerunners in SEPA migration. It successfully migrated its credit transfers to SEPA by the end of October 2011. Domestic credit transfers have become SEPA credit transfers and the legacy domestic payment file standards being replaced by the ISO 20022 standard. Altogether, 90% of Finnish companies have concluded the migration.

Figure 9.4: SEPA Direct Debit

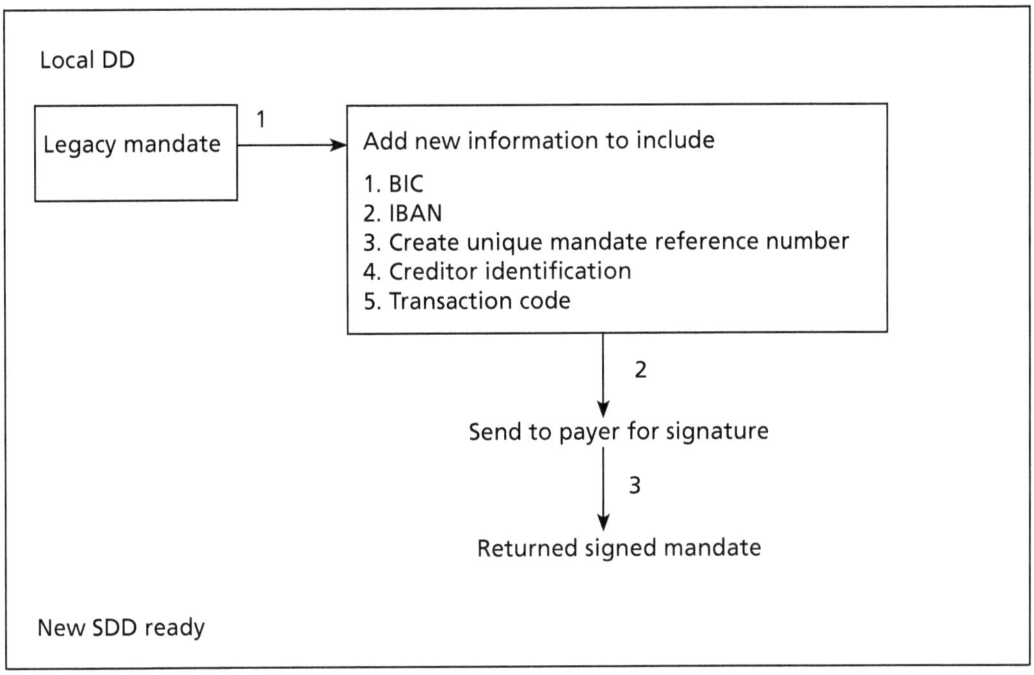

Source: Author

Payment solutions for corporates

Figure 9.5: Banks' payment solutions for corporates

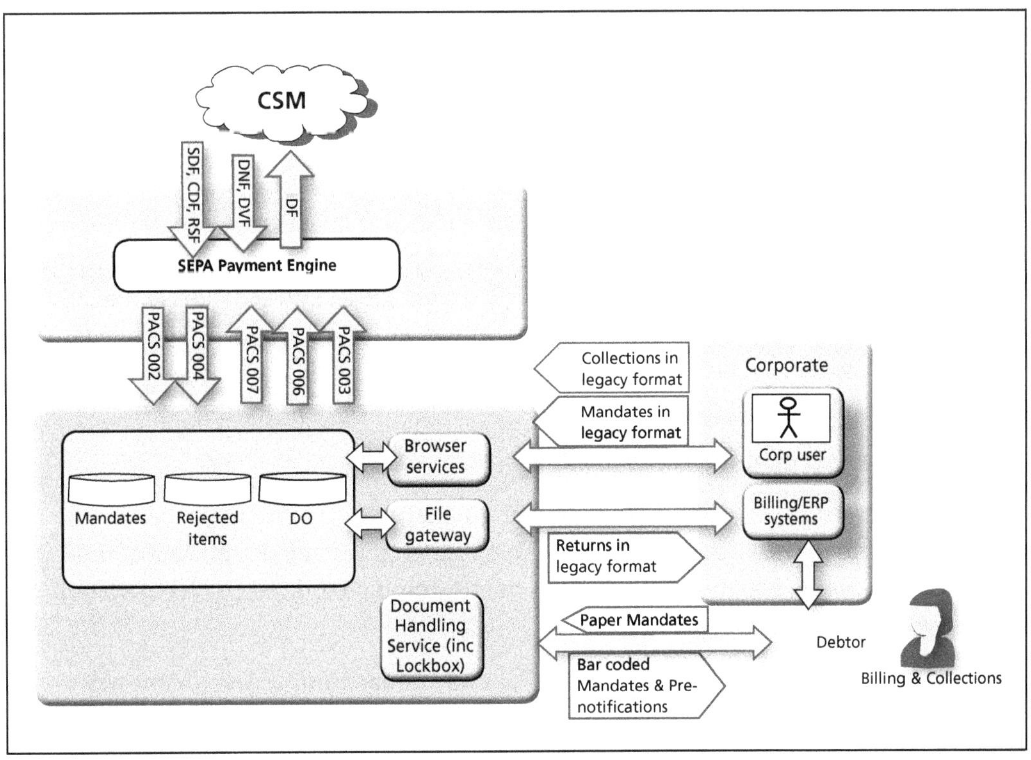

Source: Sentinel

E-payments

The term e-payments is often used to describe the online payment services offered by banks. It is an electronic platform that can process a variety of payments over the internet. The platforms are designed to be secure and available for credit and debit cards. Benefits are real-time authorisation and fast payment. A merchant acquirer account number is needed when selling goods and services requiring card payment. Specialist companies look after merchant payments through credit and debit cards, as the merchants themselves are constantly monitored for credit, ethical and moral reasons.

M-payments

Mobile payments are tipped to be the fastest growing area. Research company Juniper noted in June 2011 that mobile payments users are set to grow by 40%, to reach 2.5 billion globally. Research undertaken by an independent company ACCORD around the same time held 10,000 interviews which suggests the following for mobile payments:

- Strong appeal from 42% in the UK to 56% in Malaysia;
- SME appeal in each country was 70%;
- SMEs liked the ability to be paid straight away;
- Security is required alongside the convenience;
- Willingness to incur a fee for immediate payment especially in Canada (49%), Germany (47%) and the USA (47%).

Steve Jobs once commented that he rarely used focus groups as people could not see or grasp a new product until it was there. Mobile payments probably falls into this category.

In the UK, Barclays is offering Pingit, an instant account-to-account application for a smartphone user. Within 48 hours of the launch in February 2012, over 20,000 applications were downloaded. Barclays is not charging for the service and has completed the technology to interface smartphones with its core systems. Barclays expects to make its money through cross-selling products and adding new clients.

A number of countries have established industry bodies to take the lead in developing a non- priority platform. These include Japan, South Korea and France. In the UK, the UK Payments Council has appointed VocaLink to provide a central database that allows bank customers to link their mobile numbers to their account for mobile payments. The reason for this move is to create a common infrastructure for all banks and non-banks.

Warehouse accounts

Warehouse accounts held by non-banks offer an alternative payment process to the banking structure. The largest provider of this approach is PayPal with 230 million accounts worldwide, which competes with the traditional banking payment system known as correspondent banking.

By using a warehouse account held by PayPal and similar companies, the money coming out of a bank account or off a credit card is first lodged in that account. The holder of that account can then move money to another person with a warehouse account. Benefits include prompt and convenient payment.

Figure 9.6: Warehouse account process (1)

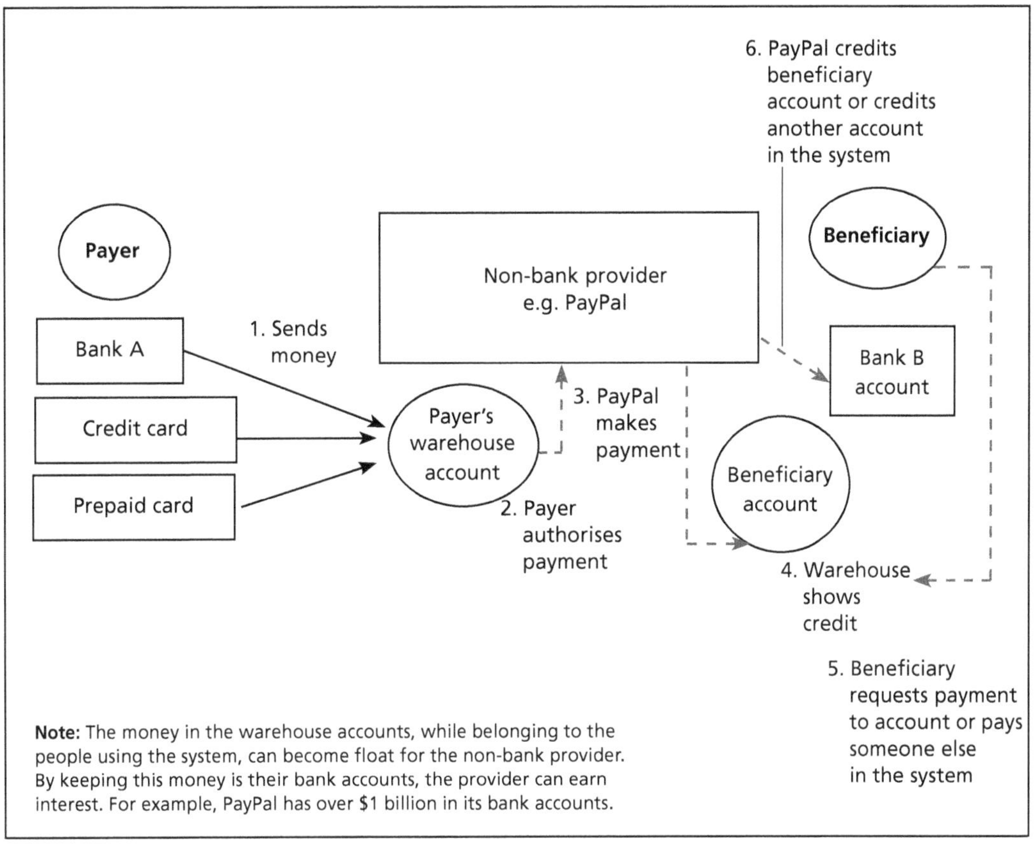

Source: Author

Figure 9.7: Warehouse account process (2)

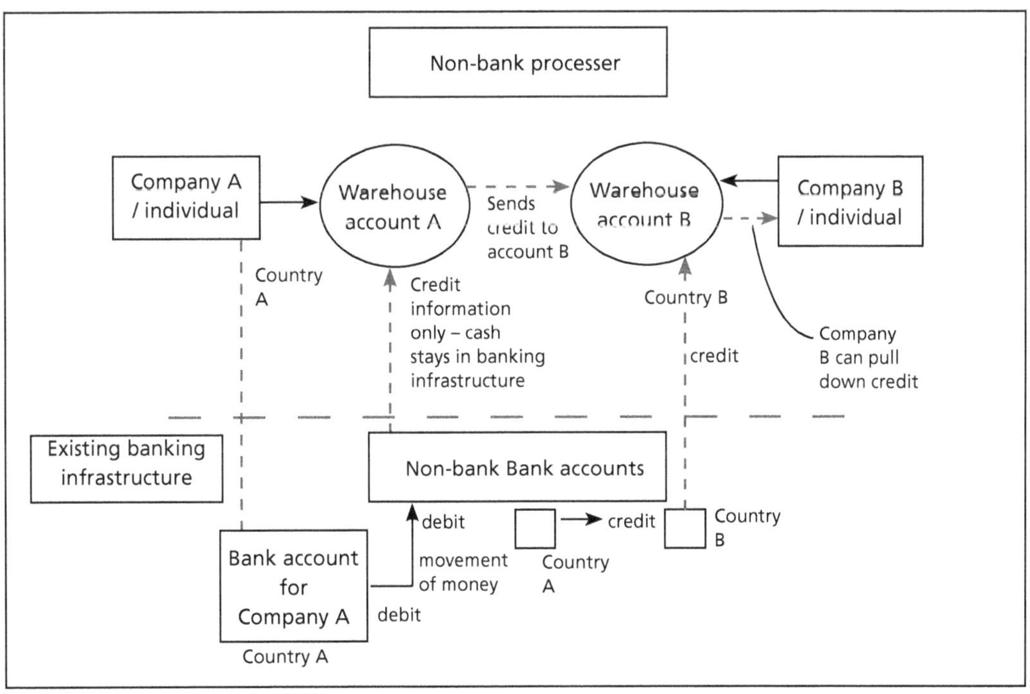

Source: Author

International payments for corporates

Correspondent banking payments

As a company moves into international cash management, it needs a bank to support its business across countries. In banking this used to be the function of the 'International Department' connected to their correspondent bank.

Correspondent banking was a very profitable business until electronic banking arrived. The move from manual to electronic cost money and reduced the time the bank held onto the money. Hence, there are many fewer banks with electronic international cash management than those offering domestic cash management, as many domestic banks did not make the necessary changes. In one way, for a domestic bank, it was an easy decision to make not to provide international cash management, as most countries have less than 2% of their payments made internationally.

Instead of being routed through a domestic company bank account, foreign exchange payments should be made through the company's account in that country.

Figure 9.8: Foreign exchange payments

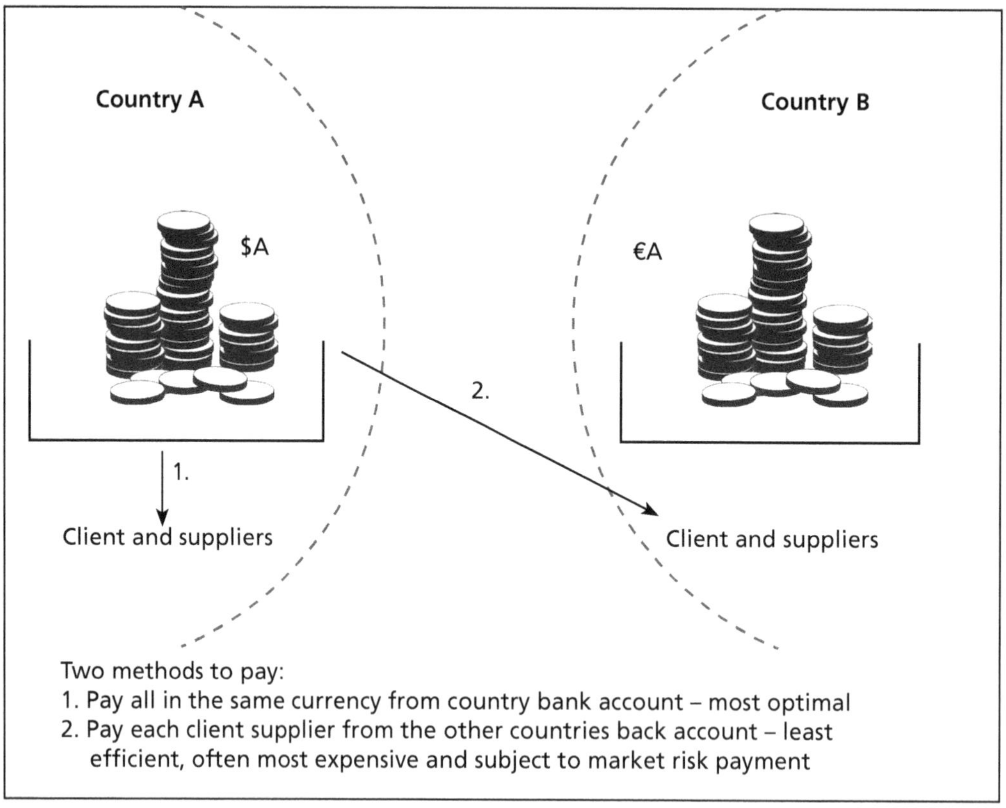

Source: IBS Publishing

Other international payment options

This relationship can be made either by the company directly – the most time-consuming – or through their domestic bank, usually their correspondent bank or through a domestic bank in an international association e.g. IBOS Association, or directly through an international bank.

Both options are limited to the areas covered by the Association or international bank. For example, Equens, a European bank-owned organisation based in the Netherlands, handled €9.7 billion payment transactions and 3.9 billion Point of Sale (POS) and ATM transactions in 2010, yet only covers a small group of countries.

The best option is to have connected banks making international bank transfers across in-bank accounts. In other words, if a company uses the same bank in two countries then a growing number of international banks will permit money transfers between accounts regardless of location as they are held within the same internal infrastructure.

Figure 9.9: Options for international payments – independent domestic banks

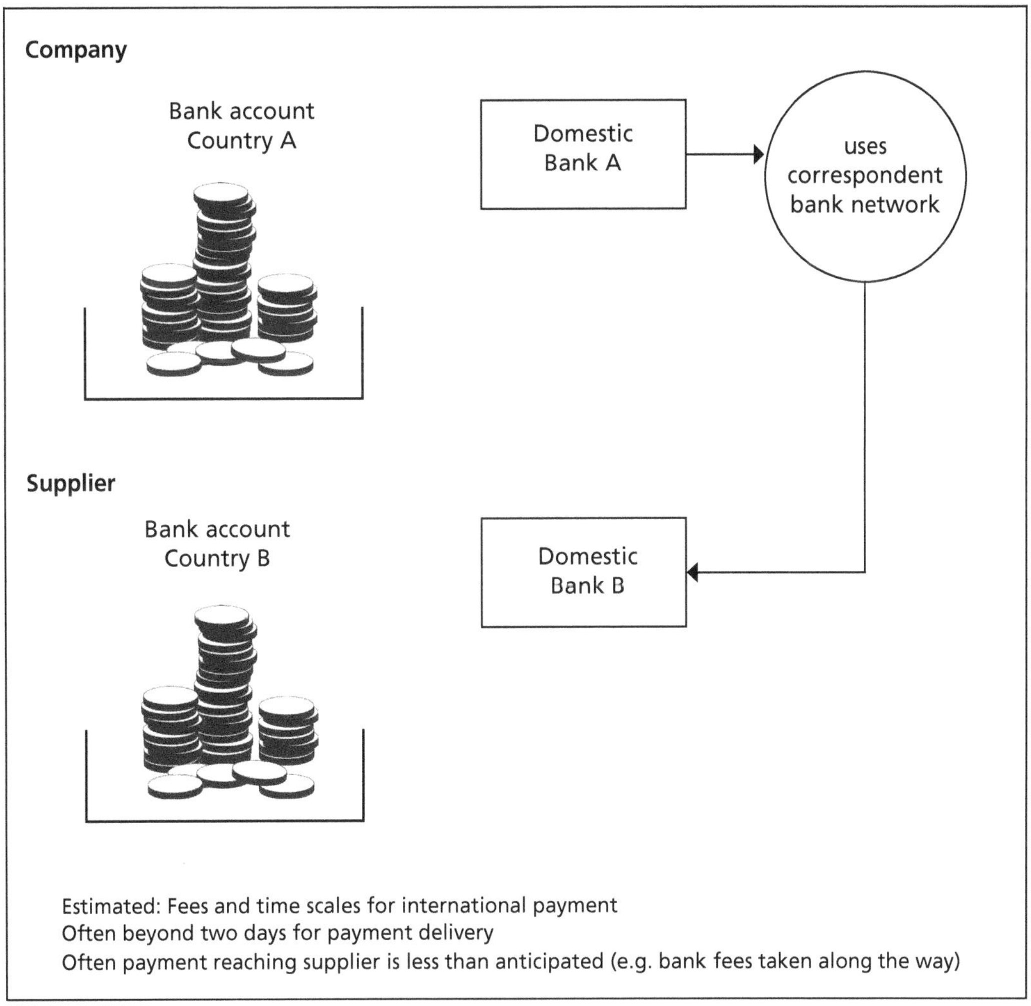

Source: IBS Publishing

Figure 9.10: Options for international payments – domestic banks in an Association

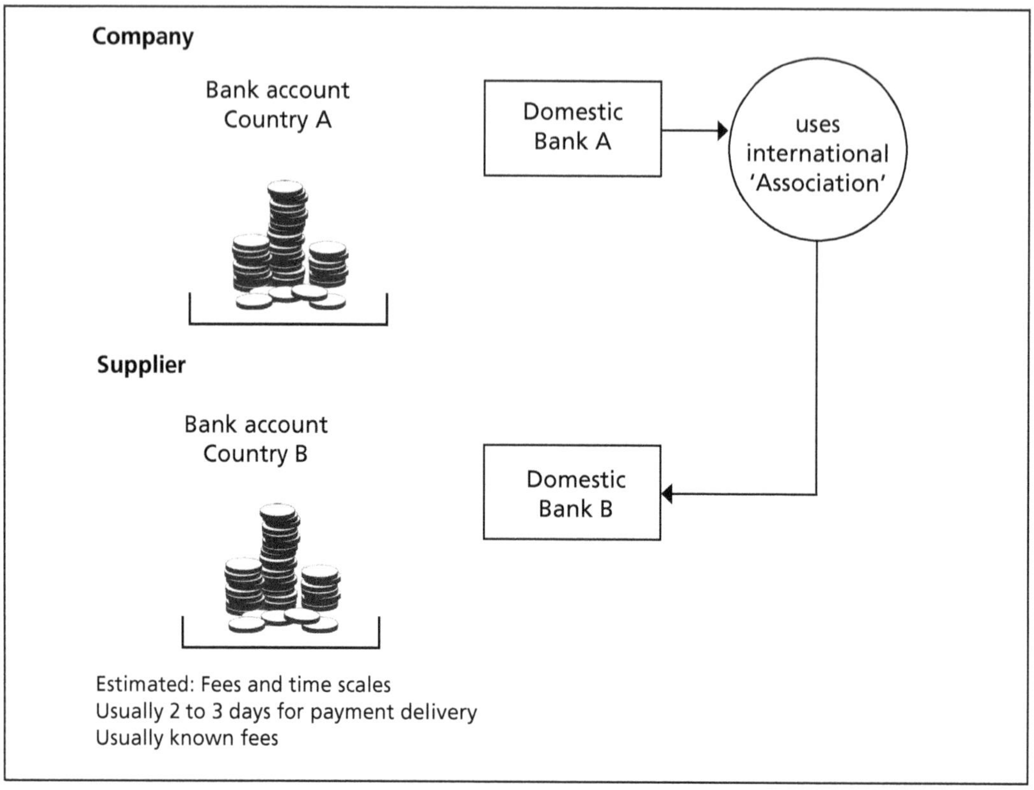

Source: IBS Publishing

Figure 9.11: Options for international payments – international bank

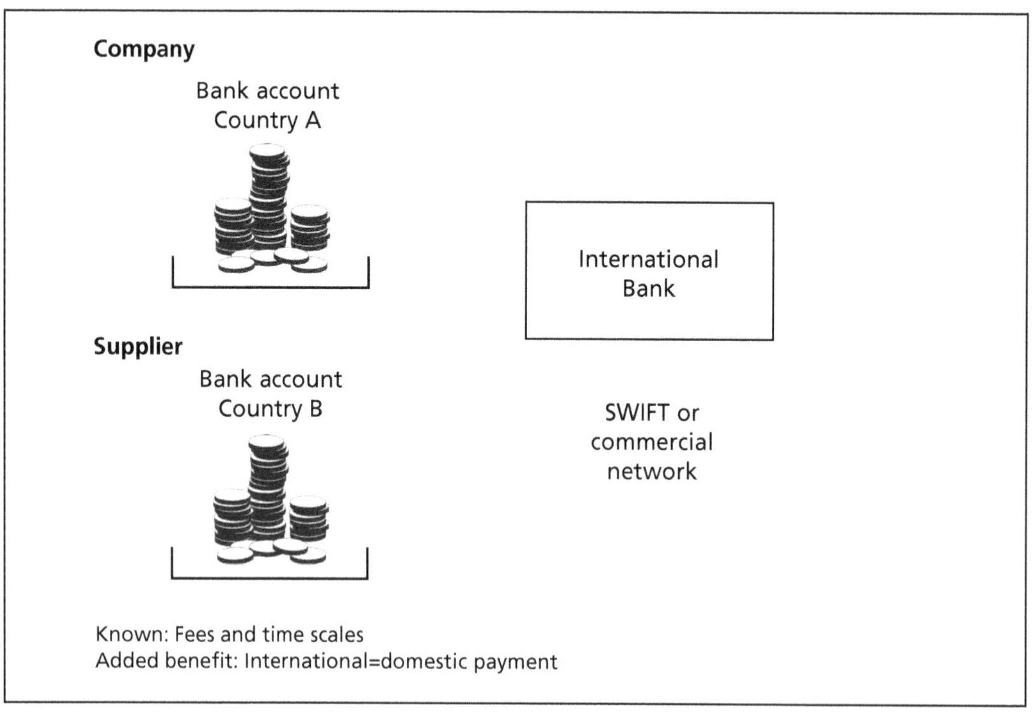

Source: IBS Publishing

The banking infrastructure for cross-border payments

The traditional banking infrastructure for cross-border payments has typically involved four banks. These are the bank of the payer, its correspondent bank, and the bank of the biller and its correspondent bank.

Figure 9.12: Traditional cross-border payments

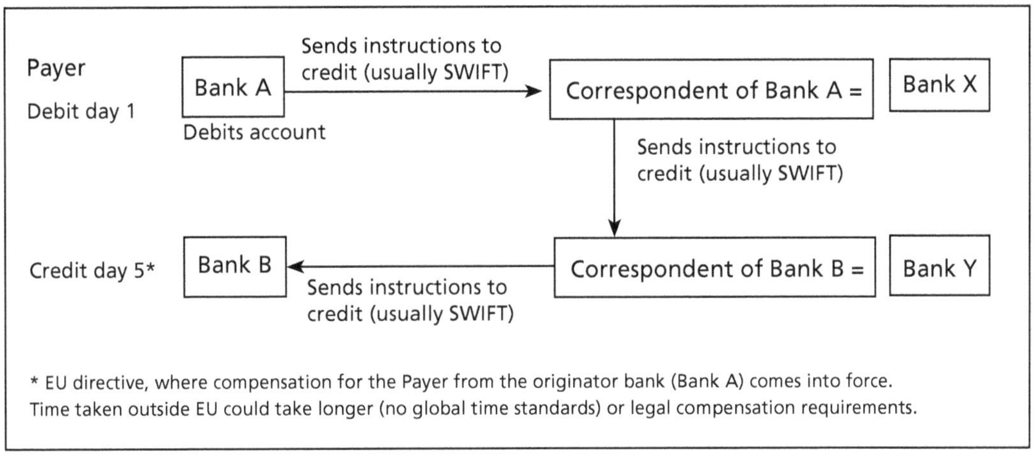

Source: Author

The correspondent banking system is well established worldwide and the infrastructure of many institutions only permits this type of routing. SWIFT was initially established to bring standard formats and telecommunication to international payments.

Third party account managers

Third party account managers can use any form of payment. The one that is most used is the DD for collecting money at source and paying the recurring bills. By adding an 8-digit customer reference number to the incoming or exiting DD (complete with the IBAN and BIC of the third party) the payment flows through the process automatically. On request for payment of a DD, the requestor's reference number is added.

Figure 9.13: Direct debit to a virtual account

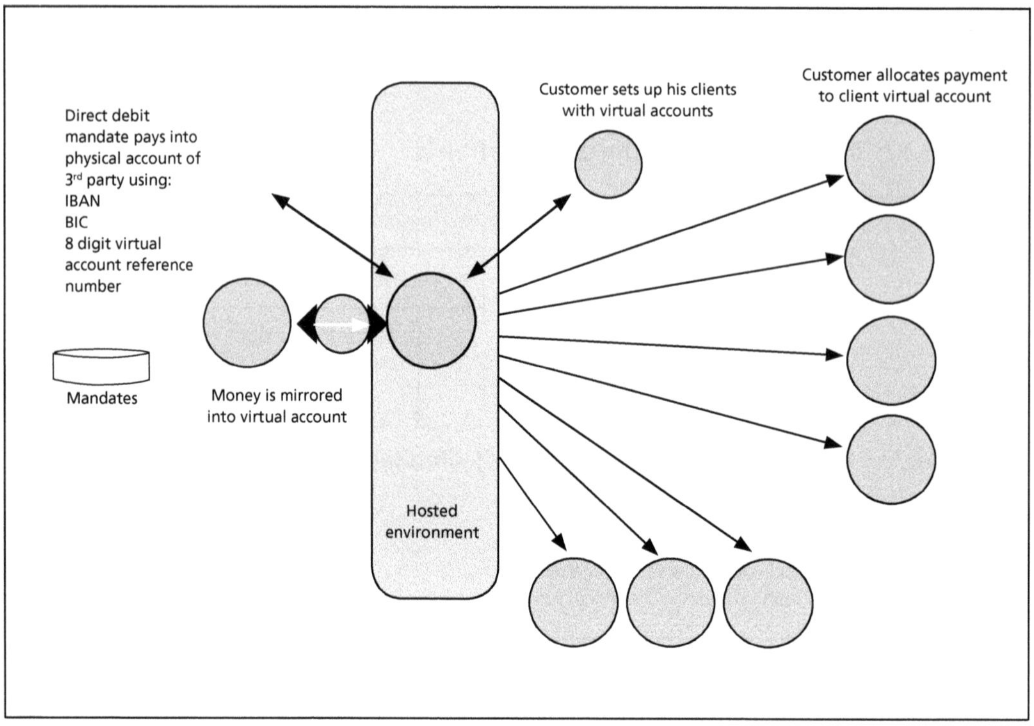

Source: Author

Figure 9.14: Direct debit from a virtual account

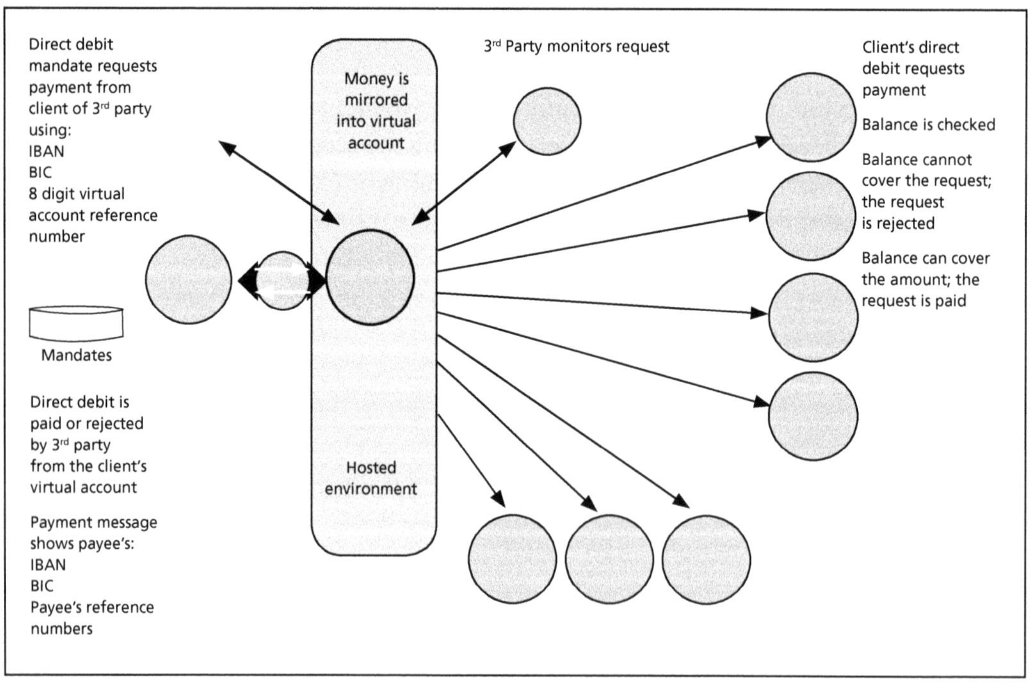

Source: Author

Payment fees

Transaction fees charged by banks may be explicit (a known amount per each kind of transaction), or implicit (dependent on the overall relationship with the bank). The more banking services are used, the lower the fees charged. Each bank sets its own rates. In Europe, payment fees are limited by law to encourage market price stability and prevent excess fees being charged.

In correspondent banking payment it is often commonplace for each bank in the chain to take a fee. This has also been addressed by the EU, which allows the originator to pay all the fees along the payment path, instead of the beneficiary receiving less money due to fees being deducted.

Transactions for warehousing are usually based as a percentage of the amount transferred into the warehouse that can vary from 2.5% to 5%. Once the money is in the warehouse, additional explicit fees for transferring the money to other accounts can be levied. PayPal, for example, charges a percentage of the amount ranging from 3.4% for £1,500 per month dropping down to 1.4% for over £55,000 per month, plus a transaction charge of £0.2.

SEPA has developed a common set of rules and has suggested a three-day standard for the banks to pay from one account into another at a different bank in the EU. By 2010 all banks in the EU were capable of processing incoming SEPA Direct Debits.

The EU Parliament has set the end date for SEPA to be in place by February 2014. The EU's legally binding date is to ensure EU-wide rules to make the payment service fair, eliminate hidden charges, and accelerate transfers. In doing so, this could save as much as €123 billion within six years. All the banks will finally be able to receive and send SEPA Direct Debits..

The level of domestic cash management sophistication and services offered is determined by a country's approach to the rules and regulations surrounding payments and the competition to banks themselves. Outside SEPA, the terms and conditions of payments are determined at the country level. For example, certain countries are considering SEPA-like standards.

Real Time Gross Settlement (RTGS)

The RTGS payment system is normally maintained or controlled by the central bank of a particular country. There is no physical exchange of money between the banks within a country. The central bank makes adjustments in the electronic accounts, e.g. Bank B's account is reduced and the same amount increased in Bank A's account. Settlement is immediate, final and irrevocable. Credit risks due to settlement lags are eliminated.

The RTGS system is used by 70% of the central banks in the world. That is, the central banks have an electronic system between themselves and their banks. For example, the Hong Kong Monetary Authority was the first central bank in Asia to introduce RTGS in 1996. The RTGS system is suited tor low-volume, high-value transactions. It lowers settlement risk and also gives an accurate picture of an institution's account at any point of time.

The implementation of RTGS systems by central banks throughout the world is driven by the goal of minimising risk in high-value electronic payment settlement systems. The World Bank and the EU are committed to funding RTGS systems, as these systems help to stabilise the world's financial markets.

The total market for RTGS comprises 174 central banks. While SWIFT supports over 200 countries, a number of central banks have payment reporting authority over a number of countries, e.g. The Central Bank of West African States unifies 101 banks in eight countries.

Figure 9.15: Real Time Gross Settlement process

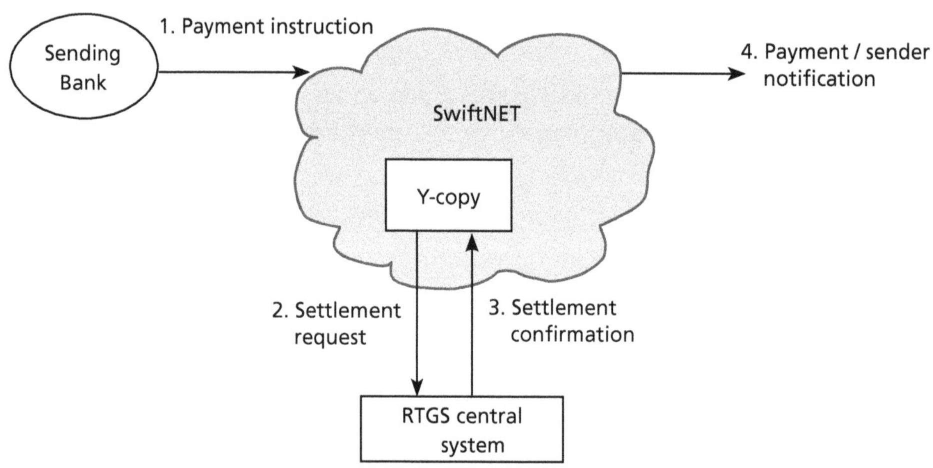

Note: Finality of the funds transfer between sending and receiving banks is achieved at the moment when the payment is settled in the books of the Central Bank.

Source: Bank of England

The credit card process cycle – key players

Credit cards are another of the payment methods available, with the largest providers being Visa, MasterCard and American Express. Like any payment scheme, there are a number of parties involved. Let's start with the credit card holder making a purchase.

Figure 9.16: The credit card process cycle

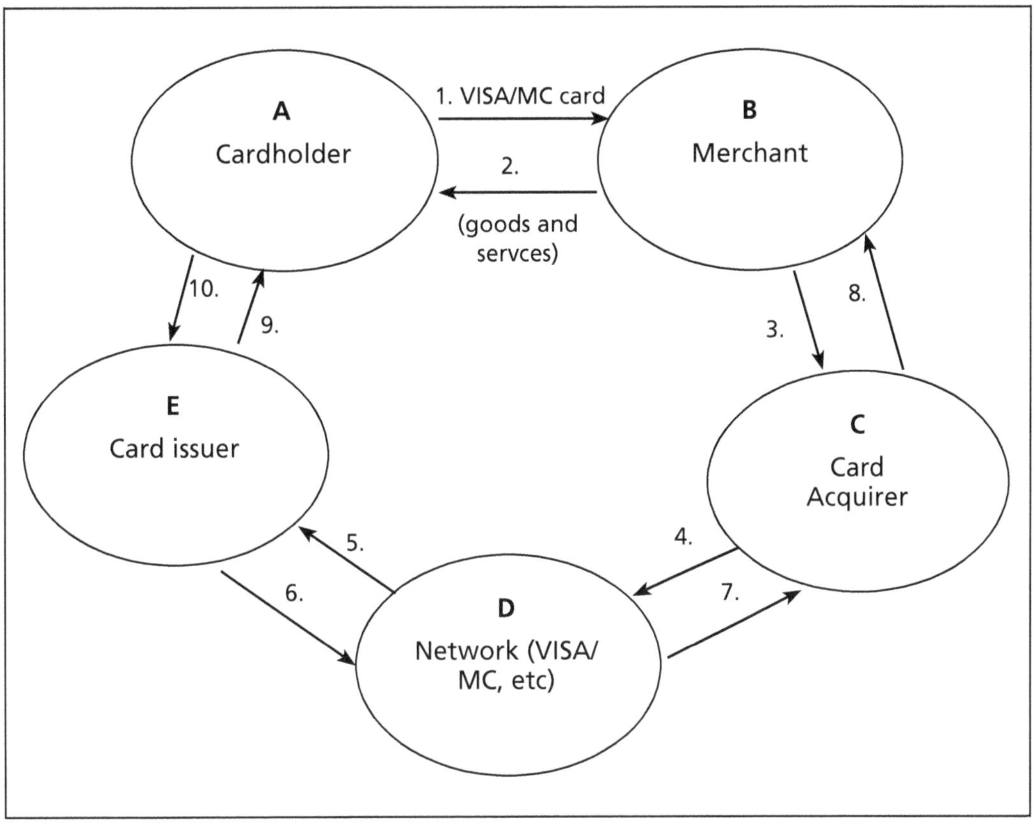

Source: Author

Sample transaction and stakeholders

A. *Cardholder makes a credit card purchase (step 1) and pays for it at step 10 of the cycle*

The time between purchase and payment can be up to 56 days and with no interest charged if paid in full. Interest charges on the balances after that time can vary up to 35%. In Canada, for example, the average fee is 19.99%.

B. *Merchant provides goods and services to the cardholder (step 2) and receives payment from the card acquirer (step 8)*

The time between the merchant sending in the transactions for payment and receiving payment is a negotiation between the merchant and the card acquirer, usually 28 days. The fees are usually between 1.5 –5%; for example, the Canadian Competition Bureau in 2009 reported 1.5–3% with the premium card brand, for example MasterCard Premium, at the top end of the pricing. As cardholders can reject transactions up to nine months after purchase for immediate credit, acquirers often hold back payment from the merchant as a cash cushion. Cash cushions can often reach 10% of the merchant's turnover. In addition, new merchants may see reduced payments until the cash cushion has reached acquirer acceptable levels. Merchants in the higher risk categories often pay in excess of 5% transaction fees.

C. *Card acquirer sends transactions into the network provider (Visa, MasterCard and American Express are the main ones) (step 4) and the network provider pays the acquirer (step 7) less interchange fees*

   The network provider pays the acquirer on terms; both the timeliness and fees are usually in the rulebook of the network provider. Visa and MasterCard have sub-second processing speeds per transaction of 20 and 47 milliseconds respectively.

D. *The network forwards the transactions onto the card Issuer (step 5) and receives payment for them (step 6)*

   The network provider has a set of rules including fees by which both the issuer and acquirer must abide, otherwise they could lose their membership.

E. *The issuer invoices the cardholder (step 9) and receives payment or query from the cardholder (step 10)*

In its 2010 Annual Report, Visa Europe noted gains in the commercial card business of 10%, which increased the number of cards to 12.4 million per year. While this is less than 5% of the total cards issued (Visa issued 408 million) the corporate did charge €61 billion in the year.

On direct debit cards, Visa reached agreement with the European Commission in relation to cross-border interchange fees for immediate debit card payments based on the 'Merchant Indifference Test'. The cross-border direct debit card transaction fee is set at 0.2% per item. Visa regards deferred debit and credit transactions as more comparable to other instruments that provide a line of credit, as opposed to cash and cheque.

Prepaid cards

Prepaid usage was first driven by expatriates, the unbanked, migrant workers, credit deprived people, gift-giving and loyalty cards. The use of prepaid mobile phones was a key promoter and educator of the concept. The sharing of the fees between the banks and the telecommunication companies led to the ability to top up the mobile telephone account at ATMs.

Prepaid cards are offered by the major card scheme providers (Visa, MasterCard, etc) to their customers; customers can put money on a card and dispatch that card to the recipient. The recipient can then use the card at ATMs and POS worldwide. The card can be used until the amount loaded onto it is used up. There are two types of card – disposal and reloadable. The disposables are thrown away once used. The reloadables, like 'pay as you go' mobiles, can have new money added at any time. Table 9.3 shows typical prepaid card charges.

Table 9.3 Prepaid card fees

Account set-up	Free to £30	One time
Monthly	Free to £15	Per month
Transaction	Free to 3%	Per request for authorisation
ATM	0.5% to 3%	Per £100 taken
Internet purchases	Free to 3%	Per purchase
Overdraft charges	Free to 30%	Monthly fees; request for transactions are tracked and deducted when new money is added to the card

Source: Author

There can be many different types of pricing, and the permutations are many. The Canadian Financial Consumer Agency, an independent government financial watchdog, described prepaid products as "an expensive way to spend your own money".

In 2011 Visa noted that if growth in prepaid and debit transactions continues, it could account for more than half of Visa's global purchases business in the next five years. The possibilities for the introduction of prepaid are vast; at the moment, there are even incentives being developed whereby the prepaid card system can be used on a mobile phone to purchase something like coffee. The retail sector can offer prepaid cards to their customers. Loyalty schemes implemented through the prepaid cards can bring in cash now and retain the customer. For example, Starbucks estimates that 25% of purchases in the US are now completed using its prepaid loyalty card.

One of the most popular uses of prepaid card is the travel card. Here the card is loaded with different foreign currencies. It is a win-win for all. The provider makes the fees through the FX spread, the corporate can see what and where their money and exposures are, and the user can access cash and make payments in local currencies.

For corporate or FI with international activities, the funding of small, local activities can be done through a prepaid card. As prepaid is competing against cash, a corporate using a pooled prepaid account can move the cash virtually immediately across to those accounts that need it. Control of internal staff expenses can be improved and the resulting paperwork decreased. In addition, management information on where the money is going and how it is being spent is available electronically. Using prepaid at the right fees has its advantages for a corporate. Banks are beginning to offer prepaid services as part of their suite of cash management offerings.

Near Field Communication (NFC) payments

NFC is a high frequency application allowing exchange of data between devices that are less than 20 centimetres apart, often referred to as contactless payment. An international standard has been established (ISO/IEC 14443) and the need today is to establish an infrastructure within which NFC can be readily used. The mobile phone market is a strong backer of this technology and in the UK the four major networks – Orange, O2, T-Mobile and Vodaphone – are NFC-compliant.

NFC payments often referred to as 'tap and go' and come in two forms – closed or open loop. An example of a closed system is payment for public transportation. Here entry to that system is by physical POS devices and a prepaid NFC-compliant card created by the carrier. An open system is one in which the NFC-compliant prepaid, debit or credit card or mobile phone can be used anywhere. One example of this is 2012 Olympics, where Visa, LloydsTSB and Samsung are provided preloaded credit for the athletes and officials. The Visa contactless payment option is called Payway; MasterCard's is called PayPass.

Reconciliation

It is well understood by financial professionals that profitable businesses fail every day if cash flow is negative and the 2008 credit crunch brought this home to even the largest conglomerates such as GE that had borrowed short and was unable to roll over credit lines. Most corporate Treasurers and CFOs don't have the luxury that GE had of tapping into emergency funding programs such as TARP and have to rely on their bank.

In the UK, after bailing out the banks, the government insisted the banks lent money to the SME market under 'Project Merlin'. The Bank of England's official assessment of Project Merlin found that lending to small businesses was £74.9 billion, £1.1 billion short of the target. Credit lines are being squeezed and overdraft rates are up, so understanding the numbers has never been more important. Bank of England Governor Sir Mervyn King in February 2012 spoke against the "harsh treatment" of small and medium companies being starved of the funds they need to grow, create jobs and drive the economic recovery. Bank of England figures show that net lending fell by £10.7 billion in 2011 – in other words, the banks received £10.7 billion more in loan repayments than they gave out in new loans. That took the total fall in credit outstanding since the end of 2008 to £82.7 billion.

Reconciliations are the end of a long process which may have been strung out over a number of months and include winning an order, receiving a purchase order, delivering of the goods/services, issuing an invoice and receiving a payment without having to chase for payment. The final step often gets less focus, as payment has now been received and typically staff that carry out reconciliations have many other duties which are more visible to their colleagues and are often prioritised as more urgent.

Timely, accurate reconciliations are vital part of the process because:

- Business decisions lean heavily on <u>accurate</u> financial decisions;
- Credit control processes can only be activated with confidence once unrecognised items have been accounted for ;
- Fraud (in-house or by customers) can be identified (and deterred) by timely reconciliation of ledgers and bank accounts;
- Incorrect bank charges, fees, interest or FX conversions can be identified and addressed early – it can be a significant amount of work to recalibrate the books if there is a long-standing error that has not been identified;
- Regulations are obligations that if left undiscovered can lead to significant fines –
    - PwC failed to notice that JP Morgan Securities Ltd had not properly

segregated an average of $8.6 billion of client funds from the firm's accounts; the UK FSA fined the bank $33.3 million pounds in 2010;

- The FSA fined Towry Investment Management Ltd £494,000 for providing misleading information to the FSA and client money breaches. The FSA set out clear rules on how firms need to treat client money in its Client Asset Sourcebook (CASS).

Reconciliation is often one of the last functions to be done on a timely basis as it often compared to looking for needles in haystacks. It is also time-consuming, costly and boring with often little gain in terms of value for money. Most reconciliations result in less than a 10% error rate. However, those 10% or fewer errors could be a high-risk business, especially when those needles turn out to be unmatched payments, internal fraud or payments applied to the wrong account which, when reversed, open up a negative black hole. It's common that the favourable cash position is often with one of the worst payers.

As volumes of payment traffic grow, the chances of mismatched transactions occurring increase. To offset these chances without automation of the process requires additional administration in terms of people to resource the reconciliation process. Reconciliation of the bank accounts to that of the corporate back office helps prevent losses in financial and customer service terms. No-one, especially the regulators, likes to see payments not recorded against the right account and for the right amount.

The issue is the historic information structure that surrounds the early days of the Automatic Clearing Houses (ACHs). Many ACH payments have limited remittance information that can be forwarded to the beneficiary due to the 18-character remittance advice field started when electronic payments begin. A beneficiary receiving the limited remittance information cannot apply the funds automatically without first finding the customer and then the invoice being credited. Often the remitter's reference number is shortened or not present at all. The payer often has not included its payment details or has transcribed them wrongly. Just ask British Telecom (BT) as it tries to and post similar amounts across their millions of clients. There are also complications in terms of fees and charges by the bank, the addition of interest and, with foreign exchange, the rates being used pre- and post-correction.

To overcome these issues, reconciliation should take place is daily and be as highly automated as possible. The process should highlight only the exceptions (usually less than 10% of the volume but often representing 80% of the cost) and suggest matches through business intelligence built into the process. For example:

- Highlight possible matches;
- Traces by source;
- Multi to one and one to multi entries possible matches;
- Automating accounting entries for correction (with dual sign-off).

The automation reduces the cost of administration and customer service is much improved. The need for further automation is clearly reflected in a survey from the Aberdeen Group in April 2011, where 29% of companies had fully automated the procedure to pay (accounts payable – A/P) and 25% of companies had fully automated the order to cash (accounts receivable – A/R).

Those companies which had automated the A/P and A/R noted:

1. Processing of Day Sales Outstanding (DSO) dropped to 21 days versus the industry average of 53 days; and
2. Cash flow forecast rate was 84% accurate as compared to the industry average of 49%.

Therefore, by performing best practice it is clear the organisation benefits. The areas that should be focused on are as follows.

Table 9.4: The reconciliations process

	Today	Future
Process	1. Manual – paper-based (storage, future referencing) 2. Complexities – errors (self-compensating errors) with no systematic priorities 3. Administratively expensive, boring work flow – ideal for inertia and mismanagement 4. Data taken out of secure systems (in-house fraud risk and additional audit checks required)	1. Automated 2. Exception management and prioritisation – degrees of difficulty and amount size 3. Automated workflows showing segregation and timing of changes – time stamps, full audit trail 4. Data held in secure and monitored environment making it harder to defraud
People and training	1. Low value activity, while important task, rarely seen as a priority 2. Problem solving people required, understanding the business and making the right decision. Often on the job training – sit with Nellie, stand with Sid	1. With reduced volumes and the right tools, less unskilled work required 2. Skilled people to get to the bottom of the problems quickly rather than waiting for escalation with suggested online solutions
Ownership	1. Low grade administrative with limited escalation unless a crisis	1. Moving up organisation often to board level as liquidity is paramount – accurate cash forecasting and liquidity management are increasing in importance
Technology	1. Fantastic technology used today, Excel spreadsheets – now what numbers would management like! 2. Macros can help, colour coding etc 3. Format and flat files (pre-defined rigid structures) – now where is that tub file filed with paper ledgers?	1. Real time updating – link e-banking to internal automated systems, installed or through cloud technology 2. Splits out fees, charges, interest into separate items, FX – midpoint days rate versus actual 3. e-invoicing and XML
Metrics – measure it to manage it	1. List common metric e.g. DSOs outstanding prepared manually before reconciliation 2. Reconciliation timeliness is often monthly or even quarterly	1. List common metric e.g. DSOs outstanding reported after reconciliation 2. Reconciliation timeliness is daily

Reconciliation is the last stage of the payment process. One reason it is not automated is that, while everyone acknowledges that is very important, the resources needed within the corporate are frequently working on higher prioritised activities. The need to automate is critical to give an internal closer and more timely view of the monies collected and paid. What prevents the automation is the paper process; the lack of standards around invoices and the number of ways payments can be gathered and sent.

Figure 9.17: Integrated and hosted virtual account solutions

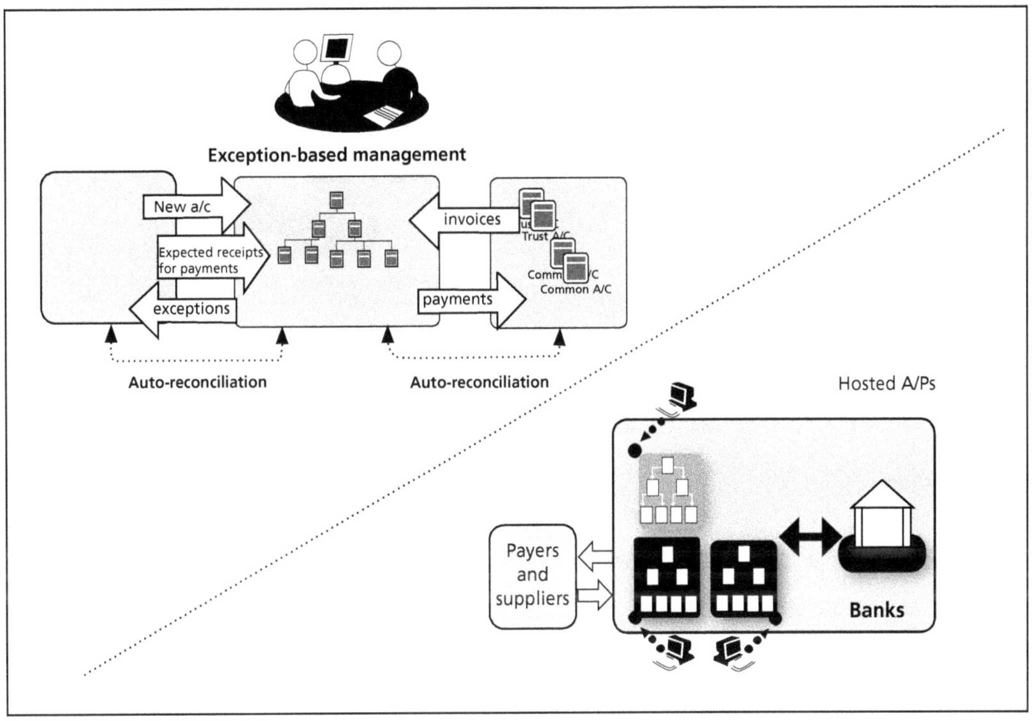

Source: Author

With multi-banked companies there are a number of approaches. One is to have a bank become the centre for gathering the information and then making payments to the other banks upon instruction. Another is to do it in-house; a third is to use third party virtual accounts.

The use of virtual accounts enables every account payable client to have an account per invoice. The incoming invoice is then paid either electronically or by cheque. The resulting transfer of funds is then reconciled between the virtual accounts, the company's back office system and the bank. The bank is taken as the golden source as to where the money is, and the virtual accounts as the golden source of the information. As Walter Wriston, former Chairman of Citibank noted: "Information about money will become more important than the money itself."

Figure 9.18: Corporates – the paper trail

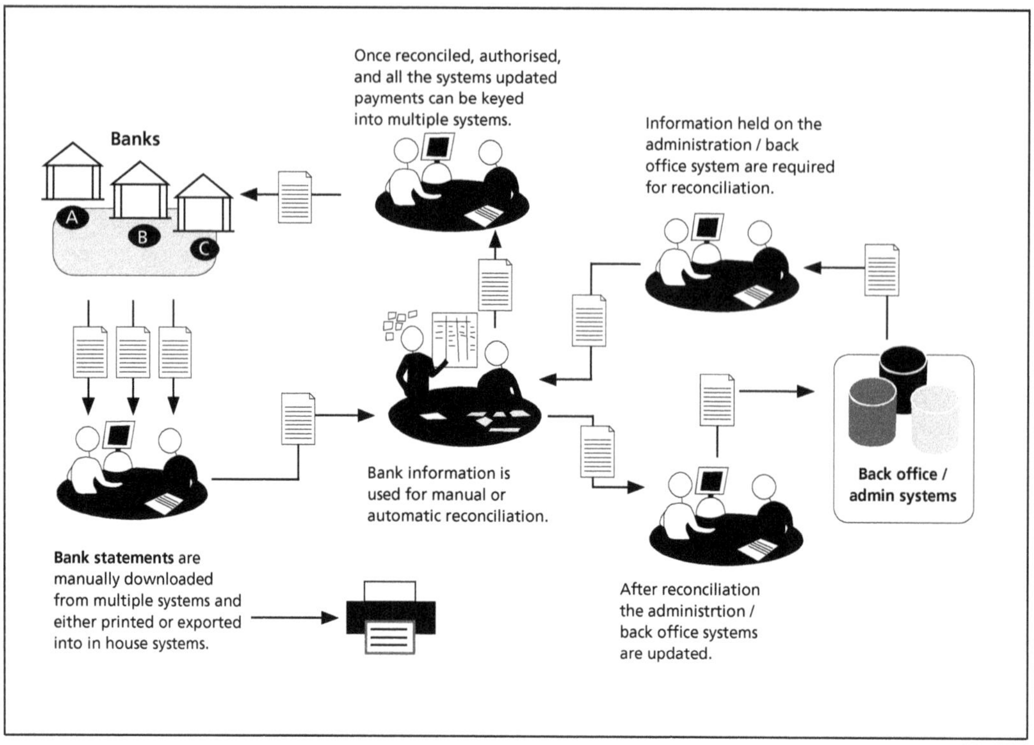

Source: Author

Figure 9.19: Corporates automated using virtual accounts

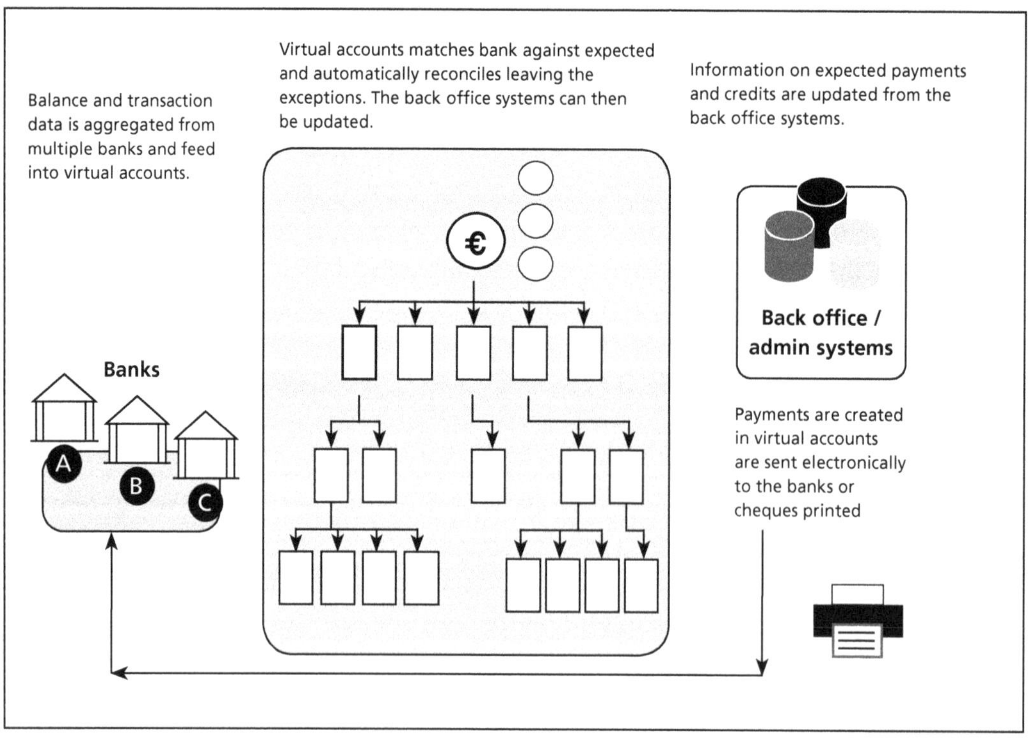

Source: Author

The future

Same-day electronic payment from a personal or smartphone for one-off payments will become the norm over time. Similarly, the receipt of recurring payments such as payroll will be via direct debit.

For banks, this is a crisis. They lose float and will fight the movement to shorter timeframes. Only regulators and legal provisions such as the SPA Directive of payment by D+1 will overcome the resistance.

For corporates, electronic payments are best, particularly because of receiving the money on the same day, and will become commonplace. Paying out money can cause the corporate to act like a bank and hold onto it for as long as possible. This tendency has to be restricted, as regulators may turn their attention to the corporate market. The cost of future compliance is far more than following best practices now.

Cheques will continue to drop in volume as immediate payments and DD programs remove much of the need for paper.

CHAPTER 10

FOREIGN EXCHANGE

Questions for the CFO, Treasurer or Cash Manager

- Who is looking after the foreign exchange, is it done using the internet or through the bank, and how do we establish the rates?
- Have we taken out hedging positions against the major currency exposures?
- Has anyone looked at the historic rates we have been charged against market rates at that time, given the spreads can exceed 10% in many currencies?
- Which currencies with the potential for appreciation should be maintained for payment?

Key considerations

- Considering foreign exchange options;
- Managing currency exposure;
- Using automated FX dealing;
- Monitoring currency movements, particularly Euro appreciation and depreciation against a group of currencies.

International cash management and FX

With international cash management, the level of complexity increases dramatically. Also, a particular bank's corporate customers' commitment to the international arena is reflected in the level of commitment towards international cash management. Large corporates can have significant influence over what services their local banks provide. The reason is, like any good service provider, the bank wants to meet the specific needs of its clients.

The first sign of international cash management is foreign exchange. Companies often price their services in their home currencies, putting the onus on the buyer to sort out the currency risks. Others price in their home currency and one other major currency, which is often USD or euros.

Most banks offer a FX 'branch' rate, usually for amounts up to $50,000 for transactions from one currency to another. The rate is changed once a day and contains a substantial spread, often 6% (depending on currency) either side of the mid-point market rate, plus a transaction fee.

FX rates for a pair of currencies are now easy to establish using the internet. Some corporate internal policies insist on three quotes. The corporate's main function is to make payments and these tend to occur at the end of the month.

Managing foreign exchange options

Cash management goes international once a company starts buying or selling a product or service involving a second currency. Now there is another currency to be tracked, measured and valued in the cash flow.

Effective management of foreign currency risk stabilises the company's performance. Currency risk management programmes can structure a cost-effective currency management strategy to match the risk exposure. A comprehensive set of currency management services would include derivatives, spot, forward and options contracts.

Derivatives

Derivatives are a financial instruments used to reduce risk. The price of the derivative is derived (hence the name) from an underlying asset, index or rate. A derivative is a security in its own right and its value is dependent upon the price movement of the underlying asset. For example, a derivative in the form of an option can be used to hedge a currency position by buying a future value for that currency. The option represents a contract between two parties. To buy at a specific price is called a 'call'. The right to sell at a specific price is called a 'put'. Options have an expiration date and come in two forms: American style, which can be exercised at any time; or European, which can only be exercised at expiration.

Most banks with significant corporate business offer some form of derivative.

Basically derivatives cost a premium, which enables the corporate to certain rights over the transaction. The derivative contract, over time, is compared to market conditions and at some point either allowed to elapse or is exercised. That point is determined as the most beneficial financial condition for the corporate.

e-options

The ability to purchase options is becoming easier with banks and others offering e-options. The price of the option is derived from the difference between the reference price and the value of the underlying asset, plus a premium based on the time remaining until the expiration of the option. See Table 10.1.

Table 10.1: Example of currency option pricing based on basis point spread

Currency		**1 month**	**3 months**
Against GBP	Mid point of currency	Option Premium added (Basis point spread)	Option
Euro	8.9	5	15
US	1.55	5	14
Japan	119.7	9	32

Source: The Times, 31 December 2011

Regulatory changes

The derivative market is undergoing extensive regulatory changes, as at the height of the market, derivatives traders over-estimated the liquidity available and failed to acknowledge that companies would default on the obligations. Derivatives issued on OTC (Over the Counter) are being repositioned onto an exchange-based system that will bring more transparency to this trillion-dollar market.

The Office of the Controller in the US reported in the 1st quarter 2011 that 1,047 insured US commercial banks reported derivative activities. The activity is concentrated in five banks, which represent 96% of the total banking industry notional accounts and 83% of the industry net currency exposure. Derivatives remain concentrated in interest rate products that comprise 82% of total derivative notional values; Credit derivatives represent 6.1% of total derivatives notions of $14.9 trillion.

Other options

Forwards

Forwards are a way to manage exchange rate risks or to make payments of foreign currency payments that are needed in the future. Forward transactions enable the buying or selling of a currency at a fixed rate on a specified future date. By linking this date to the date of the currency payment, the future exchange rate is locked and eliminates the risk of further volatility in that transaction.

Interest rate swaps

Interest rate swaps are used when a company is borrowing in foreign currency and may want to manage its exposure to fluctuations in interest rates in that currency. An interest rate swap allows management of mix of fixed- and floating-rate debt synthetically, without the need to refinance.

Currency exposure

It is essential to cover future currency movements – once a company has two or more bank accounts in different currencies currency exposure is created, as any two currencies are rarely static over their values of exchange at any particular time. The market establishes its own value of a particular currency and changes can be dramatic. Every company has a statuary currency – its home currency – in which accounting and audit reports have to be filed. Consequently, accounts in a currency other than the statuary currency have to be shown, usually under the term 'currency exposure'.

Currency exposure can affect the profit and loss account, especially if there is a major currency movement both up or down; the value of international assets; the risk in long-term international contracts; sales revenues; borrowings in international currencies; and the timing of payments being made and received.

Here a rolling schedule of incoming fees and expenses in various currencies can show where the market risk is at its strongest. Trading with a country that has consistently high inflation often results in lower net revenues coming out of that country due to the difference in exchange rates. In dealing with the UK, a country such as Australia has seen its currency rise in terms of what the UK pound can buy. Hence, if income is coming out of Australia, the revenue is increased, but if costs are being incurred there, these too will increase.

Buying and selling FX

There are a couple of ways to ensure the exposure is well-managed and the cash needed in the future is predictable.

The currency rate quotes have two figures – the buy price and the sell price. The mid rate is often quoted, giving an idea of the currency value as judged by the market at that particular time. Currencies can become volatile and can move upwards or downwards of 5% in a day. The currencies themselves are divided into prime, secondary and tertiary (exotic) currencies. The prime currencies are the most liquid, e.g. USD, and the tertiary are the least, e.g. Kenyan Shilling. The US dollar is the world's currency of choice, with 50% of all trades having a dollar component. The margins, or gap, between the quoted buy and sell rates quoted also reflects the lack of liquidity in a particular currency.

Once a corporate moves to active from infrequent FX transactions then the bank, depending on the amounts involved, permits access to the 'Corporate FX desk' or introduces them to automated foreign exchange (e-trading). The FX desk is located on the trading room floor. This enables the corporate to buy or sell currencies at more favourable rates.

Through a dealer with a phone, a corporate can see and trade (execute) on a moving market FX rate (the rate is usually held for 30 seconds by the trading party) from an online FX service. These services are readily available through banks and non-banks. Often, local banks can brand an FX service from a major financial institution, with the market risk covered by that institution. The corporate, though, now has an exposure in another currency if it is not a straight one-off payment.

Credit line from the bank

The key to buying and selling FX is a credit line limit from the bank. The reason is the settlement process that governs the surrounding currency movement. A spot trade in a currency takes two days to settle. In that time, the currency purchased can increase or decrease in value. The risk is that one leg of the currency may not occur on time, or if a bank fails, not at all. The risk of a bank failing has been greatly reduced by Continuous Linked Settlement (CLS). A consortium of banks owns CLS with governance under the Federal Reserve in the US. CLS has reduced this risk to banks across a range of currencies. This in turn safeguards the client's customers.

Spread and commission-based pricing

Some traders prefer trading on commissions over spread based trading, and, sometimes, the other way around. Clients often mention the fact that commission-based pricing allows them to get a better feeling for the markets' price action, while others prefer all costs of trading to be included in the bid/ask quote, as this may be more transparent.

Continuous Linked Settlement (CLS)

Sixty financial institutions around the world were involved in creating the Continuous Linked Settlement (CLS) system. Initially designed to reduce the settlement risk between currencies, it also streamlines the foreign exchange transaction process between trading parties. Banks enable non-CLS settlement members to access the benefits of CLS.

CLS Settlement Services supports CLS participation, payments, and foreign exchange trade matching. This solution can be integrated with existing accounts at the bank. Enabling the execution of foreign exchange settlements on a 'payment versus payment' basis, CLS offers final and simultaneous settlement of all foreign exchange transactions. These services provide:

- Real-time access to CLS transaction and balance information;
- Integrated matching and reconciliation services;
- Reduced settlement risk.

Automated FX (e-trading)

According to *Euromoney*, the multi-bank and independent platforms are growing rapidly and now handling $48 trillion a year in foreign currency value.

To begin automated trading of FX the retailer needs the money being traded to be in an account with them. Similar to the warehouse payment movement, money is transferred into an account under the FX providers' authority. Once money has been put into that account then the client is ready to buy and sell currencies.

Today, clients are often given prices off the same pricing feed. A pricing feed is the capture of the price of a currency in real time and offered to a client electronically. The major price feeds for the full range of currencies are provided by the larger global banks. Vendors such as Reuters and Bloomberg provide rate information on screens. The global bank price feeds are used as the wholesaler price. Vendors and the smaller banks take the major price feeds and offer them to their clients.

The banks provide the currency prices with a built-in spread. The retailer aggregates the clients' amounts and when a currency amount has been reached and the credit lines established with the global bank, a trade is executed. The vendor or bank then gives the trade to the global bank to trade that currency back into the currency of the home currency. This gives the retailer limited to virtually no exposure to the market. The positions being created by the aggregation of the smaller trades are covered once they reach a certain size, and as such, do not expose the retailer to suffering major market shifts in the wrong direction.

FX roles

The responsibilities and roles for providing automated FX are:

- The administrator;
- The dealer;
- The trader;
- The customer;
- The compliance officer;
- The support team.

The administrator

The administrator is responsible for managing trading parameters of the currencies, rate feeds, margins, users, groups, permissions as well as administration activities such as password resets, and creation of new users.

The dealer

The dealer's objective is to achieve maximum flow of trades through the system from the customers. They are responsible for the administration of customer settings such as margins, and intervening on customer deal requests where necessary. The best customers receive the most favourable margins often based on a matrix of rates by customer level. The rates are usually an add-on to the spreads shown and can be varied by client.

The trader

The trader's role is to manage the currency positions by buying or selling with the liquidity providers. Traders also manage the preferred liquidity provider for each currency pair. The liquidity provider is often a bank and gives credit facilities for the retailer to provide the service to their clients.

The customer

The customer is anyone who is willing to trade with the retailer and is over 18 and has passed through compliance.

The compliance officer

Before a customer can trade currencies they need to pass due diligence, and the compliance officer makes certain all clients are screened and with proof (usually a passport) of who they are and pass the ongoing compliance checks on a frequent basis.

The support team

The support team is responsible for ensuring any enquires from clients and regulators are quickly resolved. For example, some clients have concerns about unexplained spikes or sudden market moves in the price feed that may trigger orders but do not correspond to moves in the underlying market. This is particularly important if spikes trigger the execution of stop-loss orders (a pre-set level agreement which is set to reduce the size of the loss in a falling market).

Currency movements

Margin, or increased leverage

The retailer can provide the client with a margin account that enables the client to buy more currency than he has in the account. The reason for this is that the retailer is looking at the movement that particular currency is making in a day. It is rare for a major or secondary currency to move by 10% in any one day. Consequently, the retailer with the authorisation over the account can sell out that currency when required should the money in the account not be sufficient to pay if the rates move downwards.

Depending on the retailer, the client's profile and the past practices, the following margins can be issued for a major currency:

- Assuming 10% daily historic movement, the retailer could give a margin of 10 to 1. That means the client can buy 10 times the amount in the account. By putting in £1,000 into the account, the client can buy £10,000. The retailer probably has a stop-loss order.
- Assuming a 2.5% daily historic movement, the retailer could give a margin of 40 to 1. That means the £1,000 becomes £40,000.

In setting the margin for the account, the retailer takes into consideration the currency pair and the currency in the account.

A client could have the account in GBP and has bought EUR and sold USD. The client could be looking for short-term gains and closing out the position at the end of the day. This way, no market risk is taken overnight.

Comparing euro performance

Taking a view over the last two years of market trading of the euro's performance against other currencies, Table 10.2 shows the Australian Dollar, Chinese RMB , Swedish Kroner, USD and GBP rose 20%, 15.57%, 12.93% 9.7% and 5.68% respectively. Poland's currency, on the other hand, declined 8% in value. That means the euro could buy 8% more goods in Poland that in 2009, whereas goods from Australia cost 20% more.

Consequently, if any surplus cash were kept in either the Australian or Chinese currencies, a two-year appreciation of 20% and 15.67% over the euro would have been realised (less the currency exchange fees). In certain countries, the use of holding cash in currency other than the home currency is commonplace. An example of this is Zimbabwe where the US dollar is preferred over the local currency, which has lost most of its value over the last few years. In that period, the price of a car in local currency five years ago would now, five years later, buy a loaf of bread.

Table 10.2: Euro changes as reported by the European Central Bank

Currency	Dec-09	Dec-10	Dec-11	2 yr change	Largest daily Movements
Australia (AUD)	1.60	1.31	1.28	-20.00%	-2.40% 3.10%
Great Britain (GBP)	0.88	0.86	0.83	-5.68%	-1.80% 3.0%
USA (USD)	1.44	1.33	1.30	-9.72%	-2.70% 1.90%
Poland (SLN)	4.10	3.97	4.43	8.05%	-2.30% 3.10%
Sweden (Kroner)	10.29	8.96	8.96	-12.93%	-0.90% 1.10%
China (Renminbi - RMB)	9.83	8.82	8.29	-15.67%	-2.10% 1.90%

Asian currencies and the RMB

Traditionally, companies have kept their global cash surpluses in USD, EUR or GBP. This process is now undergoing a review, especially by those companies that see their Asian operations growing and becoming a larger part of their revenues and expenses. The Asian people have historically maintained far more currencies than those in the US and Europe. The reasons are often high interest rates in a particular currency and high inflation that in turn creates volatility of that currency. Most Asian bank accounts clients use five or more currencies, whereas in the US and Europe, the majority stays with one currency. The reason for reviewing the choice of an Asian currency is the chance of long-term appreciation.

The Chinese authorities are encouraging the RMB to be used as a settlement currency for international trades. With its deposits in RMB doubling in the last few years, Hong Kong is a major beneficiary of this policy, and has the largest offshore deposits of RMB in the world. A European Central Bank report shows the RMB has become a key driver of currency movements in Asia since the mid-2000s and even more so since the financial crisis. China's dominance in the region and the role of the RMB in the international monetary system makes it already a tri-polar currency; that is, the USD, EUR and RMB are now equally acceptable in the market.

The future

The FX market is one of the most transparent markets in the world, with price availability across the web. The next phase is the move to same-day payment or D+1 and the removal of spot timing of D+2 for the major currencies. Nordea provides this for the Nordic currencies today. The use of options will also become common as they become demystified and easier to purchase and monitor.

The banks will continue to dominate this space, as extra-large credit lines are needed to attract the trading volume. The trading volume will continue high as algorithmic trading (mathematical formulae that are aimed at predicting currency prices) becomes commonplace. Computers perform algo trading to take advantage of price differentials and trading trends. The greater the volume, the greater the chances of accurately forecasting which way the currency prices are heading.

Corporates will become increasingly aware of their FX exposure and take precautions against taking too great a loss in a particular currency. For example, GlaxoSmithKline has been sweeping cash from banks in the eurozone back to the UK. This is to reduce their risk of exposure to the euro monetary system. Many may well use a reporting currency; for example, HSBC reports in USD to meet the needs of its worldwide shareholders. Others in countries with fragile currencies may adopt another currency. Here USD is often used, and coming up fast is the Chinese Renminbi, especially in Asia.

CHAPTER 11

SUPPLY CHAIN MANAGEMENT

Questions for the CFO, Treasurer or Cash Manager

- Are our accounts receivable and accounts payable automated; what is the aging and the amount expressed in terms of working capital at a 10% interest rate?
- How much of our receivables exceeds the agreed terms of our contracts and how can it be reduced?
- Does it make commercial sense to use invoice factoring to help cash flow?
- How many of our invoices received and sent are electronic?

Key considerations

- Automating the supply chain;
- Determining the size of the supply chain;
- Using various types of invoice financing;
- Moving to e-invoicing.

The supply chain and liquidity

The goal of supply chain management is to coordinate the movement of goods and services with the movement of money for the greatest efficiency.

The supply chain is full of potential to release liquidity for the parties involved. The best way to do this is to better understand the supply chain structure. Start by breaking down the process into the following components:

- Days Sales Outstanding (DSO) – the time it takes to collect payment once the service has been sold;
- Days Inventory Outstanding (DIO) – the time it takes to replenish the initial inventory;
- Days Payable Outstanding (DPO) – the time it takes to pay for the goods sold.

While all three can be influenced by the corporate, only DPO is fully controlled by the corporate. The goal is simply to reduced DSO and DIO by a third.

DPO

DPO often has a corporate guideline giving a sense of when the average payment will be made in terms of days lapsed. Many organisations, especially large ones, have service level agreements (SLAs) for payment, for example the National Health Service in the UK has promised to pay invoices within 30 days. Currently the NHS is achieving over 80% of its monthly accounts payables within 30 days of the invoice receipt.

DSO

DSO is often noted in credit reports as an indicator of the credit health of a company: a high level of old receivables outstanding viewed against the normal for that industry's sector could flag a concern. In addition, the older the receivables the less likely they will be fully collected.

Some Boards and/or management teams focus on DSO numbers, while others do not. One example of a change in management was in the international software sector Misys (UK FT250 company), which had less than 40 days outstanding in 2005; by 2011 this had grown to 86 days. The company mantra in the early 2000s was 'cash is king'; any receivables over 60 days were actively addressed and any receivable hitting 120 days were written off against the business. Today Misys has £69.4 million in trade receivables awaiting collection.

DIO

DIO is the working capital tied up in the inventory pending sales. The longer it takes to replenish the inventory, the longer it costs to fund. This is particularly the case in areas where tax and tolls are taken at the point of acceptance. For example, governments often put tax on alcohol, cigarettes and gas (petrol). This has lead to active inventory management especially if the tax is actively collected. In the UK, for example, the tax on petrol represents over 80% of the cost and as such most garages only carry one week's supply. Hence the 'just in time' methodology is being applied to non-manufacturing industries to save money and increase margins.

Supply chain management developments

The next major change in global cash management looks to be the electronic supply chain. Both the global banks in the case studies in this book (Citibank and HSBC – see Chapters 14 and 15) have supply chain management teams.

Financial supply chain innovation has tended to be bilateral, with a bank creating a specific solution for a customer without integrating the customer's trading partners. This is especially evident on the payable side, in which the buyer and the bank control the cash flows with relative ease. This approach does not permit the inclusion of others in the supply chain, which has been ably addressed by SWIFT's Trade Services Unit (TSU), especially since its the move to open accounts. Recent estimates suggest that more than 80% of global trade is now conducted on open account, moving away from the traditional forfaiting practices.

SWIFT's TSU

SWIFT's TSU is a centralised matching and workflow platform available to the SWIFT community. The platform provides timely and accurate comparison of data taken from underlying corporate purchase agreements and related documents, such as commercial invoices, transport and insurance.

The TSU supports the exchange of a 'Bank Payment Obligation' (BPO), an irrevocable conditional obligation from one bank to pay another bank, subject to the presentation of compliant data in the TSU. The "Notice of Intent to Pay" message is an additional information message indicating one corporate's intention to pay another corporate. Together, these two features provide a strong backbone for banks to offer alternative forms of financing, including pre-shipment, post-shipment and reverse factoring.

Forfaiting

Forfaiting (a French word meaning to surrender or relinquish the rights to something) enables a corporate to receive a cash payment on a without recourse basis and all risks associated with the transaction are transferred to the bank. The corporate receives immediate payment and surrenders the right to any further claim for payment. The benefits are:

- The receipt of cash upfront;
- The receivable is settled and removed from the balance sheet;
- All risks are removed including, sovereign, commercial bank, and corporate.

The bank providing the forfeiting makes certain the risks involved are covered and affects the transaction with one of the following debt instruments:

- Letter of Credit;
- Bills of Exchange;

- Promissory Notes;
- Standby Letters of Credit;
- Letter of Guarantee.

Forfaiting credit terms can vary from 90 days to 10 years, providing the underlying country and credit risks are acceptable. The minimum amount is $500,000 (or the equivalent in a major currency). Forfaiting is used extensively in Asia, with the most active markets being China, Korea, Japan, Taiwan and Indonesia.

Size of the supply chain

In 2011, REL Consultancy estimated there was $800 billion in 'trapped capital' in the US corporate supply chain That is money that a company may not know about and therefore is unable to reinvest or deploy to another part of the business. The 13th annual report by REL (July 2011) showed for Europe's top 1,000 companies the following key changes from 2009 to 2010:

Days Working Capital (DWC)	46.5 days in 2005
	42.9 days in 2010
	Improvement was 7.6%

DWC is composed of the accounts receivable added to the inventory and subtracting the accounts payable. This total is then divided by the total per day. (DWC = (A/R + Inventory – A/P)/(Total Revenue/365)) and shows how many days it takes a company to convert its working capital into revenue. The faster it does this, the better the cash flow and efficiency of collecting money within the company. The shorter the working capital ratio, the better is the timeliness of the cash flow.

In 2010 SWIFT researchers Zanders' Report on Working Capital based on research on 4,127 companies worldwide from October 2009 to September 2010 from public reported financials estimated there was €3.67 trillion in trapped capital in the corporate supply chain. Since 2008, this has increased by €183.5 billion as debtors have slowed payments by 4.3 days of sale. In addition, Zanders found that:

- Asian companies had added 15 days to their funding from 2004 to 2010;
- Receivables and Inventory had increased to 88.5 days of sales;
- The above increase equated to €128.7 billion or 5% more liquidity needed.

In the US, the Aite Group research firm has shown that one of the top challenges for American companies is the need to move from paper to a fully automated process. In September 2011, it was estimated that nearly 60% of accounts payable were still paper-based.

Top 20% of companies achieve efficiencies

The Aberdeen Group in 2011 noted that the top 20% of companies could:

- Process an invoice from receipt through settlement in 5.3 days against the average of 10.2 days;

- Discounts for early payments were achieved in 60% of the time against the average of 9%;
- The average cost to process the invoice was $7.78 against the average of $12.05.

The common characteristics of the top 20% are:

- 3.8 x likely to establish pre-negotiated, fixed early discounts;
- 2.6 x likely to have automated alerts to notify managers of payments exceeding pre-defined thresholds;
- 1.4 x likely to have segmented their supply base for electronic payments.

The technology used across the process by the top 20% is:

Function	Usage by top 20%
Document imaging	56%
Electronic approval workflow	52%
Scanning	52%
Electronic bank account management	48%
Invoice networking	31%

The methodology used by 47% of the companies surveyed is paper and spreadsheets. 20% use internal Enterprise Resource Planning (ERP) systems; 17% use a module added on to the ERP system or a third party offering, with 3% outsourcing the process. The remainder is a mixture of stand-alone workstations, software designed for their specific industry, and a wide variety of packaged software.

The Aberdeen Group in 2011 also conducted a survey of 20 US banks on the type of payables and disbursement offerings across the supply chain and the bank revenue generation, which produced the following results.

Product	Banks offering product	Bank revenue
ACH	100%	85%
Wire transfer	100%	70%
Account reconciliation	95%	35%
Cheque Issuance	90%	30%
Electronic invoice presentation	40%	5%
Supplier management/liquidity	30%	5%

Payment services are used pretty much universally across the banks. The electronic invoice presentation and payment services and the supply chain are offered by approximately a third of banks. One reason could be that the level of bank revenue is significantly less than what can be achieved through the payment products. These two areas are complex, and absorb a large amount of manual resource and demand higher pricing that is difficult to justify.

The physical supply chain

Products are being manufactured in one country and sold to another country. As a result, uniform standards and formats are evolving, as is the automation of the accompanying paperwork. The following is taking place:

- More than 50% of goods by value are delivered by air, often days before the cash is moved;
- Common standards for documentation are beginning to appear across the various standard setting groups;
- Electronic preparation of documents (the move from paper to electronic) is being strongly encouraged, which eliminates errors and omissions;
- The process is becoming increasingly transparent.

The electronic financial supply chain

As the products are being made, the money involved in the manufacturing and transportation of them follows them. Each party in the chain requires payment or guarantee of payment before moving the products. The following improvements can be seen:

- Payments delivered by banks range from same day to three days;
- The opportunity to finance collateral and invoicing cross-border;
- The ability to move the financing with the goods, i.e. from buyer to seller to buyer;
- The process is becoming increasing transparency across the whole flow, both bilateral and multilateral.

Technology creates efficiency

The complexity of the supply chain creates difficulties in achieving standard workflow control when manual activities occur or are introduced. Often the manual activities result in work-around in the financial flow. This often results in ineffective cash management positions as the process becomes opaque. Cash movements then become unpredictable. Ongoing operational efficiencies are created by establishing open standards and using technology that prompts for the right data at the start of the process chain. The operational efficiencies include STP (straight through processing), which, in turn, leads to predictable cash flow.

The introduction of new Extensible Markup Language (XML) based payment initiation message, combined with the associated advices and bank statement, beings to address components of the corporate and bank messaging – see further below and Chapter 3. The XML approach helps eliminate the use of proprietary bank standards and provides the necessary data consistency for banks to provide debit advice and financial statements.

Figure 11.1: Supply chain growth

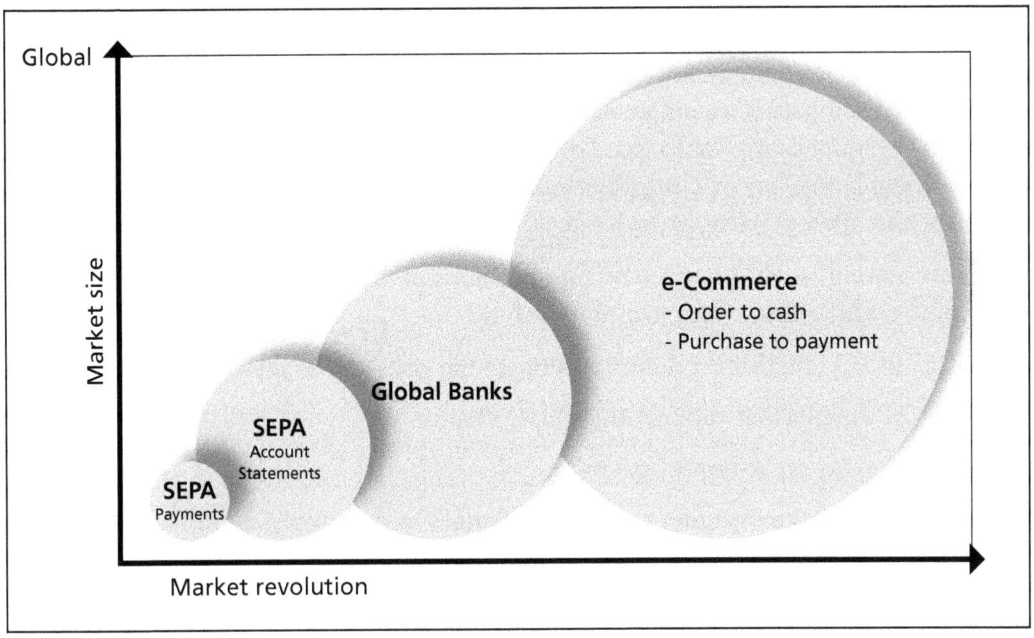

Source: XMLdation

Finally, there is a legal commitment on the banking community to support banking specific BIC and IBAN, which are unique strings of alphanumeric characters. Ultimately these strings need to pass through the many underlying clearing systems. The new banking codes, if correctly used, along with STP transactions and automation of the reconciliation process will greatly improve the timeliness of the payment.

Logistics and the supply chain

There is recognition among buyers that they cannot afford to have goods in transit or inventory for any extended length of time. In the UK, for example, the entire country's petrol supply at service stations is about seven days. The cost of inventory carry is not economically prudent, as duty has to be paid immediately (duties in the UK are over 80% of the price of the fuel). Not only does the cost of inventory accelerate the movement of goods to 'just in time' production and marketing, but the party that owns the goods and at what stage also changes. In addition, by reducing the number of stockholding centres, the savings on inventory can be substantial. In the US, for example, the inventory carrying cost as a percentage of the gross domestic product fell from some 8% in 1980 to slightly under 4% by 2000, freeing cash to invest in other ventures.

Supply chains and the role of the financial services industry

Recognising the need for an all-encompassing approach to a supply chain, many large sophisticated companies no longer accept the provision of banking services on an individual product basis. Banks that fail to provide an holistic approach to the supply chain will put at risk any existing payments, cash management, trade finance, foreign exchange and other services provided to supply chain members.

Banks are getting much closer to the supply chains of their customers and provide many non-traditional services that may include:

- A broad range of products to mitigate the risks across the supply chain;
- Investments that support the supply chains;
- Same-day cross-border payments;
- XML-based messaging to support changes in the supply chain;
- Daily reconciliation of transactions involving payments and receivables;
- Online cash forecasting;
- Electronic document preparation services.

Information obtained throughout the process is stored, reused and passed on to bring about even greater efficiencies throughout the process.

Automation and standards

The supply chain for the larger companies represents a challenge for all parties to make it as liquid as possible. To do so the supply chain has to move from physical to electronic.

Figure 11.2: Supply chain management

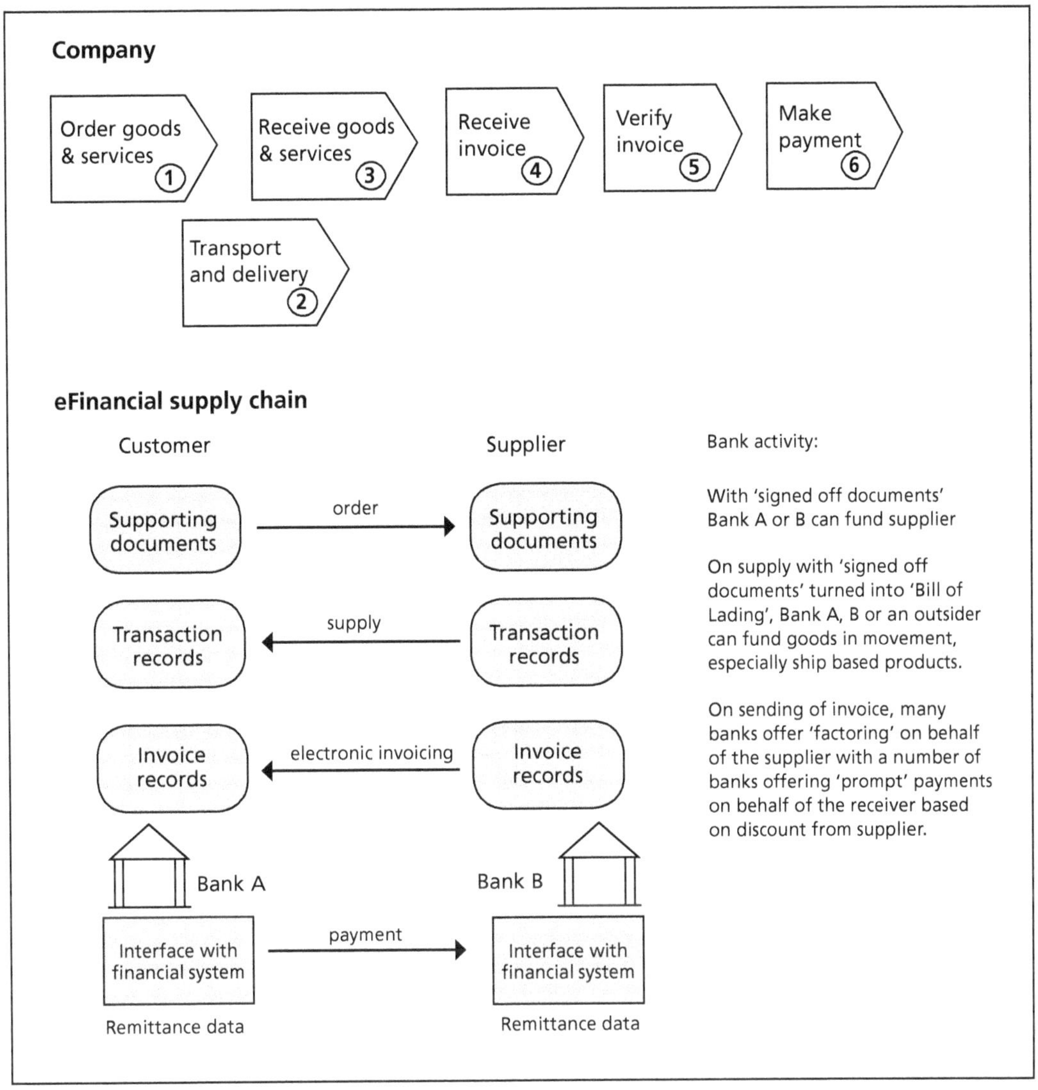

Source: IBS Publishing

The complexity of the landscape creates difficulties in achieving standard workflow control, introduces manual dependencies and hampers the entire chain, resulting in an ineffective cash management position. From a cash management perspective, establishing open standards can facilitate improvements in operational efficiencies, achievement of STP and the optimisation of corporate cash.

The introduction of the XML-based payment initiation message, combined with the associated advices and bank statements, addresses one of the three core components of the client-to-bank interface (the other two being the underlying file security and the communication interfaces). As the banking community supports this new standard, this will enable the corporate to use more than one bank. In simple terms, the corporate now has the required portability and is no longer locked into a bank through proprietary standards. However, banks' legacy internal infrastructure technologies make disconnecting from proprietary standards a slow process.

The underlying message structure has been designed to enable the corporate community to maximise its STP rates by clearly defining what information is required to facilitate automated processing. The XML message definition also provides the required data consistency around the debit advice and financial statements. Finally, there is a commitment from the banking community to support the provision of a unique18-character Uniform Resource Identifier (URI) which the underlying clearing systems have the required capabilities to pass along. The changes provide the opportunity to automate the reconciliation process through the receipt of the unique reference indicator and to introduce standard, automated workflow control.

Collectively, these changes will enable the corporate community to achieve operational efficiencies through the elimination of the manual reconciliation process, which typically can require three to five days for the application of funds. Ultimately, in order to gain ultimate efficiencies, the reconciliation process should occur daily.

This then allows the invoices to be quickly turned into cash. Each invoice is tracked by sales days outstanding and the cost if it was an 8.5% per annum loan or through the use of invoice financing at 25.5% per annum.

Figure 11.3: Sales days outstanding

Classic dunning

Days	0-30	31-60	61-90	91-120	121-150	151-180	180+*
Month (dunning)	1	2	3	4	5	6	write-off

*Write-off policy for many companies

Cost of £100,000 in bills outstanding

Days	0-30	31-60	61-90	91-120	121-150	151-180
Cost:						
Loan	700	1400	2100	2800	3500	4200
Invoice financing	2,100	4,200	6,300	8,400	10,500	12,600

Assuming:
1) Cost of 8.5% loan rate to the company.
Cost of money to each company is different as is cost of money by country.

2) Invoice finance of 25.5%

Note:
The company is extending credit to the supplier through sales days outstanding.
A number of companies offer a discount for prompt payment, uasually within 10 days.

Source: IBS Publishing

The difference is that cost is based on the cash needs of the supplier. A cash-rich or poorly managed A/R results in an opportunity cost of £2,100 after 90 days. The company financing the invoice will charge £6,300 for the same timeframe.

The supply chain for an investment grade company can use the advantage of their credit rating to support their clients through a bank willing to work with them.

Figure 11.4: Supply chain financing for large companies

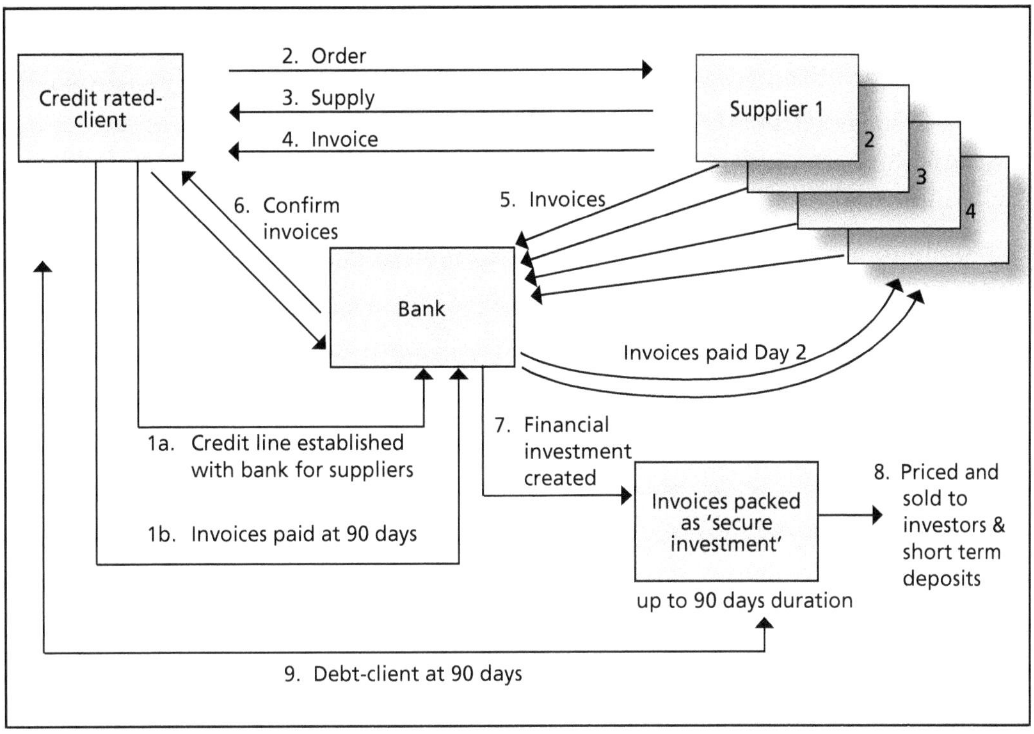

Source: Author

Figure 11.5: Accounts receivable financing

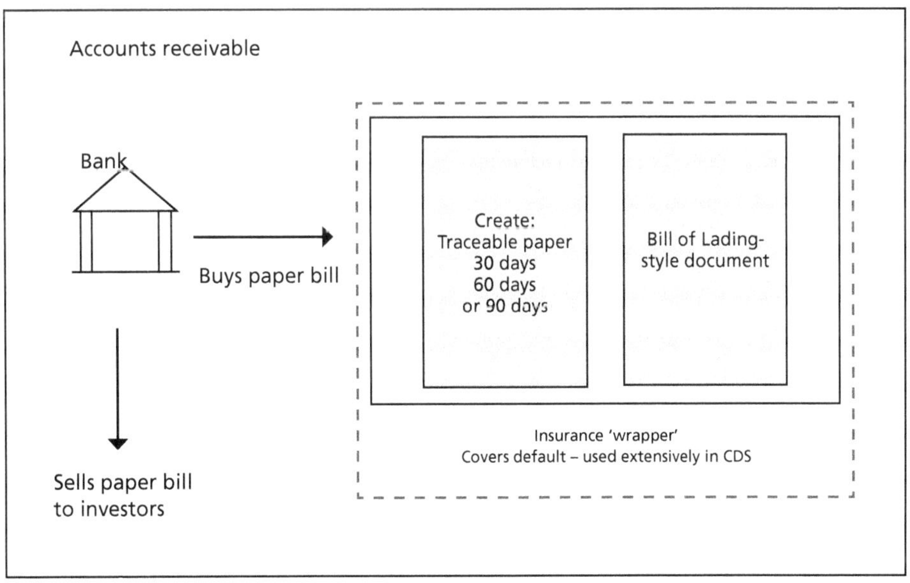

Source: IBS Publishing

Invoice financing

In times of tight credit, the use of invoice financing in all its forms increases, especially when banks do not want to open additional credit lines on their books. Invoice financing is riskier; for example, fraud in terms of 'fresh air' invoicing is a common event used by suppliers to boost the cash flow. It is also labour-intensive, as each invoice has to be verified, so the interest rates are higher than a credit line, reflecting the additional administration and the risk costs in the process.

Corporations with good credit ratings tend to pay all in 2–3% per month on the money extended. In addition to the credit reports and the credit assessment, Personal Guarantees (PGs) are often also required (see Chapter 7).

Invoice financing comes in a variety of forms; the two most common are invoice factoring and invoice discounting. The difference is that in invoice discounting, the financial company is kept confidential and the supplier (biller) performs the back-office functions of:

- Chasing the invoice for payment;
- Providing monthly statements;
- Cash allocation.

The benefits of invoice discounting for the three parties are:

- Supplier – sole relationship with the customer;
- Customer – no changes internal procedures; no changes in credit control;
- Bank – less administration.

Figure 11.6: Invoice factoring

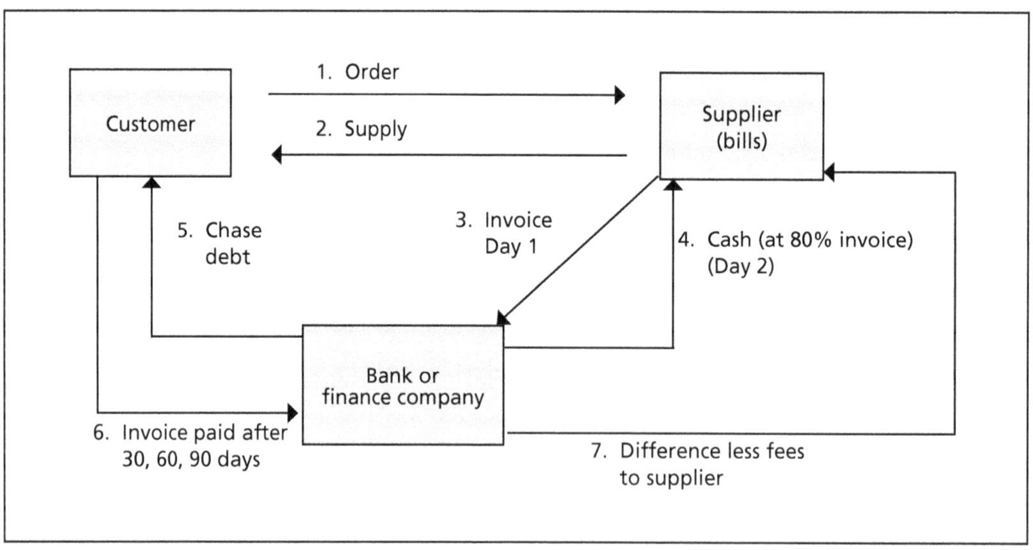

Source: Author

Figure 11.7: Invoice discounting

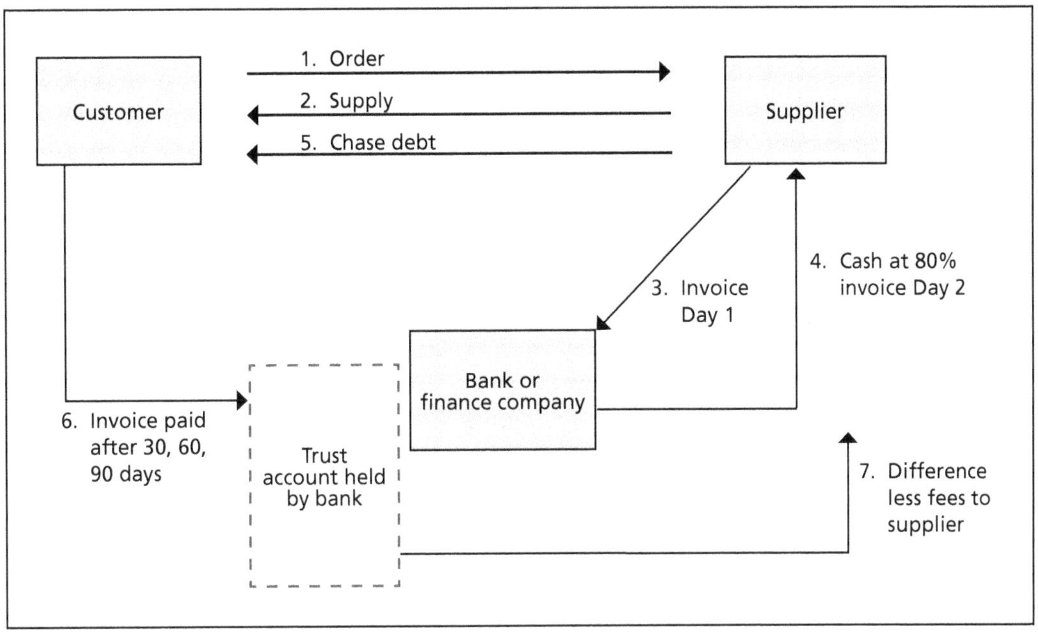

Source: Author

A bank (or finance company) takes a view on the invoices being generated by the supplier. These are checked for validity and often an additional check is made to determine who the customer is and their credit rating. The amounts requested are compared against the supplier's credit rating and within the conditions agreed to at account set-up. The bank issues a credit to a level somewhat below the value of the invoice. For example, a £10,000 invoice often is reduced by 20% and the £8,000 paid to the supplier. The money is advanced to the company and offset as money comes in from the invoices. Often the money coming into the bank is kept in a separate account, reconciled with the invoices outstanding, and then passed onto the client's account.

Value dating on the money being received in the bank's account for invoice factored invoicing is first posted to the company's 'in trust' bank account and then money moved once the payment clearing period is over. Then and only then is the money 'factored' reduced.

Factoring charges include a percentage of the invoice and/or interest charged on monies outstanding. The reason it works is that the bank provides the money to the company upfront while the suppler waits for the invoice to be paid. Payment is most often contractually set at 30 days, but often this is extended to 60 or 90 days. Some industries, such as publishing, can go to 120 days before payments are received. Wholesale movement of terms for a company from, e.g. 90 to 120 days, reflects the deteriorating financial health of the company. Suppliers experiencing such a situation need to decide whether to continue to supply and whether or not they can recover the 30 days of free credit in the future. The supplier company relationship also plays its part. In difficult times the suppliers tend to simply go along and make the appropriate internal cash decisions. Often a company experiencing some degree of financial difficulties will part-pay an invoice. This is referred to as 'throwing them a bone'.

Historically, the way banks and corporate measure the performance of accounts receivables is in days outstanding (DOS) or sales days outstanding (SDO). It is not unusually for certain industries, e.g. retailing, to have a norm of 90 days from point of payment to receipt of money. This way the suppliers indirectly provide the cash for the retailer to manage the business. The product is sold from Day 1 for cash or on a credit card and then paid in total on Day 90. This is termed 'negative working capital' and used by businesses that generate cash straight away, for example, retail chains.

The EU and other governments are trying to establish standards for the timeframe between invoice and payment. The goal is to have a 30-day standard. The UK government has key performance indicators (KPIs) for many of its services; the NHS KPI is to pay invoices in 30 days. The current level is around 80% are paid in that timeframe. The issue at hand is that one person orders the product, it is delivered to one location, and a third person pays the invoice. The time taken to verify delivery and complete the administration for payment to be made can take over 30 days.

Many companies offer a discount on their charges if the payment is received within an agreed timeframe. This can be a discount from 2–5% if payment is received in 10 days.

E-invoicing

Electronic invoicing (e-invoicing) is the electronic transfer of invoice information (data on billing and payment) between business partners (supplier and buyer). It is part of the supply chain linking the corporate's internal processes with the payment systems. The EU estimates that replacing paper invoices with electronic generated invoices can save €64.5 billion per year for businesses. The issue has been the legal and infrastructure challenges by country and within the corporate internal environments. The EU has a goal to make e-invoicing the norm rather than the largely manual process it is today through the use of standards including ISO 20022.

E-invoicing provides massive cost savings for large corporates' supply chain management, where costs can be as much as €60 per received invoice. Any e-invoice solution can be of immediate added value to customers in terms of faster payment, especially if it requires no major investment in their infrastructure.

E-invoicing is suitable for companies of all sizes, and implementing it in the internal system can be simple and economical. It also brings the following advantages:

- E-invoice processing significantly reduces invoicing costs;
- The number of invoicing errors is reduced because the invoice information is delivered to the customer after being fully checked automatically;
- Delivery of e-invoices to customers is fast;
- E-invoicing cuts down the use of paper and fuel as printing and transportation are eliminated;
- The invoice can be processed automatically with little or no rekeying of data.

Figure 11.8: Paper vs e-invoicing

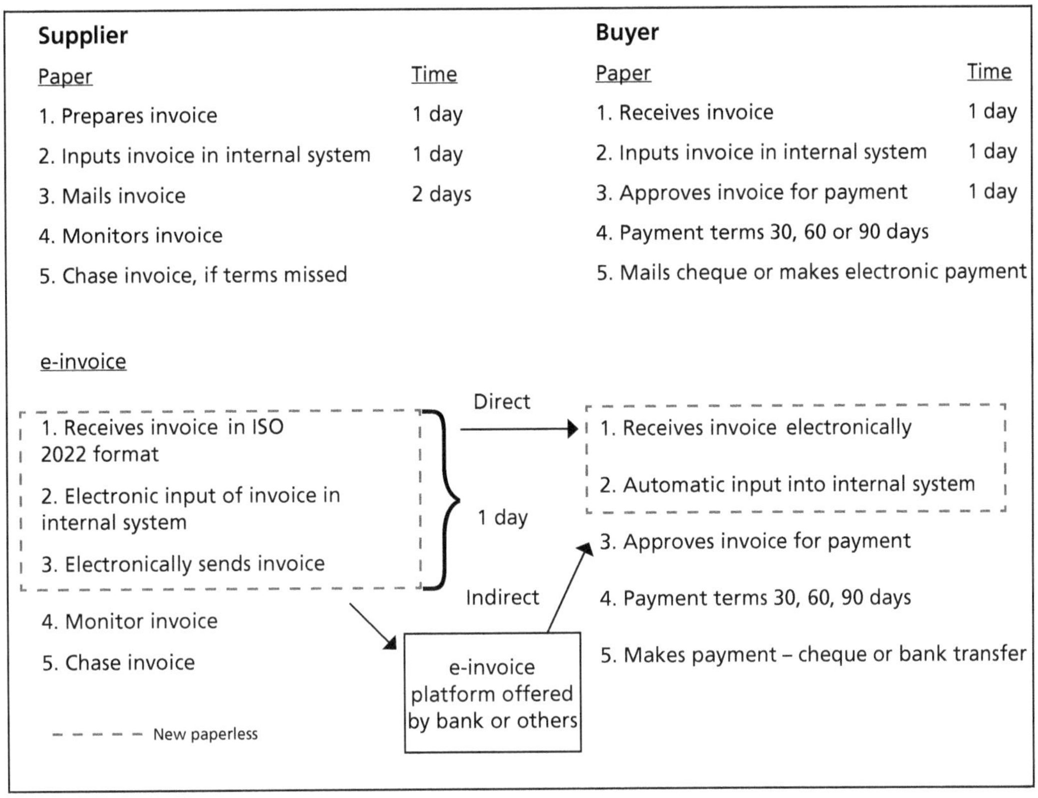

Source: Author

Global adoption of e-invoicing

While e-invoicing adoption is growing at 35% annually in Europe, it has a long way to go in terms of dominant market share. Scandinavia leads Europe, with 15% of all invoices being issued electronically.

In addition, European e invoicing service providers recently created a trade association to represent the industry in the public policy debate, and to jointly carry out projects in the cooperative space and promote adoption. In other global regions, progress is being achieved. Key examples are Brazil and Mexico, where the government sector is leading the way, as well as North America and the Asia-Pacific regions.

Following a requirement by the Finnish state in early 2010 for state agencies and institutions to receive only e-invoices from their suppliers, the state Treasury is leading the way in e-invoicing adoption and uptake. The Treasury offers companies that do not yet have an e-invoicing capability a free-of-charge service for sending their invoices to the state in electronic format. So even the smallest suppliers can shift to e-invoicing and start to benefit from optimised cash flow, better working capital management and lower processing costs.

The Finnish state agencies currently handle 13 million sales invoices and 1.9 million purchase invoices annually, and have over 230,000 suppliers on their database. The Treasury estimates that incoming paper invoices costs €30-50 for the receiving company. Companies can reduce these costs to €10 by semi-automating the invoice process, and reduce further down to just €1 by fully automating the process – a significant level of savings when applied across all invoices the government sends and receives. A recent report from the Federation of Finnish Financial Services estimates that, by switching from paper to electronic invoices, there is a 43% time saving per outgoing invoice and 50% for an incoming invoice. In addition, the report found that the carbon footprint for an outgoing e-invoice is less than half of that of an outgoing paper invoice.

In Europe, there are similar initiatives ongoing in Sweden and Denmark. In Mexico it is now mandatory to issue invoices electronically if the invoice sum is higher than 2,000 pesos, and, since 1 January 2011, businesses are required to perform regulatory compliance checks for senders' and receivers' invoices.

Changing supplier and buyer processes

The major block for e-invoicing is the changes needed to supplier and buyer processes. E-invoicing has been around for many years, with the two biggest and earliest proponents being General Electric (GE) and General Motors. These companies created the EDIFACT standard, but apart from a few major companies there was little uptake. Suppliers doing business with these two companies had to send in their invoices in prescribed formats as part of the terms and conditions of the contract. Basically, if there was no electronic format, then no payment of the invoice was made. The suppliers therefore had to adopt their internal systems to be EDIFACT compliant.

Rosettanet

The Rosettanet organisation is a self-funded, non-profit 500 member consortium dedicated to creating and implementing open and industry wide e-business process standards in information technology, electronic components and semiconductor manufacturing. This program is aimed at reducing processing costs through automating accounts receivable reconciliation and improving the flow of payment information to facilitate the efficient and timely use of available funds.

The corporate standards community is supported by the banks. Its use is starting to show some real benefits for its members. Intel, for example, highlighted some of the benefits since adopting this new standard as follows:

- Increased cash availability from $0 to $0.5–$8 million per day;
- Time for cash availability from three days to 30 minutes;
- Automatic credit availability from 0% to 81.5%;
- Reconciliation labour: manual – $50 per payment, to automatic – $0.

Bill payment in the US

Bill paying in the US has set of procedures established by the National Automated Clearing Houses Association (NACHA). The standard formats and intra-operability rules allow banks to offer a multibank option for businesses. The ACH payment message formats allow banks, billers and e-billing provider to standardise transactions. Business can now present bills in standard format through multiple banks so their customers can view and pay their bills though their own online banking site via PC or mobile phone.

The goal has always been to reduce the paperwork associated with accounts receivables and payables. The bills can be emailed to a central paying agent, for example, Citibank, by the company. The client then logs in and sees the bills to be paid. Payment can then be made electronically. Consumers in the US pay over 50% of the bills they receive electronically each month in 2011 and this trend is estimated to grow 7% in 2012. The consumers use the internet to locate their bill and then pay it online. Basically the billers post their invoices online and e-mail or text the buyers. The buyers log on through a secure web site and pay their invoice. The buyer often has to go to many web sites to pay for many different bills.

The corporate in the US issues electronic invoices virtually 100% of the time. Of these invoices only 43% are paid in the same manner as the consumer. The reason for this is that the corporate has to integrate e-billing and e-payment technologies into existing processes and technologies. The adoption of e-procurement and Financial Electronic Data Interchange (FEDI) technologies is only financially viable with the larger corporates.

Citi processes nearly $5 billion per annum in bill payments through their electronic invoice presentation and payment (EIPP). The platform also allows any disputes to be settled online. Citi has noticed that on average Sales Days Outstanding can be reduced by 10 days. In addition, the dispute rate drops by 45%. The electronic cost is significantly lower than the range of $0.50 to $0.90 per transaction for the paper equivalent. Electronic payment is also faster – two days against five to seven for a cheque – and electronic payments have lower delinquency rates.

The future

The automation of the supply chain will continue. The level of capital trapped within the chain needs to be released and a community approach by industry bodies is probably needed. SWIFT, the banking infrastructure provider, has worked on a Trade Utility platform and its acceptance has been slow.

The really large companies with many suppliers can use their often-excellent credit rating to facilitate invoice financing for their suppliers from their bank. The banks encourage such initiatives as they can create the funding needed to liquefy the supply chain by selling high qualified credit rated corporate paper to other corporate treasurers with surplus cash.

By balancing the needs of corporates with surplus cash and those in need of cash in a secure and credit-sound way with a trusted third party, the money in the supply chain can be released.

CHAPTER 12

ILLIQUID MANAGEMENT

Questions for the CFO, Treasurer or Cash Manager

- What is the best way to keep the cash flowing, retaining the assets and handling the creditors, while undergoing a significant change in course?
- Have we been trading while insolvent?

Key considerations

- Bankruptcy;
- Pre-pack administration.

In October 2008, Royal Bank of Scotland failed and was part nationalised. From 7 October it relied on the Bank of England to fund the bank. On 13 October, the UK government announced it would provide up to £20 billion of new equity to recapitalise RBS. Subsequent increases in capital brought the total to £25.5 billion, reflecting the lack of control, reporting and understanding of the fund allocation within the company.

In the UK, it is illegal to trade while insolvent. In other words, if there is no money in the accounts, then adding new debtors is against the law. For major companies reaching this point there are avenues to keep the company alive while the credit issues are addressed. Governments will save very few companies and only those critical to that nation. The financial crisis was a new experience, resulting in countries investing taxpayers' money to prevent their banks from going into liquidation and thus saving the global financial system – failure to do so could have sparked another Great Depression.

Governments will save few banks from bankruptcy, as the UK did for RBS, but for any with poor or deteriorating financials, or in receivership (a third party who is looking after the company), bankruptcy probably awaits.

Bankruptcy

Bankruptcy is one way of dealing with debts that cannot be met and the creditors are unsympathetic to the situation. Bankruptcy is a form of insolvency and therefore debts need to outweigh assets. There are a number of approaches in this situation. Bankruptcy involves the handing over of assets to help pay off the debtors under a court partition. A trustee to administer this activity can be nominated by the court (Official Receiver) or an insolvency practitioner (an authorised debt specialist) appointed by the directors. Once the court order has been served, the creditors have to deal with the trustee as well as the debtor. The trustee is there to ring-fence the financial situation and resolve it as best as possible.

For corporates that enter bankruptcy, it means the end of the business and the dismissal of employees. It happens suddenly, often with little warning. The receiver calls a meeting of the staff, explains the situation and then tells everyone to go home. The Official Receiver in the UK will advertise the bankruptcy in the 'London Gazette'.

The UK permits a corporate to put a subsidiary into bankruptcy without affecting the company parent. This is does affect how the UK banks look at lending to the subsidiary. The company parent may be fine credit score-wise, but the bank looks at the viability of the subsidiary. Banks will often require legal documentation around funding to the UK subsidiary to protect the credit being extended in case of default of the subsidiary.

In the US, filing for Chapter 11 bankruptcy allows corporations to retain ownership of the assets and agree to operate under the supervision of the court. The success rate of Chapter 11 reorganisations is estimated at 10%.

Liquidation in the UK

The winding-up process

In the UK, more creditors are using winding-up orders to encourage and force payments. Any creditor with at least £750 owed to them can issue a winding-up petition. The procedure is as follows:

- File an application to the Law Court;
- The Court will determine if it is reasonable, and if so will issue a winding-up petition to the company;
- The company has seven days to resolve the petition by
  - Paying the debt and costs in full;
  - Reaching an agreement to settle the debt;
  - Request the court to stop as, a) the debt is in dispute, or b) the filing is inaccurate;
- If the company does not respond then the winding-up petition will be advertised in the 'London Gazette'.

This is the point that winding-up of the company has started under the Insolvency Act 1986, section 129 (2). The company can still either pay the debt owed or argue that the petition is unreasonable at this stage. If the Court upholds the debt then the petition and issuance of a winding-up order is granted.

The process to close or liquidate the business then begins. A liquidator is appointed who will be responsible for closing the business. Any employees can be made redundant immediately. The liquidator will then try to sell any of the company's assets to generate cash. This cash is used to repay outstanding debts to the company creditors once the liquidator's fees have been paid.

Liquidation

Liquidation or winding-up is basically the end of the limited company as the assets are taken and sold and the company ceases to function. It is legally dead. There are three liquidation approaches:

1. Shareholder-led where there is enough assets to cover the debts;
2. Creditor-led when the shareholders acknowledge debt is greater than the assets.

   Either of these options can be a voluntary liquidation. A voluntary liquidation, which can be either a members' voluntary liquidation or a creditors' voluntary liquidation, is brought about by resolution of the company and is conducted by a qualified practitioner;
3. Compulsory liquidation, when the court makes an order for the company to be wound up on behalf a creditor or the directors of the company.

In the UK the costs of putting a company into liquidation in 2012 are:

- £1,165 deposit to the Court;
- £220 Court fee;
- Cost of an advert in the 'London Gazette';
- Any legal or accounting costs of professional services being used in the liquidation by the person pursuing the winding-up of the company.

The compulsory order results in the appointment of an official receiver. The receiver has the right to investigate the financial situation and the directors' behaviour to establish the cause of failure, as well as sell off the assets. The usual practice is to call a meeting of the creditors to appoint an insolvency practitioner (liquidator) when the company is of sufficient size. The official receiver then concentrates on the company and a report is made to the Secretary of State for Business, Innovation and Skills under the Company Directors Disqualification Act 1986. The report covers the conduct of the directors and recommended course of action.

An example of liquidation is the Glasgow Rangers Football Club. Under a former owner, Sir David Murphy, the 140-year-old club was sold to Craig Whyte for £1 plus liabilities. Whyte then raised up to £24 million by selling blocks of future tickets, thereby establishing a body of creditors. These creditors would later be asked to agree to a Company Voluntary Agreement to receive a percentage of the money they have advanced to the club.

The money from the future sales of the tickets was then used to pay off the most pressing debt, £18 million that was owned by Lloyds Bank. The club subsequently went into administration over an unpaid tax bill of £9 million within nine months of Whyte's ownership.

In 2000 the UK Insolvency Service banned Whyte from being a director of a British company for seven years. The assets of the club allegedly belong to Whyte's company, and may be worth millions in terms of residential and commercial property – not bad for £1.

The previous owner, Sir David Murphy, did not fully utilise the assets at his disposal (see Chapter 5), and if he did follow Know Your Customer procedures, he chose to ignore indicators on the potential character of Whyte (see Chapter 2).

Pre-pack administration

One approach to bankruptcy is the 'pre-pack'. This covers the process of selling the assets immediately after it has gone into administration. It is a process conceived and put in place by the directors that allows the best assets of the company to pass through the administration while leaving the creditors out. It also is contingent on the directors finding the necessary funds to pay the administrator and fund the company going forward. An example of a pre-pack is Cobra Beer, which was sold to Coors immediately after Cobra Beer entered administration. While saving employee jobs as well as the brand, this move left suppliers (debtors) out of pocket by £75 million.

CHAPTER 13

CASE STUDY: NORDEA

Questions for the CFO, Treasurer or Cash Manager

- Can we use any of the services offered by this bank?
- Do they cover the corporate geographic areas in which we operate?
- Is there anything we can copy that will improve our performance?

Key considerations

- Safety of your money;
- Using same-day foreign exchange settlement in Scandinavia.

Profile

Nordea is the largest financial services group in Northern Europe with a market capitalisation of €25 billion, total assets of €671.0 billion and a core Tier 1 capital ratio of 11%. Nordea is a cross-border creation of four national banks in Scandinavia.

Nordea plans to use all funding programs to ensure the bank is well capitalised and has a liquidity buffer (cash cushion) which can be used anywhere, any time across the group should an event of illiquidity strike. The average funding gap, when it occurs, averages €10 billion. This liquidity buffer is to fund situations where Nordea is in urgent need of cash and normal funding sources do not suffice. The buffer ensures a total positive cash flow defined by the funding risk measures and consists of high-grade liquid securities. These securities can be sold or pledged as collateral to raise funds. After the €33 billion long-term debt issued in 2011 Nordea believes that it will be more than one year before it needs new market funding.

Nordea has leading positions within corporate, retail and private banking, with 1,400 branches, call centres in Nordic countries and an e-banking service. It has the largest distribution network of any bank in the Nordic and Baltic region. Nordea has 10 million customers including new European markets, of which 8.3 million are active households and 0.7 million active corporate customers.

Nordea is a leading user of SWIFT. It is among the top 50 user institutions on SWIFT, primarily transmitting the MT (Money Transfer) 103 Single Customer Credit Transfer, the MT 940 Customer Statement Message, and the MT 548 Settlement Status and Processing Advice.

The Nordic countries have some of the most developed electronic infrastructure, with all four countries being in *The Economist's* Top 10 and offering some of the most advanced cash management services. At Nordea, 90% of its cross-border payment traffic is derived electronically from customers, either on the internet or on proprietary systems; 90% of that traffic is processed without intervention, and 100% is sent out via SWIFT.

Client base

Nordea corporate client geography 2010	
Sweden	320,000
Finland	123,000
Norway	82,000
Poland	57,000
Denmark	47,000
Rest of the world	33,000

Nordea has a network of international branches and representative offices providing services to shipping, offshore, and oil services companies.

Nordea Finance is the 10th largest leasing company in Scandinavia, with €522 million revenue in 2010.

Cash management and trade produced revenue of €523 million per year in 2010.

Nordea's customers received over 120,000 e-invoices a month in 2011. In 2010, Nordea reduced the number of printed correspondence to customers by 48 million pages and 27 million pages over 2009.

Cash management products

Group accounts

Group accounts is a balance netting service within Nordea that concentrates group funds into one account (the top account) on a real-time basis. The top account is normally held by the parent company. A number of summary levels and/or sub-accounts are connected to the top account. Sub-accounts are used for day-to-day transactions even though legally they are not real bank accounts. All funds in the group account are bank balances on the top account. When funds are paid in or withdrawn from a sub-account, the total available balance on the top account is instantly adjusted. This gives total overview of the group's liquidity in real time.

Sweeping and topping

Sweeping and topping is a cash pooling service for the concentration of bank account balances belonging to a company or a group of companies. On an agreed regular basis the balance of the sweep account is automatically swept to the concentration account. In the case of a negative balance, funds can automatically be topped from the concentration account to the sweep account. Concentrate group's cash balances are pooled by currency.

Zero balancing

Zero balancing is a cash pooling service for the concentration of funds within a company, or a group of companies, into one account – the top account. The balances of the sub-accounts are transferred to the top account at the end of each business day with original value days. The top account will therefore hold the overall net cash position of the company or group of companies. The parent company or a group treasury company normally holds the top account. Any number of sub-accounts can be linked to the top account. Sub-accounts are used for normal cash management transactions and are actual bank accounts.

SWIFT statements

Nordea provides automatic message generation, routing and management services to the bank and their corporate customers. The solution is able to generate MT101 and MT103 messages, and allows for the optional generation of MT202 cover messages, ensuring that the relevant information is available to assist corporate customers in their financial decision making.

Value dating and currencies

The payment service is virtually unique as it enables funds in currencies between accounts across borders to be settled with same-day value. The money is available for use without having to wait the normal 2-day clearing time across a spot price currency. Funds in Nordea currencies are transferred with same-day value if the payment order is received by the account-holding Nordea unit not later than at 15.30 CET.

Few banks offer this same-day service as the foreign exchange market works on 48-hour settlement for spot trades. That is, the money is moved same day between a pair of currencies across Scandinavia.

Direct debit

Alongside e-invoices is a direct debit service offering companies' access to the direct debit infrastructure common format for the Nordic countries. Files with direct debit information are sent via Corporate XML/EDI Gateway to the individual service suppliers. Nordea and the service suppliers make sure that the payments are debited to the right accounts at the right time. The Nordic Direct Debit service has been extended to include Poland in addition to the four Nordic countries.

Same-day cross-border money

Request for Transfer is an instruction sent via the electronic banking system to debit an account held with another bank. The request may include payment instructions, such as intercompany payments, third party domestic or international payments.

With Request for Transfer, payments are controlled centrally and via a corporate's own electronic banking system; the solution offers one point of contact and simple access to all Nordea's accounts held abroad. Money can be transferred in all units of Nordea. These cover the Nordic countries (Denmark, Norway, Sweden and Finland), the Baltic region (Estonia, Latvia and Lithuania) and Poland, Germany, Singapore, the United Kingdom and the United States.

Inter-company payment

The Nordea inter-company payment is a cross-border payment between companies belonging to the same group and holding accounts with Nordea. The Nordea inter-company payment improves liquidity management as all the company's accounts are held centrally. Cash movement between the inter-company accounts occurs in real time.

In-house bank for a corporate treasury

Historically, global cash management was only possible in some circumstances, and usually the treasury departments of a multinational company had to repeat the same work in every country. The central treasury department can now be organised like a bank. The corporate treasury maintains an interest-bearing account with every foreign subsidiary or domestic subsidiary, and all transactions can easily and electronically be processed using these accounts.

Netting

The netting of inter-company invoices can be carried out on the same day for all subsidiaries. Various dates, or daily netting of inter-company invoices, are also possible. The affiliates can also have foreign currency receivables with third parties. The affiliates have the opportunity to close forward contracts with the corporate treasury. The corporate treasury is informed about the exposure and can close hedging transactions with the banks involved. Instead of closing inter-company forward contracts, Nordea could also apply factoring with the affiliates. The affiliates can sell immediately or on an agreed date the currency positions resulting from sales to third parties to the corporate treasury. The discounted amounts are converted into local currency and are credited to their interest-bearing inter-company accounts. It is no longer necessary to manage the inter-company forward contracts portfolio as the exposure is immediately booked into interest-bearing inter-company accounts and corporate treasury can easily manage the group exposure.

Mobile banking

The Nordea mobile banking application is available for the mobile telephone. A cell phone with WAP (GPRS) is enabled and the bank is immediately open all day long. In Lithuania Nordea mobile banking uses Omnitel, Bitė and Tele2 and is available to subscribers with a mobile internet connection. To become a user, the customer signs a Corporate Internet Banking Agreement that covers both internet and mobile banking services.

Nordea mobile banking enables:

- Changing currencies;
- Performing local and international money transfers;
- Checking the balances and operations performed in all the accounts;
- Sending queries to the bank.

Prices for banking transactions performed on Nordea mobile banking are the same as for Internet banking services.

e-invoicing

Nordea's Netbank enables e-invoices to be sent to corporate customers that use Netbank and file transfer, and also provides paper invoices to companies not yet capable of receiving e-invoices. The invoice is paid in Netbank with a click of a button, giving the convenience of not having to rekey in account and reference numbers. Adding to the ease of use is that the invoices are registered for automatic payment on due date and then the debit is taken.

Nordea's customers receive two features to the e-invoice. An e-invoice alert sends a message on a received e-invoice to a mobile phone and/or e-mail. By replying to the text message confirmation, the invoice can be confirmed and the payment is made.

Factoring

Factoring – the payment of receivables by Nordea for its customers before the client has paid by its debtors – is available across the whole supply chain. The various subsidiaries can advise the customers to pay directly to the bank accounts of the corporate treasury. With such a procedure, treasury always knows the currency position of the entire group. Nordea can implement factoring of receivables with third parties, inter-company settlement and cross-border payments to third parties in such a way that no transaction exposure arises in subsidiaries' books.

Re-invoicing

If re-invoicing is used as an instrument to manage taxable income, then it cannot be replaced by the concept of the interest-bearing inter-company accounts. The corporate treasury can be established in a low tax country and contribute to the results of the group not only operationally, but also from a taxation point of view. Dublin and Belgium provide opportunities to minimise taxes.

Working capital

As the supply chain becomes more automated, Nordea is not only able to assist the corporate with working capital requirements but also, if the corporate client is a Nordea customer, a symbiotic relationship can be nurtured. For example, by ordering components from another company, that company needs short-term financing to complete the order. Consequently, once completed, the company which ordered the components needs short-term financing to pay for them. The legal ownership is transferred from one company to another throughout the process. The ownership can be tied back to the bank with the details and ownership transferred electronically to provide collateral for the short-term financing. It fits very well if the corporate and its clients both have accounts with Nordea. The cash is moved by Nordea for all the parties in their database on an interbank transfer base.

Achievements and initiatives

The bank distinguishes two aspects to its cash management activities:

- Those provided to its own corporate customers, either via the Nordea international network or through cash management relations with other banks;
- Those provided to other banks, for which it acts as an underlay bank, in particular to their multinational customers with accounts or operations in the region.

Nordea has a unique, strong position in all four Nordic countries – Denmark, Finland, Norway and Sweden – and a nationwide presence in the three Baltic States – Estonia, Latvia and Lithuania – as well as in Poland.

Its goals are to:

- Earn money on the cash for the clients' benefit;
- Share services and/or other administration structures with the clients;
- Provide easy and fast opening, closing and maintenance of accounts;
- Strengthen capacity to manage and forecast working capital needs;
- Provide solutions that are easy to understand, implement and adopt;
- Clarify the high volume of details associated with cash management; and
- Continue ongoing automation of cash management services.

Client case study – Tele2

Tele2 (www.tele2.com) is a fast-growing telecoms provider in many European countries with over SEK 20 billion in revenue and 33.5 million customers. As of September 2011 the net debt position was SEK 11.2 billion and the company has a medium debt target of 1.25 to 1.75 multiple of EBITDA. Two currencies – the euro and the Rouble – are monitored and hedged, given the size of the cash flow in those two currencies. The year on year difference between 2011 and 2011 showed the Kroner had appreciated 6.6% against the euro and 8.3% against the Rouble. That is, it costs 6.6% more in euro to buy the same thing 12 months ago.

Tele2's primary telephone service and mobile networks plans to deliver improved quality in service and speed. These elements are growing in importance and pave the way for Tele2 to continue to deliver superior value as a wireless operator.

These improvements can be achieved through Tele2's strong operational performance that is creating solid cash flow. Solid cash flow is the basis for strategic and disciplined flexibility and significant shareholder remuneration.

To gain control of liquidity – both surplus and deficit – a centralised account structure was established. This is reflected in the 3rd quarter 2011 interim report showing sales and EBITDA over 11 specific countries.

Table 13.1 Report for external sales less exchange rate fluctuations (external sales, total in Swedish Kroner)

	2011 Q3	2010 Q3 *	Growth	2011 YTD	2010 YTD*	Growth
Sweden	3,124	3,058	2%	9,255	8,792	5%
Norway	694	735	-6%	2,029	2,178	-7%
Russia	3,015	2,503	20%	8,475	6,874	23%
Estonia	221	206	7%	619	617	0%
Lithuania	333	330	1%	918	928	-1%
Latvia	288	303	-5%	821	897	-8%
Croatia	382	360	6%	982	921	7%
Kazakhstan	115	34	238%	185	71	N/A
Netherlands	1,430	1,334	7%	4,368	3,987	10%
Germany	265	352	-25%	824	1,092	-25%
Austria	346	373	-7%	1,034	1,132	-9%
Other	127	143	-11%	401	552	-27%
	10,340	9,731	6%	29,911	28,041	7%
FX effects		258	-2%		1,472	-7%
One off items	-	-		-	542	
Total	**10,340**	**9,989**	**4%**	**29,911**	**30,055**	**0%**

* Adjusted for fluctuations in exchange rates including acquisitions.

Tele2's treasury centre

As a company with headquarters in the Nordic Tele2 needed a banking partner that could give it financing commitment, process large payment volumes, and supply a cash pooling solution. Based on these requirements Nordea was the partner chosen as it has:

- The capability to handle large volumes of payments in all countries in the Nordic region;
- A presence in all three Baltic states;
- The ability to provide a good working cash pooling solution.

The incoming payment flows in Sweden, Norway, and Denmark amount to many millions of transactions each year, through many different payment types and direct debit transactions. The major parts of the transactions are in three different currencies.

A multi-currency credit is connected to the master cash pool to make it possible for Tele2 to dispose of the excess liquidity of the group the same day as it is generated in the local cash pools. Tele2 has multi-currency disposal of the balances in the master cash pool. The credit limit in SEK is the counter value of the combined balances in the master cash pool. By this, the group liquidity in the Nordic countries is concentrated to one account without the constant use of FX transactions. It also means that Tele2 can minimise the size of the credit line in the master cash pool.

Tele2 is provided with real-time balance information from all accounts via the electronic banking system (Corporate Netbank). Daylight limits (intra-day credit facilities) are used in the local pools to allow withdrawals. The daylight limit is the maximum negative balance that is allowed in the account during the day. A negative balance is always settled to zero at the end of each day. The payments in Finland are also handled by Nordea, but connected to the European Euro-pool solution.

CHAPTER 14

CASE STUDY: CITIBANK

Questions for the CFO, Treasurer or Cash Manager

- Can we use any of the services offered by this bank?
- Do they cover the corporate geographic areas in which we operate?
- Is our money safe worldwide?
- Are we big enough for Citi?

Key considerations

- Innovative bank with $10 billion in revenue per annum from a wide array of cash management services aimed at the larger and multinational corporate.

Profile

Citigroup has Tier 1 common of $115.1 billion and a Tier 1 ratio of 11.8%. Citi has segregated the cash management product and services into its own division. Global Transaction Services (GTS), offers integrated cash management, trade, and fund services to multinational corporations, financial institutions and public sector organisations around the world. The network spans 100 countries, supporting 65,000 clients. As of the second quarter of 2011, it held on average $365 billion in balances. In 2010 GTS provided Citi with 15% of its $65.6 billion annual revenue: i.e., trade and cash management is worth close to $10 billion a year, a large proportion of which is in reoccurring revenues.

Cash management products

CitiDirect (e-banking)

Launched in 2001, CitiDirect is used by 50,000 business entities worldwide and is the access point for e-banking. CitiDirect is based on a 'one-click' methodology. Once through the security level, the following menu items are shown:

- Payments;
- Payment services;
- Administration messages;
- Purchase FX payments;
- Import transactions;
- Direct debit services;
- Trade services.

Click on one of the services and a menu pops up, e.g. 'Payments':

- Input from preformats;
- Quick entry from preformats;
- Input new outgoing;
- Input new incoming.

Plus a subset of process workflow:

- Modify;
- Verify;
- Authorised;
- Fund FX payments;
- Release;
- Batch release;
- Repair.

All other menu items are similarly navigable.

CitiDirect online banking provides access and execution capabilities to funds, credit monitoring and access to real-time information. With the CitiDirect platform a company can:

- Create, change and cancel payment mandates online;
- Prepare standing instructions to collect fixed amounts from customers on a scheduled basis;
- Validate and reconcile direct debit transactions against approved mandates;
- Request customer approval of a reversal;
- Access comprehensive receivables reports.

The CitiDirect platform provides many direct debit reports and inquiry features that show key details and summaries of transaction activity. With the CitiDirect data import capability, a corporate can upload and integrate direct debit initiation files in virtually any format into existing applications and systems.

CitiDirect contains an event notification service. The service alerts clients to specified transactions and events via email, telephone and personal digital assistant (PDA) devices. CitiDirect has a payment investigations function and file management capabilities.

CitiDirect BE Mobile

In 2011, Citi's Global Transaction Service unit launched CitiDirect BE Mobile, a mobile browser-based application allowing clients to receive notifications and authorise payments using their mobile phones. CitiDirect BE Mobile has been made available to 50,000 clients and 300,000 users worldwide.

CitiDirect BE Mobile brings core transaction functionality, available with Citi's online banking platform, CitiDirect Online Banking, directly to clients' mobile phones. With CitiDirect BE Mobile, clients can receive SMS alerts that complement email and fax notifications, and authorise payments pending approval in every payment type supported by the online banking platform.

Leveraging the proven security of CitiDirect, CitiDirect BE Mobile offers an alternative access channel to the traditional PC. Designed to work with the world's most popular devices, CitiDirect BE Mobile gives clients a flexible, safe and easy-to-use solution that addresses the changing business landscape and allows them to transact business on the move. With on-the-go access to business and financial data, clients can enjoy the convenience of a mobile channel and the value-add benefit of improved productivity.

CitiDirect BE Mobile is live in 24 countries around the world, and will be rolled out globally as clients increasingly need the ability to connect and access real-time information wherever they are.

WorldLink

WorldLink Payment Services beneficiary deduct enables the company to instruct Citigroup to deduct transaction fees from the principle (beneficiary) amount of the WorldLink payment. This flexible feature allows the company reduces transaction costs and customises fee deductions to meet specific market or client needs. For example, the EU directive on cross-border payments also has the option of the company paying the transaction fees on behalf of their supplier.

The WorldLink Payment Services beneficiary deduct capabilities have been expanded to include many currencies. Fees from cheque currencies and from funds transfer currencies can now be deducted via SWIFT or file. The WorldLink Payment Services beneficiary deduct fees structure offers the corporate the flexibility in determining the amount to be deducted from eligible payments.

WorldLink Payment Services reporting and tracking online

Companies can view, print and download reports and statements via a secure internet environment. The reporting includes:

- Online access 365 days a year, seven days a week;
- Multiple users can access the same report at the same time;
- Reports retained for one year from date of generation.

WorldLink also offers the corporate:

- One payment consolidation – a single currency amount for many foreign currency payments;
- Automatic account management – sweep of idle multiple currency accounts balances;
- Foreign exchange contracts independent of payment initiation;
- Pre-issue contracts for the purchase of currency on a spot date or future date.

Group accounts

Citigroup has a wide-ranging group of accounts, starting from a single currency non-interest bearing account through to multi-layered 'liquidity structured' accounts.

Citigroup's Automated Investments allows balances to be swept and invested every day and invested in:

- Automated end-of-day overnight balances swept for US demand accounts (Citibank New York) and invested overnight in a Citibank Nassau or Puerto Rico branch time deposit, an International Banking Facility (IBF), or Fed Funds purchases – funds returned start of next day;
- Funds invested into a variety of money market mutual funds offered by Citigroup Asset Management as well as selected third-party providers. The funds offer low risk, high liquidity and a high level of current income, designed for the preservation of capital.

Citibank Electronic Cheque Deposit (ECD) in the US

The US Cheque Clearing for the 21st Century Act ('Check 21') gives the reprint of a scanned cheque legal equivalence to the original paper cheque. Citigroup has partnered with Electronic Data Systems (EDS) to provide ECD for efficient, and cost-effective cheque deposits. ECD enables companies to scan cheques in their own office, and then electronically transmit the images to Citigroup. The benefits include:

- Time saved by not going to the bank to make paper deposits;
- Improved cash flow by shorten clearing times through efficient processing as cheques enter the banking system electronically.

Payment

Citibank Funds Transfer provides same-day execution and settlement for payments such as investments, treasury payments, foreign exchange settlements and third-party settlements. The corporate can have same-day movement of funds and immediate availability, with payments processed by CHIPS, FedWire or Book-to-Book transfer. The benefits are:

- Initiation of payments electronically, via electronic banking, file transmission, computer to computer (CPU) or SWIFT;
- Ability to move US dollars around the globe on a same-day basis, with immediate availability;
- Intra-day liquidity, especially in the broker-dealer market;
- Immediate advising options to parties involved with and outside of the transaction.

Alongside the payment transaction a corporate can send the following advice:

- Funds transfers;
- Funds transfers in the future;
- Funds transfer timed payments.

Notional pooling

Notional pooling is offered to corporations, especially those with decentralised operational structures that want to preserve the autonomy of their subsidiaries and accounts.

Pool participant accounts in a single currency are aggregated for interest compensation purposes. Funds are not physically moved, but are instead notionally combined. There is no commingling of funds, and the integrity of the individual account position is maintained. Net excess pool positions both in the US and offshore can be invested in a variety of financial instruments.

Notional pooling enables a company to:

- Minimise interest expense by offsetting debit and credit positions;
- Preserve autonomy, control and record keeping;
- Benefit from offsetting without movement of funds;
- Automate interest reallocation.

Notional pooling is often used in conjunction with target or zero balancing and automated investments. Notional pooling is offered in those jurisdictions where it is permitted by regulation.

Data aggregation

Data from client bank accounts, investments and bank debt is collected from all sources and stored in a Global Information Warehouse. Data can be aggregated from both Citigroup accounts as well as from other banks.

Analytics

Analytic tools, such as cash forecasting and currency risk can be used by the client to understand their positions from the aggregated information on cash, investments and debt. For example, treasurers can view their global cash position as well as breakdowns by region, country, financial institution or legal entity.

Target balancing

Target balancing is an automated process that concentrates end-of-day balances from a source account to a target account. These services can be maintained in-country, regionally or globally and encompass structures operating within a single branch or multiple branches throughout Citigroup. Target balancing enables:

- Maximising cash efficiency;
- Minimising interest expense by offsetting debit and credit balances;
- Maximising return on excess liquidity.

One of the most common forms of target balancing is the Zero Balance Account (ZBA) structure, a basic cash management technique to consolidate account balances and reduce overdraft costs and risks.

Netting

Citigroup offers a wide range of netting services. In addition, a corporate has the flexibility to choose either a payables- or receivables-driven netting approach. CitiDirect Online Banking enables the corporate to automate processes and create simplified intercompany settlement procedures. Netting creates significant savings in foreign exchange and transaction-related costs, as only a few transactions move and then only the netted amount.

Netting is available as self-service, allowing the corporate to run reports first on the netting participants' approximate and final positions and then, after determining the subsequent foreign exchange required to bought or sold, complete payment instructions. The data needed is extracted from the corporate accounting systems. Citigroup netting experts develop the right web-based strategy to meet the individual's corporate needs.

Electronic supply chain

Citi's supply chain management provides small and medium enterprises with early settlement of invoices at a financing cost related to their client's credit rating instead of their credit rating. That is, it pays the supplier on Day 1 to 3 and collects the money from the client on the agreed contract terms, usually 90 days. The client is the lender of last resort, should one of the SMEs default on Citi in some way. That means that Citi is protected from credit risk from any of the suppliers. Citi then takes these invoices and creates a short-term investment that it sells through treasury. The short-term instrument is an investment vehicle for clients with surplus money. This enables Citi to fund the invoice process without funding from elsewhere. Citi makes a margin from the suppliers and takes in deposits based on the client's credit rating, which may be higher than Citi's, resulting in favourable cost of funds.

The Citibank Electronic Account

In response to the balance of working capital and cash conversion Citibank developed the Citibank Electronic Account. The Electronic Account creates a closed loop exchange between the buyer, its suppliers and Citigroup. Consider the example of a US national discount retailer, which routinely pays its manufacturers in 56 days, despite being offered 2% discount for payment in 10 days (the corporate gains more by delaying payment). Through the Citibank Electronic Account, the buyer gets to extend payment beyond the current 56 days, and the manufacturer benefits by receiving payment in 10 days, less the 2% discount. Both companies reduce the cost of financing their working capital needs. The supplier has a reduced DSO while the DPO of the retailer (buyer) is increased.

The account works in the following way. The corporate sends the suppliers payment instructions to Citibank. Citibank pays the suppliers within 10 working days less the 'fast pay discount' – usually 2% of the total invoice. The corporate makes one consolidated payment to Citibank in 30, 60, 90 or 120 days from the invoice date maintaining or extending DPO. Based on payment patterns, the corporate may receive a rebate from Citibank if the corporate payments arc madc earlier.

The advantage for the corporate includes one payment to Citibank rather than multiple payments to suppliers, saving cost and the opportunity for additional revenue if payments are authorised early to suppliers.

The benefits to the suppliers are early and predictable payments reducing the cost of collection and improving cash flow.

The key to the above is having a process that can have all the parties needed to approve the invoice within the 10-day timeframe. Often this includes a number of disparate departments. The only way this can be achieved is through electronic invoicing.

Citibank e-Billing

Citibank e-Billing allows the corporate and suppliers to ability to manage the entire invoice and payment cycle electronically. Citibank offers a complete solution to the corporate, assisted by an experienced team that facilitates the process – from treasury, operations and IT departments to marketing and customer service.

The process is as follows. To access to Citibank e-Billing, corporate and supplier require Internet Explorer or Netscape. Citibank e-Billing extracts the data from the corporate invoicing file and presents the invoices on the Internet. An e-mail is sent to the supplier to alert them that an invoice is waiting.

The corporate uses a browser to view the invoice, process it through payables and initiate payment. The corporate maintains control over what is paid and when the payment is to be made. Citibank e-Billing automatically batches and transfers payment to meet the scheduled settlement date. In the event of a dispute or changes to an invoice, the corporate has the ability to adjust the invoice, using designated reason codes. The resulting payment reflects the adjusted value, but the content of the invoice remains intact so the supplier can apply the resulting payment appropriately.

Both corporate and supplier can export the billing and payment data into their accounts payable or accounts receivable systems. Citibank can combine netting capabilities with Citibank e-Billing services, offering the corporate further benefits.

The above process is known generically as Electronic Bill Presentment and Payment (EBPP). This process has so far failed to capture significant market share because the process and supporting software does not deal with customers' traditional mail which, for most companies, forms near 100% of their current billing and their internal systems. Email solutions are starting to make headway but e-billing/invoicing requires a behavioural change. Even sending email notifications requires the supplier to go to the corporate' designated website to collect their bills.

CityFXPro

CitiFX Pro endeavours to provide the most competitive target bid/ask spreads available under normal market conditions. Citi may adjust the target spreads and auto-execution amounts at any time. This is due principally to market conditions. In times of high volatility or little liquidity (few to no trades), the spreads may be increased and auto-execution amounts may be reduced or stopped. In such cases manual execution could be available.

The bid/ask price at the time of the transaction reflects the maximum transaction cost for the transaction: whether a buy or a sell. To be clear, the 'spread' being paid to the national bank for a purchase or a sale is exactly one half of the total bid/ask spread as is displayed in the bid/ask price at the time the transaction is entered into. This bid/ask price may vary depending on the underlying market conditions and other factors, and clients should be careful to examine the total width of the bid/ask spread in order to assess their total transaction cost.

CitiFX Pro surveys the bid/ask spreads offered by most major margin FX providers and sets its spreads to ensure its pricing is competitive. In addition, CitiFX Pro may be able to offer narrower bid/ask spreads to some clients based on the volume they trade through the platform.

CitiFX Pro offers some of the largest auto-execution amounts in the margin FX market. This means that clients get competitive prices even for larger sized trades. This allows clients to efficiently execute larger trades in single lots rather than having to break them up and run the risk of having the market move against them as they execute their entire order.

Pricing on 130+ currency pairs

CitiFX Pro offers three different pricing models dependent on client needs and initial account opening size. These are tradable prices, available under normal market conditions. For example, the target spread in basis points above and below mid point.

Currency Cross	Max Auto-Execute Amount	Target Spread	Margin Requirement*
EUR/USD	EUR 10,000,000	1.6	2.0 / 2.0 / 2.0 %
USD/JPY	USD 12,000,000	1.9	2.0 / 2.0 / 2.0 %
GBP/USD	GBP 10,000,000	2.3	2.0 / 2.0 / 2.0 %
USD/CHF	USD 7,500,000	2.4	2.0 / 2.0 / 2.0 %
EUR/JPY	EUR 8,000,000	2.5	2.0 / 2.0 / 2.0 %
AUD/USD	AUD 10,000,000	2.4	2.0 / 2.0 / 2.0 %
EUR/GBP	EUR 10,000,000	2.4	2.0 / 2.0 / 2.0 %
EUR/USD	EUR 10,000,000	1.2	2.0 / 2.0 / 2.0 %
USD/JPY	USD 12,000,000	1.7	2.0 / 2.0 / 2.0 %
GBP/USD	GBP 10,000,000	2	2.0 / 2.0 / 2.0 %
USD/CHF	USD 7,500,000	2	2.0 / 2.0 / 2.0 %
EUR/JPY	EUR 8,000,000	2.1	2.0 / 2.0 / 2.0 %
AUD/USD	AUD 10,000,000	1.9	2.0 / 2.0 / 2.0 %
EUR/GBP	EUR 10,000,000	1.8	2.0 / 2.0 / 2.0 %

Outsourcing treasury functions

Citi's Treasury Solutions Group can service on an outsourced basis a company's treasury, risk management and/or regulatory reporting. The web-based treasury management platform, which consolidates services from Citigroup and third parties, provides a complete picture of a corporate treasury position.

The Treasury Solutions Group gives the company online access to treasury applications, providing benefits from STP, inputting of deal requests and authorisation of transactions, to accessing real-time positions worldwide.

By outsourcing the treasury functions the corporate receives from Citigroup:

- Access to the latest treasury applications online;
- Expert management of liquidity and exposure positions;
- Reduced operating costs as Citi performs the operations.

Online investment

Citigroup offers a wide variety of investment choices, including:

- Citibank Time Deposits;
- Cash Reserve Accounts (money market deposit accounts);
- Commercial paper;

- US government repurchase agreements;
- Money market funds.

Investment transactions initiated through Citidirect online platform are automatically settled against the Citibank account.

Liquidity desks

Through its network of liquidity desks, Citigroup provides a central point of contact to facilitate investment transactions in every major region. Citigroup supports regional desks in New York, London and Tokyo that are supplemented by country desks in other countries. For clients, the benefits of actively investing through Citigroup's liquidity desks include:

- Potentially higher yields for large incremental balances;
- Real-time market updates and trade execution personally provided;
- Customised investment maturities;
- Increased opportunities for clients whose investment period is beyond overnight.

Achievements and initiatives

WorldLink was started by Citi in 1984 and offered cheque processing in three currencies for clients, thus providing clients with the benefit of not holding cheque books in multicurrency that could only be cleared by their bank. WorldLink allowed cheques to written and processed locally in that currency. Initially, this allowed international bank branches to outsource the cheque processing to a centralised cheque processor. The pricing was a transaction charge on each cheque written and a percentage split on the float.

Since the 1980s WorldLink has moved with the automation of payment and now offers:

- Cheques in 100 currencies;
- Cross-border funds transfer;
- File transfers;
- Online FX capabilities covering 100 currencies;
- Non-account based into cross-border ACHs in 40 countries;
- Embedded into CitiDirect in 2001.

Citibank is one of a handful of banks that can truly claim to be a global cash management bank. However, it too needs to partner with other banks to provide in-country services, especially physical branches that their corporate clients require to handle physical cash.

In *Euromoney*'s 2011 Annual Cash Management survey, Citi was voted the #1 Cash Management Bank globally for the fifth consecutive year.

CHAPTER 15

CASE STUDY: HSBC

Questions for the CFO, Treasurer or Cash Manager

- Can we use any of the services offered by this bank, especially in Asia?
- Do they cover the corporate geographic areas in which we operate?
- Is there anything we can copy that will improve our performance?

Key considerations

- A strong bank with Tier 1 capital of $140 billion and a ratio of 10.6%;
- Offering extensive cash management services across Asia, especially in the Chinese currency offerings out of Hong Kong.

Profile

HSBC Holdings plc serves 89 million customers worldwide, through 7,500 offices in 87 countries and territories. While HSBC started in Hong Kong, the purchase of the Midland Bank in the UK resulted in the head office being moved to London. The US dollar is used as its presentation currency as it is the major currency for its worldwide operations. The financial reporting reflects the closing rates for the euro and GBP. With assets of $2,691 billion, virtually doubled in seven years, HSBC is one of the world's largest banking and financial service organisations with a Tier 1 core capital ratio of 10.8%. Over 70% of its profits are realised in Asia. The HSBC logo was rated the 32nd most valuable brand in the world by Interbrand in 2011.

HSBC is a top US bank holding company and one of the top five movers of US dollars internationally. HSBC's mostly middle-market US companies came through the acquisitions of Marine Midland Bank and Republic National Bank of New York.

In cash management, HSBC offers a wide array of products from a single chequeing account for payment and receivables to multinational, special-purpose accounts in multi-currencies.

HSBC has a fully automated treasury, which enables corporates to mix and match their foreign exchange requirements online. The FX products on offer cover a wide range of offerings, including derivatives.

Cash management products

Exposure management

The level of exposure management starts as soon as trading with partners using other currencies than the company's main currency begins. Many companies entering into a new country select a currency to price their services which may not be the currency of that country; for example in Russia or Argentina the US dollar is frequently used. While this may not cause an exposure to currency risk for the seller, it does so for the buyer. Hence there are several approaches to exposure management available, as follows.

Receivables solutions

Converting receivables into cash is a critical process of any company's cash flow. Depending on the company and its internal procedures, many receivables can exceed 100 days. Also the time and effort it takes to collect and manage receivables, across all channels and from different locations (paper or electronic, local or cross-border), can become a full-time occupation. HSBC offers Integrated Receivables Solutions (IRS), which enables corporations to outsource their accounts receivable management. IRS integrates the corporate back-office/ERP system and automatically reconciles and reporting receivables at a country and regional level. The process is accessed and managed by HSBCnet.

Currency dealings as and when

A possible strategy for a currency being received or paid out, for example USD to GBP, is to leave it until it needs to be converted. However, to avoid market risk (the currency going down) a spot FX is traded (settlement in two days' time) – the cash flow receives the market rate of that day. This means the corporate know has exactly the number of pounds needed to pay away.

Actively managing the exposure

Instead of simply taking out a straightforward future, an active programme of FX can be undertaken. Here under HSBC management, any favourable changes in FX rates could be taken as income. Other products such as currency options and FX derivatives can also be used. These enable the potential for upside benefits to be realised. The issue for most corporates is the ability to actively manage the exposure and can be a distraction from the day-to-day business of the company. In Asia, where companies often deal in 10-20 different currencies, management of currencies is part of ethos. Not so in Europe or the US, where only a few currencies are being utilised.

HSBC describes exposures as:

- Transactional exposure – this arises from business conducted with companies, where payables or receivables are denominated in a currency that needs to be converted from one currency to another.
- Balance sheet exposure – the value of international subsidiaries' assets and liabilities is affected by exchange rate movements, which give rise to translation exposure when consolidated with those of the parent.
- Profit and loss account exposure – a company with international subsidiaries needs to account for its foreign currency earnings when consolidating its profit and loss account.
- Intraday liquidity management – HSBC, in the capacity of USD Clearing Settlement Institution, provides intraday sale & repurchase ('repo') facility to the direct participating banks of the USD clearing system. Should the intraday repo go overnight, and not repurchased by 2.30pm Hong Kong time the following day, then it will be classified as permanent and subject to the conditions laid out in the Master Sale & Repurchase Agreement.

The minimum amount for an intraday repo is US $1 million and the repo repurchase will be done on a last-in-first-out (LIFO) basis. For operational simplicity, repurchase funds sent via CHIPS in New York time will be returned to the participating banks' accounts at 9.00am Hong Kong time. This repurchase will be carried out prior to the start of the opening of the USD system at the beginning of the day's operations, by utilising the credit balances of the accounts.

Interest rate offerings in other countries

HSBC offers a wide range in interest rates, for example the New Zealand International Cash Management Account is offering high interest rates per annum on surplus business cash on balances over NZD 50,000. To take advantage of this rate without currency risk, a forward contract is taken out for the period of investment, for example, three months. The pricing principle assumes that HSBC buys NZD now, paying for the dollars with another currency, taking advantage of the interest rate and repatriating the currency plus interest in three months' time. This is advantageous if a company is trading with another company in New Zealand and needs to make payments within certain timeframes.

Cash concentration and multi-currency receivables

The two-layer account structure is used for cross-border sweeping or cash concentration in a single currency, usually US dollars, when more than two countries are involved. Surplus funds from multiple legal entities within a single country are concentrated into a main account. Each main account within a country is swept cross-border on a regular basis into a central treasury account usually in the multinational corporation's home currency.

For example, a German company can operate domestic euro cash pools in the European Union countries, sweeping surpluses in euro back to Germany to reduce debt or invest. By operating an in-house bank, receivables in multiple currencies can be managed and netted centrally.

By adding an exchange margin and amount to standard cross-border sweep for each currency pair, the target or pegged balancing can be adjusted on a daily basis. Specific legal agreements are required to authorise the bank to apply the agreed to FX conversion and settlement on behalf of the company. The tax issues have to address prior to actual money being moved.

Online banking – Direct Connect

HSBC Connect (formerly Hexagon ABC) is designed for the requirements of regional treasury centres and shared service centres, providing transmission of a high volume of transactions through a host-to-host channel. Given the potential to the corporate of the cost of developing and maintaining multiple bank interfaces, most banks have unique and specific electronic connections, HSBC has joined with SAP and SWIFT to provide a multi-bank corporate solution. This will enable a corporate to have real-time access to bank balances throughout the world at various banks

HSBC*net*

The internet global portal offered on the web comes with no software downloads. All new changes to the software are independent of the client and are automatically made centrally. Any changes are made as simple as possible to the end users. It is the consolidated platform for the client activities with HSBC worldwide. The software maintains who the contacts on the account are and authorisation procedures. The security includes a separate device, which provides unique one-off passwords per log-on. This creates a multi-layer log-on verification complete with 128-byte encryption.

The key functions include:

- Language of choice;
- Balances and statements;

- Establishment of preformatted payment instructions;
- Approval levels for payment – up to three levels including other countries;
- Assignment of payment limits;
- Various payment types – Priority Payments, Inter-Account Transfers and ACH debit/credit;
- Option to send email confirming payment has been sent to HSBC to the beneficiary.

HSBC offers an outsourcing function for the issuance, mailing and tracking of cheques by country for its clients. Cheques are regarded as non-urgent payments.

A full suite of standard reporting is available as is the capability to provide company-specific reports. The reporting capability includes filtering, thus making individual transactions easier to find. This information can be downloaded into spreadsheets or XML formats for internal systems.

HSBC*net* Mobile

Once a client is established on HSBC*net*, a mobile banking service is on offer. The major features of the mobile are:

- Balance and statements;
- Authorised select payment instructions;
- Receive notifications of payment authorisations via MyAlerts;
- Authorise cross-border payments with GetRate.

The service is available on iPhone, Blackberry and Android with the specified level of software releases. Security is the key concern. A device is used to create the unique one-off password, similar to the PC version of HSBC*net*, but the mobile user is given the following instructions:

- No storing of profile on the phone;
- Keep the anti-virus software updated;
- Never leave the phone logged on;
- Avoid using other people's phones;
- Use only secure Wi-Fi (password protected);
- Avoid strange unknown apps.

The mobile has the balance and reporting functionalities plus the filters to quickly find specific transactions. These include reference number, value date and amount range. Another filter shows countries, location and currencies. On viewing a pending transaction, that transaction can be authorised, sent to repair or rejected. Payments for South Korea can only be viewed only on the mobile and only individual payments can be authorised – the PC is needed for bulk payments.

If a payment is needed in another currency, the GetRate shows the exchange rate. At this stage the payment can be accepted and authorised or rejected.

The MyAlert key shows the pending payments and these are categorised by:

- High value payments;
- ACH;
- Low value payments.

The approval process is synchronised first with the PC and then with the mobile, enabling the mobile user to make payments away from the office at any time.

Achievements and initiatives

HSBC is one of the market leaders in foreign exchange derivatives. From its role as a major market maker and liquidity provider to the foreign exchange cash markets it offers through electronic banking:

- Spot FX – all currencies with any currency pair;
- Forwards – any time within two years online;
- FX derivatives – including collar options and average rate options;
- Exposure management.

With HSBC*net* FX and MM Trading is available for online trade execution services. HSBC provides five-day trading for 95 currencies in foreign exchange. Clients with agreements to invest into the liquidity fund can see the balances, yields, price data and the funds registered. Funds can be bought and sold in a wide range of currencies. When buying the funds, money has to be moved by the client while redemptions are automatically settled. The aim is to make trade execution as easy to use as possible with one-click online execution and automated back-office confirmation.

HSBC has applied the Henry Ford model to the FX trading process. From 1903 to 1913, Henry Ford reduced the time of car manufacturing from 540 minutes per car to 2.3 minutes. HSBC has taken the time to complete the whole cycle from price request through to FX confirmation from 21 hours in the 1990s, to seconds.

Client case study – Korean Air

Korean Air, one of the world's largest air cargo operators, generates nearly $1 billion in post-cost surplus cash annually from its five main operating areas: North America, Europe, Japan, China and the rest of Asia. Treasury policy is centralised, with the control of all collection accounts worldwide residing in Seoul. As is the case with many airlines, much of the significant costs and debt for aircraft financing is located centrally in Seoul. Therefore the speedy and efficient centralisation of surplus cash is vital.

The initial focus was narrowed from Europe, China and Asia Pacific, to just Asia-Pacific. Other than in exceptional cases such as Indonesia, where all billing is done in USD, Korean Air's passenger ticket sales and cargo receipts are all in local currency.

Korean Air had many bank relationships in Asia Pacific, usually more than one per country, and surplus funds tended to be remitted back to Seoul on a weekly, bi-weekly or monthly basis, depending on the timing that the balance being reached.

HSBC's solution for Korean Air in Asia-Pacific revolved around the debit of local currency in-country and the credit of USD to Seoul on the same day. Given the size of cash surpluses generated by Korean Air, the transfer of funds was implemented on a daily basis. In this way, the centralisation of Australian, Hong Kong, New Zealand and Singaporean dollars could be achieved at least seven days earlier than under Korean Air's previous arrangements.

Figure 15.1: Korean Air's FX outsourcing solution

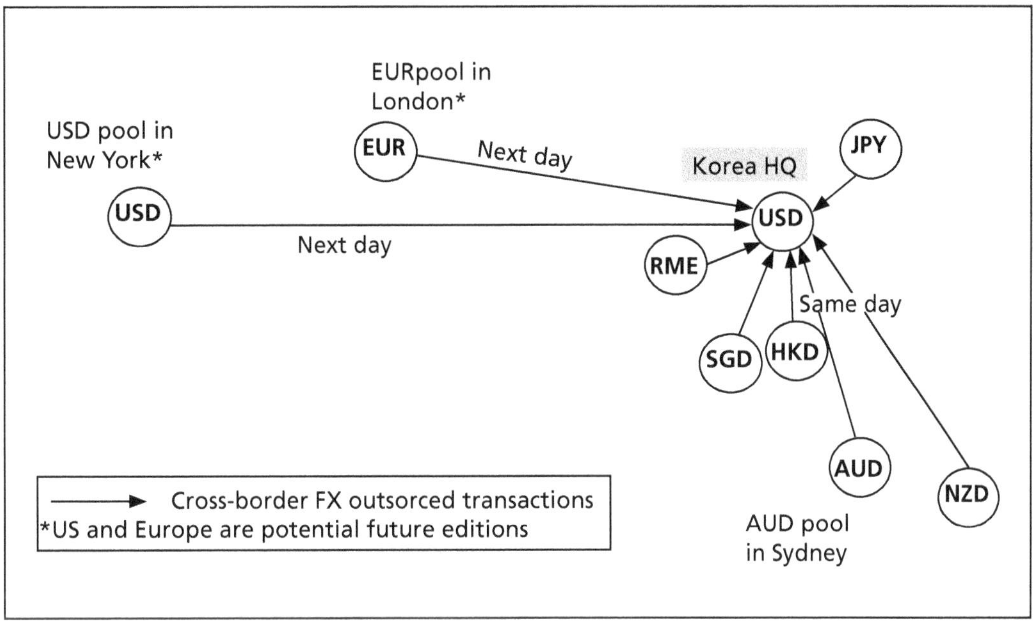

Source: Korean Air, HSBC

Having taken the decision in early 2004 that a significant depth of change in cash management policy was required to meet the goals envisaged, the final structure implemented realised a number and variety of tangible benefits: 50% of Asia-Pacific receivables now arrive in Seoul at least seven days earlier than before. Benefits include the following:

- Reduced bank charges – economies of scale have driven FX margins down and moving to a single regional bank for collections, payments and liquidity management has brought further savings;
- Increased interest income – improved availability of funds in Seoul has realised seven to 14 days in float savings. Management of both cash and the information relating to cash can now be done across the region in real time.

HSBC made all in-country offices branches the same legal entity: Korean Airlines Co. Ltd. This created the following benefits:

- Withholding tax and inter-company lending issues were minimised;
- Fund transfers were automatically improved. So, for example, in China, all sales proceeds can be remitted outside the country as long as sales lists and tax certificates are provided.

CHAPTER 16

CASE STUDY: WELLS FARGO/WACHOVIA

Questions for the CFO, Treasurer or Cash Manager

- Can we use any of the services offered by this bank, especially in the US?
- Is there anything we can use that will improve our performance?

Key considerations

- A large US bank offering extensive cash management services;
- Focused on automating the flow of information and transactions from the corporate to the bank(s), especially around the accounts receivable and payable and converting payments from paper to electronic.

Profile

Wells Fargo has Tier 1 capital of $91.9 billion and a ratio of 9.35%. Wells Fargo acquired Wachovia on 31 December 2008. Prior to that, Wachovia was rated the fourth largest bank holding company in the US based on assets. Wachovia's client base totalled 13 million household and business customers. In addition, it had 9.9 million online product and service enrolments and 3.3 million active online customers. The customer base is highly electronic; of the 10.4 million customers; 4.1 million are also e-customers, serviced by 1,160 bank branches and 28,800 employees. Wachovia Treasury Services was the nation's third-largest cash management provider.

Wells Fargo with Wachovia is a $1.3 trillion organisation, with 9,000 stores and 12,000 ATMs serviced by 270,000 people; it services one out of three US households. 19.7 million clients use online banking, with 6.7 million using mobile banking.

Its Tier 1 ratio under Basel II is 9.35% (30 September 2011) and under the proposed Basel III is reduced to 7.41%. Net interest income declined from 4.01% to 3.8% due to exceptional deposit growth in the 3rd quarter of $42 billion. The average deposit cost was 25 basis points.

Cash management products

Wells Fargo believes strongly that there are four key hurdles to overcome before cash management can flourish:

1. Inefficient manual processing;
2. No real-time visibility;
3. Inaccurate cash forecasting;
4. Increased exposure to fraud.

Inefficient manual processing

Manual processes include 'cut and paste', rekeying of information, no control of the incoming or outgoing information, payments constantly needing repair (the addition or changes of data) and paper-based reconciliation. These processes are time-consuming, error prone, prevent transparency and are an expensive overhead in terms of administration. This is particularly true in the US where research by the Aberdeen Group has showed that 93% of companies still receive and process invoices manually, and only 8% of companies have automated procedures to pay and receive. reducing the time to pay a single invoice by 92%

No real-time visibility

Wells Fargo is driving real-time across its systems and procedures. The extensive use of its online banking and mobile channels by customers requires their accounts to be updated immediately, with alerts being activated if required when funds are moved out of these accounts.

The global consolidation of cash with multiple banks and currencies is being worked upon to give a global position to a client. The client has one today, but the completeness and timeliness of that position is a work in progress. The process of getting each bank in the international network to provide the information required is cumbersome.

Inaccurate cash forecasting

Wells Fargo noted from the Hackett Group's research in 2011 that in the US that 22% of companies reported forecasting over two to three months were within 5% of the actual figures produced, and that 70% of companies rely on stand-alone spreadsheets.

Increased exposure to fraud

The 2009 AFP Payments Fraud report showed that 71% of organisations experienced attempted or actual payment fraud, and 91% of experienced fraud involved cheques – the average loss was $15,200.

The automated invoice capture and routing service allows clients to send in their invoices in whatever format and within 15 days they are ready for payment. One client, Champion Technology, reported a 40% reduction in administration costs and $300,000 in payment discounts in meeting the time window to receive such discounts

Services for multinational corporates (MNCs)

Processing and consolidating cash throughout large multinational companies requires a cash management provider with size and international scope. To meet these geographic needs, Wachovia has created a service offering that blends significant domestic resources with a combination of overseas branches, representative offices, and an extensive correspondent-banking network. Worldwide, Wachovia has joined forces with banks in more than 50 countries to offer corporate clients a comprehensive range of banking services, both locally and internationally.

Wachovia is a member of the IBOS Association, an international banking alliance aimed at serving corporate clients with in-country and cross-border banking requirements. The IBOS financial institutions have committed to common service level agreements and pricing, thus making it easier to create operating accounts in a single country or a cross-border liquidity management structure.

Cash management consulting for multinational corporations

Managing global liquidity is a challenge many companies are facing as their international reach grows. Wells Fargo Global Financial Consulting services offer solutions to help manage varying global liquidity positions and transaction processing so the company can establish centralised visibility and control on decentralised cash.

Wells Fargo assists with solutions that reduce the costs of multicurrency payables and receivables, and manage inter-company funding and global liquidity. Wells Fargo has an alliance arrangement for managing global liquidity with Bank Mendes Gans (BMG).

Based in the Netherlands, and known worldwide as a niche bank for international cash management, BMG offers customised, state-of-the-art services that 'layover' the company's existing in-country cash management systems. The company achieves managing multicurrency liquidity and retaining local banking relationships through one system.

Wells Fargo helps manage a varying liquidity positions by using BMG's multicurrency cash pool service. BMG forms an umbrella on top of the existing bank accounts, enabling the company to manage liquidity positions on a global basis.

Cash pool services provide a tool to help manage short- and long-term inter-company funding requirements without the need to perform foreign exchange and/or swap transactions or create inter-company loans. Surplus cash and cash shortfalls of group company accounts are centralised with same-day value. Local bank account balances are near zero or target balanced and centralised for balance and interest compensation purposes.

The currency balances of the group of companies in the cash pool are fully offset regardless of the currency, without the need to convert funds. Interest is applied at money market conditions and interest margins on compensated balances are fully refunded to the company. The company receives simple and efficient daily reports that provide insight into the total global cash position.

The company set investment and/or borrowing requirements on the balances in the accounts. These cash pool services can reduce overdraft debit interest costs, maximise interest yield and further enhance liquidity management opportunities. The increasing complexity of inter-company transactions, risk management strategies, accounting and tax regulation create the need to set up payment systems to simplify and make global transactions more visible.

Global Financial Consulting services, with BMG, could provide tools to help companies and simplify the settlement of inter-company and third-party payments and receipts on a fixed periodic schedule. These transactions are netted and settled centrally through a system designed to yield savings and to enhance cash flow efficiency. This service reduces cash flows to just one payment to or from each of the group companies in the required currency. A single payment can cover all invoices due. Simultaneous settlement of intercompany and third-party payments and receipts can produce significant savings in the cost of remittances, while eliminating float amongst participating group companies.

ACH

Wells Fargo Automated Clearing House (ACH) solutions enable clients to conveniently and securely move money electronically, as well as save costs. Funds can be moved overnight between almost any two banks or accounts, or electronic transfers can be timed for a future date – a better option than cheques for accounts payables and receivables.

Converting payments to ACH eliminates cheque printing, distribution and reconciling expenses and the issues associated with lost and stolen cheques, including stop payments and reissues. Regardless of geographic location or unexpected transportation delays, funds can be paid or collected overnight.

Additionally, ACH transactions can be combined with lockbox transactions (see further below), and customised file outputs can be created through the receivables service, allowing automatic update to the receivables system. Any ACH transactions received from unauthorised originators are returned automatically. ACH Control with Positive Pay gives the option to review and make a decision (pay or return).

Cash collection (USA)

Cash collection from and to businesses has proven security – PIN numbers control phone-initiated coin/currency orders; cash centre processing sites are fully secured (closed-circuit cameras and security guards). Deposits and place into a tamper-evident bag with cash in one pouch and cheques in the other. Deposits are delivered to a conveniently located Wells Fargo store, or placed with a contracted armoured carrier service for delivery to a cash processing or cash vault facility. The deposits can be directed to a single account, achieving cash concentration without funds transfers.

Deposits placed in a Commercial Depository (night drop) made at a teller window or delivered to a cash vault location by 2pm local time receive same-day credit. Deposit credit generally is verified by close of business the next day. Deposits delivered by armoured carrier to a money centre facility are usually allowed extended deadlines. The deposits can be made to one account or separate accounts. If a single account is used, individual depositing/store location numbers using the deposit reconcilement option can track deposits. Deposit activity and detail can be viewed online.

Coin/currency orders can be placed and picked up or delivered by armoured carrier when the deposits are presented. Change orders placed by 11am local time are packaged for next-day delivery. Strapped currency and rolled coin are provided in the denominations specified. At the financial centre, the client account can be automatically debited on the day of the scheduled pick-up, or you can pay with cash or cheque. At the cash processing centre or cash vault, the account is automatically debited.

Remote Deposit Capture (RDC) for cheques

RDC gives customers automated cheque presentment, streamlining the operations, significantly reducing costs and improving productivity.

Commercial and corporate clients can scan cheques (themselves or through an outsourced provider) and electronically send the images and data to their bank for deposit into a DDA account, with no paper to follow. Customers use image technology to produce electronic deposits. Before transmitting the deposit, the customer will balance the deposit dollar amount to the sum of the cheques, ensuring accuracy and reducing the chance of adjustments. The deposit then is electronically transmitted to Wells Fargo through the internet, and the customer receives an acknowledgement of receipt of the deposit transmission. The customer truncates the original cheques for destruction or retention.

Once Wells Fargo receives and acknowledges the image transmission, it settles the deposit, checks for image quality and verifies the DDA account number. The bank then determines the appropriate clearing channel (image presentment via image exchange or printing of substitute cheques), assigns float to the deposit and posts the deposit to their DDA account.

Direct deposits

Electronic payments replace cheque payments for applications such as payroll, pension, employee expense reimbursements, dividends and vendor payments. Direct deposit payments are transferred through the ACH network, drawing funds from the client's disbursement account to credit the recipient's chequeing or savings account. The company must obtain the bank and account number information for all direct deposit participants (employees, shareholders, vendors, etc.).

Prior to settlement date, Wells Fargo is given the total dollar amount of the payments and delivered the corresponding payment information in the required NACHA (National Automated Clearing House Association) file format. Wells Fargo verifies that the file total matches the dollar amount reported and, as an option, acknowledges receipt of the ACH file by fax or e-mail.

On settlement date, the payees' accounts are automatically credited and the designated company account is simultaneously debited for the total amount of the ACH transactions.

The Wells Fargo single Demand Deposit Account (DDA) system allows deposits to be made to the same account from any location. Cash and cheque deposits are accepted at all Wells Fargo locations. In select markets and regions outside the US, arrangements with partner banks are available to make deposits of physical items.

Pre-authorised payments (direct debit)

This form of payment speeds up the collection of receivables and improves cash forecasting using an electronic alternative to cheque collection for recurring consumer payments. The ACH solution allows automatic debit of the debtor's accounts and access to funds on the payment effective date.

To make a pre-authorised payment, permission by the debtor must obtained, along with the bank and account number information, and a written consent to have the account automatically debited for recurring payments. The pre-authorised payment transactions are in the NACHA format.

Sweep investments for corporates

Features include automated daily investment of idle collected balances into a predetermined investment instrument, including money market sweep, Eurodollars, commercial paper, repurchase agreements, federal funds and mutual funds. Also available is online access to same-day or historical balance and transaction detail, payment initiation, account services and account reconciliation.

Global cheque clearing

Wells Fargo provides multi-currency cheque clearing and expedites the availability of foreign item deposits. The cheques, once bundled and delivered to Wells Fargo, are deposited in the US dollar account at Wells Fargo, based on predetermined foreign exchange rates. The cheques must be denominated in the foreign currency of the drawee bank (e.g. Japanese Yen drawn on a Japanese bank) or in USD on select countries. This offers the convenience of bundling cheques of varying currencies and drawee countries on one deposit ticket, with one courier or postal cost. The corporate needs to verify that each cheque has been properly endorsed, photocopy the front and back of each cheque and then forward the original cheques via registered mail or courier.

Drafts are available, as some companies need to make payments in foreign currencies or in USD to foreign payees in cheque form rather than wire transfer. Wells Fargo International Draft service offers the ability to initiate, track and modify drafts by PC. Drafts are drawn on banks physically located in many parts of the world, making negotiation much easier and often less costly.

Lockbox – the collection of cheques

Debtors can send their cheque payments directly to one of Wells Fargo's coast-to-coast lockbox locations. The remittances are collected from the US Postal Service, delivered to the operations unit, processed and deposited. All related payment information is then transmitted to the company.

Customer payments, along with any machine-readable remittance coupons, are mailed directly to the corporate customer's post office box. Incoming mail is picked up several times a day and on weekends at some sites. The mail is opened and scanned, and a cheque digit routine is used to validate captured data from the scan line, resulting in a higher hit rate and fewer errors for receivables posting.

Once cheques are encoded and endorsed, funds are deposited to the client's Wells Fargo account, and a report is produced that lists all payments received, in batch and sequence order. An image transmission is sent to the client daily so they can update their accounts receivable files automatically. With Wells Fargo image technology, corporate clients have online access to the receivables data needed. The payoffs that come from faster funds collection and reduced in-house processing expenses are the primary reason a bank's lockbox is so effective.

Client case study – Bumble Bee Foods

Bumble Bee Foods, a private company of 1,000 people provide branded, shelf-stable seafood in North America. The biggest challenges were:

Accounts payable: an extensive manual processing which included:

- Rekeying;
- Lack of remittance data leading to vender enquiries;
- 16-day time lag from the time the invoice received until it was entered into the system;
- Supplier rebates were seldom received as the rebates were rewarded for payment made in less than 30 days.

Accounts receivable: Most sent cheques, tying up $29 million each month due to mail and deposit float.

Wells Fargo assisted in Bumble Bee by:

- Cleaning up the master file and eliminating 33% of the vendors that were duplicated or inactive;
- Confirmed contact information ;
- Gathered banking data;
- Promoting automatic payments instead of cheque – 21% of A/P now use ACH, 14% of A/R moved to ACH, resulting in a 54% decrease in the cost of processing payments.

www.ingramcontent.com/pod-product-compliance
Ingram Content Group UK Ltd.
Pitfield, Milton Keynes, MK11 3LW, UK
UKHW052301280926
15471UKWH00006B/1054

9 781907 72047